The Social Construction of Intellectual Disability

Intellectual disability is usually thought of as a form of internal, individual affliction, little different from diabetes, paralysis or chronic illness. This study, the first book-length application of discursive psychology to intellectual disability, shows that what we usually understand to be an individual problem is actually an interactional, or social, product. Through a range of case studies, which draw upon ethnomethodological and conversation analytic scholarship, the book shows how persons categorised as 'intellectually disabled' are produced, as such, in and through their moment-by-moment interaction with care staff and other professionals. Mark Rapley extends and reformulates current work in disability studies and offers a reconceptualisation of intellectual disability as both a professionally ascribed diagnostic category and an accomplished – and contested – social identity. Importantly, the book is grounded in data drawn from naturally occurring, rather than professionally orchestrated, social interaction.

MARK RAPLEY is Associate Professor of Psychology at Murdoch University. His work applies discursive psychology to questions of power, in particular the interactional and rhetorical production of persons with intellectual disabilities, the 'mentally ill' and Aboriginal Australians. His most recent books are *Quality of Life Research: A Critical Introduction* (2003) and, with Susan Hansen and Alec McHoul, *Beyond Help: A Consumer's Guide to Psychology* (2003).

The Social Construction of Intellectual Disability

Mark Rapley

Murdoch University
Western Australia

PUBLISHED BY THE PRESS SYNDICATE OF THE UNIVERSITY OF CAMBRIDGE
The Pitt Building, Trumpington Street, Cambridge, United Kingdom

CAMBRIDGE UNIVERSITY PRESS
The Edinburgh Building, Cambridge, CB2 2RU, UK
40 West 20th Street, New York, NY 10011–4211, USA
477 Williamstown Road, Port Melbourne, VIC 3207, Australia
Ruiz de Alarcón 13, 28014 Madrid, Spain
Dock House, The Waterfront, Cape Town 8001, South Africa

http://www.cambridge.org

First published 2004

Printed in the United Kingdom at the University Press, Cambridge

Typeface Plantin 10/12 pt.   *System* LATEX 2$_\varepsilon$ [TB]

A catalogue record for this book is available from the British Library

Library of Congress cataloguing in publication data
Rapley, Mark.
The social construction of intellectual disability / Mark Rapley.
     p.   cm.
Includes bibliographical references and index.
ISBN 0 521 80900 2 (hardback) – ISBN 0 521 00529 9 (paperback)
1. People with mental disabilities.   2. Social interaction.   3. Group identity.   I. Title.
HV3004.R36   2004
362.2′0422 – dc22   2003060608

ISBN 0 521 80900 2 hardback
ISBN 0 521 00529 9 paperback

To my late friend and colleague
Hanneke Houtkoop

Understanding is like night. Interpretation is like day.
(Hugh Mehan and Houston Wood, 1975: 193)

Contents

Acknowledgements

This work would not have been possible without the intellectual generosity and support of a number of people. In particular, I owe an immense debt to Charles Antaki, Hanneke Houtkoop and Alec McHoul. As will also become evident, my thinking has also been much influenced by Martha Augoustinos, Derek Edwards, Jonathan Potter and Margie Wetherell. I thank them for their generosity; as always, errors, omissions, misreadings and other howlers remain mine.

This book draws together and consolidates work from a project that has spanned the last ten years. As such, versions of some of the material in this book have previously appeared in journal article format: specifically, chapter 3 draws upon Rapley and Antaki (1996), A conversation analysis of the 'acquiescence' of people with learning disabilities, *Journal of Community and Applied Social Psychology*, 6: 207–27. Chapter 4 extends Rapley, Kiernan and Antaki (1998), Invisible to themselves or negotiating identity? The interactional management of 'being intellectually disabled', *Disability and Society*, 13, 5: 807–27. Chapter 6 draws upon and extends McHoul and Rapley (2002), 'Should we make a start then?': a strange case of a (delayed) client-initiated psychological assessment, *Research on Language and Social Interaction*, 35, 1: 73–91. I am grateful to the respective publishers for their permission to re-use this work.

I should also like to record my thanks to Patrick Kiernan and Erica Usher for their invaluable contributions to my work; to Sarah Caro at Cambridge University Press for her forbearance and to Susan Beer for her tireless and painstaking work on the typescript.

Finally, I would like to thank Susan Hansen for her support, encouragement and endurance.

A note on the cover illustration

The cover picture is an image of Justin, a young man with Down's Syndrome, taken as part of a photography project directed by Mona Neumann and the Down Syndrome Association of Western Australia. Aside from simply being a beautiful image, the picture underscores the analytic point of this book. Unless one *already knows* that the man in the picture has Down's Syndrome, the cover is, simply, a beautiful image. Intellectual disability is not just there to be found, rather intellectual disability – and all that goes with that identity ascription – has to be actively constructed as defining Justin's being-in-the-world.

See www.museums.wa.gov.au/exhibitions/downs/

A note on transcription notation

The transcription conventions used here were derived from those developed by Gail Jefferson (see Atkinson and Heritage, 1984).

(.) (. .) (. . .)	Pauses of approximately, a fifth of a second, half a second and one second.
(2 secs)	A roughly timed period of no speech.
.hh	A dot before an 'h' denotes speaker in-breath. The more h's, the longer the in-breath.
Hh	An 'h' denotes an out-breath. The more h's, the longer the out-breath.
hehh hahh	Laughter syllables with some attempt to capture 'colour'.
Go(hh)d(h)	This denotes 'laughter' within words.
((slurps))	A description enclosed in double brackets indicates a non-speech sound.
cu-	A dash denotes a sharp cut-off of a prior word or sound.
lo:ng	Colons show that the speaker has stretched the preceding letter or sound.
(guess)	Material within brackets represents the transcriber's guess at an unclear part of the tape.
?	A question mark denotes a rising intonation. It does not necessarily indicate a question.
=	The 'equals' sign denotes utterances that run on.
↑↓	Arrows indicate rising or falling intonational shift. They are placed before the onset of such a shift. Double arrows indicate very marked shifts.
under	Underlining indicates emphasis.
CAPITALS	Capital letters indicate a section of speech that is noticeably louder than that surrounding it.
°soft°	Degree signs indicate that speech is noticeably quieter than the surrounding talk.

> fast <	'Greater than' and 'less than' signs indicate that the talk they encompass
<slow>	was produced noticeably quicker than the surrounding talk; the reverse for 'slow' talk.
he	⌈llo ⌊hello Square brackets between adjacent lines of concurrent speech denote the start of overlapping talk.
[ˆt]	dental 'click'.
→	Side arrow indicates point of interest in the extract.
[. . .]	Material omitted from Extract.

Introduction

The aim of a critical history of psychology would be to make visible
the relations, profoundly ambiguous in their implications, between the
ethics of subjectivity, the truths of psychology and the exercise of power.
(Rose, 1999a: np)

An ancient Chinese proverb says, 'Wisdom begins by calling things by
their right name.' During this period of flux and transition, there may be
an opportunity to get the name right for people with mental retardation.
(Schroeder, Gerry, Gertz and Velasquez, 2002: 5)

It is, by now, something of a commonplace to refer to things-in-the-
world – be they ideas, objects or categories of persons – as 'socially
constructed'. Such a commonplace, indeed, that the very idea of 'the
social construction of x' (whatever x may be), along with the entire
project of what is usually described as 'social constructionist' (or often
it appears, interchangeably, if inaccurately cf. Jacobson, 2001) 'postmodern' scholarship, has been famously parodied (Sokal, 1996) and
held up to ridicule as a mere 'intellectual imposture' (see Sokal and
Bricmont, 1999). This book seeks to retrieve something of the utility
of the notion of social construction, by way of a detailed examination of
professionalised (and essentialised) understandings of persons described
as 'intellectually disabled', and the analysis of social interactions between
members of the helping professions and 'intellectually disabled' persons,
wherein professional estimation and management of their (in)capacities
and (in)capabilities occurs.[1] It is important at this point to be clear that
the brand of social constructionism on offer here, discursive psychology,
is a very particular one, with roots in ethnomethodology and conversation
analysis. It is quite unlike other kinds of social constructionism (narrative enquiry, grounded theory, interpersonal phenomenological analysis
and so on), with quite specific theoretical and analytic differences from
these approaches. Chapter 1 offers a detailed account of my reading of

---

[1] 'Mental retardation' in US terminology, 'learning disability' in the UK.

1

discursive psychology, but for comprehensive, canonical, accounts of the area see Edwards and Potter (1992); Potter (1996); and Edwards (1997).

As such I hope to show how what has come to be a taken-for-granted social, administrative/bureaucratic and professionalised category of personhood can, rather, be understood not as some fixed object in an unchanging social world (or one of the 'static features of a pre-defined macro-sociological landscape' (Wetherell and Potter, 1992)), but instead as a status of being-in-the-world which is actively negotiated – if not always from positions of equality.[2] That is, unlike Schroeder *et al.* (2002) whose optimism about current circumstances presenting 'an opportunity to get the name right for people with mental retardation' presupposes the 'condition' and suggests that all we need to do is name it correctly, here I try to show how that 'condition' (whatever it is called) is, interactionally, brought into being. Indeed the establishment, maintenance and exploitation of power asymmetry in interaction – and the upshot of this accomplishment for the respective social identities of the parties to the interaction in question, is the central focus of this book.[3] For it is in this arena – that of social interaction, or more precisely, of talk-in-interaction – that social identities ('intellectually disabled person'; 'clinical psychologist'; (in)competent adult; member/non-member, for example) and their concomitant duties, rights, opportunities and obligations, are constructed and cemented *as such* (Antaki, Condor and Levine, 1996; Antaki and Widdicombe, 1998b; Edwards, 1997; Sacks, 1992). This book then, after Rose (1999a) seeks 'to make visible the relations, profoundly ambiguous in their implications, between the ethics of subjectivity, the truths of psychology and the exercise of power'.

However, rather than explore the negotiation of the identity of people described as intellectually disabled in and via the analysis of actual interaction, much of the debate – particularly in the psychological and sociological literatures – over the social competence of people with intellectual disabilities is based on staff- or researcher-rated standardised measures and, though more rarely, on coded observational ratings or interview-based examinations.[4] Very few reports in the literature present

---

[2] Not to mention a formally identifiable 'mental disorder' as specified by the American Psychiatric Association's (1994) *Diagnostic and Statistical Manual of Mental Disorders* (4th edition).

[3] See Hester and Francis (2002) and Mehan and Wood (1975) for a helpful analysis of the difficulties inherent in the *a priori* assumption of the influence of *structural* asymmetries in and for interaction.

[4] While it may appear to presume that which I attempt to analyse, I have not found an æsthetically acceptable way to indicate the provisional status of the construct 'person with an intellectual disability' without littering the text with quotation marks. As such, I ask that the reader keeps the presence of scare quotes around concepts such as 'intellectual disability' in mind.

data which demonstrate the moment-by-moment prosecution of *naturally occurring* social interaction.[5] The disability studies literature, with even fewer exceptions, appears often to be based on the views of theorists and/or 'experts by experience' (although see, for example, the work of Taylor (2000); Ferguson *et al.* (1992); Goode (1983; 1994) and Goodley (1997) for notable examples to the contrary). In contrast, in this book, I attempt to build on a small body of work that has attended to ethnomethodological strictures and examine naturally occurring interaction between people with an intellectual disability and their care staff and other professional interlocutors. In the studies reported here video- and audio-taped data, collected in people's homes during interactions with psychologists, nursing and social care staff, were transcribed and analysed with a particular focus on the joint negotiation of competence, and the social identity afforded to the 'impaired' party, by virtue of interactional exigencies and interactional management. To anticipate my conclusions a little, perhaps, the practices of care staff and professional assessors – in circumstances ranging from formal quality of life assessment to defrosting chickens; from structured interviewing to taking out the rubbish – demonstrably serve actively to *constrain* and to *constitute* (or, even, socially construct) the competence of people with intellectual disabilities.[6] It is also noticeable that, by the demonstrably interactionally produced underestimation of the capacities of the people with whom they work, staff may also (inadvertently) sustain their dependence and incompetence.

In order to examine this, social, construction of identity (as competent member – or otherwise) I draw upon a range of theoretical and methodological approaches which can, rather loosely, be gathered together under the rubric of discursive psychology (Edwards and Potter, 2002).[7] Discursive psychology is, at least from the perspective I adopt, as much an analytic 'mentality' as it is a set of techniques or exclusive theoretical commitments: my position is outlined in more detail in chapter 1 but, for present purposes, may be described briefly as employing the

---

[5] But see Goode (1994) for an elegant demonstration of the power of ethnographic analysis in his beautiful study of 'the world of the deaf-blind' and (1983) for a respecification of the methods by which competence may be discovered.

[6] The notion of 'competence' is slippery. Briefly my usage of the term is ethnomethodological, with 'competence' being seen as a worked-up, intersubjective, accomplishment, as opposed to an internal, psychologised, attribute of individual persons. I explicate my use of the term in more detail in chapter 2.

[7] The expression 'competent member' may be read as synonymous with membership in the category of 'morally accountable *human* agent' (Weinberg, 1997, my emphasis). Much of this book is concerned with the analysis of the practices whereby negotiation of candidate membership of this category is managed, and the practices whereby the denial of such membership is accomplished.

tools of ethnomethodology/conversation analysis (EM/CA) to develop an analytic purchase on the topic of minds (and their capacities), the world, and the relation between them, most usually approached in contemporary psychology and sociology (and, largely untheorised, in disability studies) from a Cartesian or cognitivist perspective. In rejecting cognitivism, discursive psychology is thus in company with those working from both an ethnomethodological and a Wittgensteinian/'ordinary language philosophy' position – Button *et al.* (1995); Button and Sharrock (1993); Coulter (1979; 1999); and Leudar and Thomas (2000) for example – although clearly differences and tensions exist between workers in these traditions.[8] Likewise, discursive psychology is deeply suspicious of classical, structural, accounts of persons, their capacities and their conduct.

Informed by the work of Nikolas Rose (1985; 1996) and other workers in the Foucauldian tradition on the development of the 'psy-complex', and the discursive psychological work of Edwards and Potter (1992); Wetherell and Potter (1992); Potter (1996; 1998); and Edwards (1997), such an ethnomethodologically grounded approach lends itself to (i) the adoption of an historical perspective on the construction of intellectual disability as 'otherness' by the psy-complex (ii) the examination of the interplay between social identities and professionalised knowledge and practices (iii) the analysis of the interactional production of psychologised constructions of intellectual disability in and through the enactment of professional practices and (iv) the presentation of a more respectful account of the interaction competence of persons categorised as intellectually disabled. The book is divided into two parts; an introduction to, and overview of, discursive psychology and critique of the general theoretical literature(s); followed by detailed case studies of psychological assessment practices and day-to-day interactions between care staff and people with an intellectual disability. The opening chapter offers a theoretical and methodological context for the book. Through a discussion of recent work in discursive psychology, the contingent and contested nature of social categories of persons, identities and the 'self' is discussed. The approach of conversation analysis, membership categorisation analysis and discursive psychology to the analysis of talk and texts is described. The chapter outlines the case for extending the application of discursive psychology to the study of intellectual disability. Much of the material discussed here may be familiar to readers in social psychology, but this sort of thinking appears yet to receive little attention in the intellectual disability and broader disability studies literatures. As such the

---

[8] See Potter (1996, esp. pp. 219–27) for a detailed discussion of these tensions.

patience of readers who have followed the debate in social psychology is requested.

Chapter 2 discusses 'intellectual disability' as diagnostic, social and moral category. The development of psychologised understandings of individual subjectivity and the production of 'intellectual disability' as social identity is elaborated and the discursive construction of intellectual disability as a diagnostic identity – for example in the American Association on Mental Retardation (1992; 2002) classificatory nosology – is examined. The relevance and feasibility of the discursive psychological approach is discussed in the light of existing work on language and communication in people with intellectual disabilities, and an examination of the local and rhetorical production of social and personal identities – such as 'disabled person' – in both talk-in-interaction and in official texts is illustrated. The chapter also offers a critical review of recent work in disability studies which critiques both dominant social science research practices and the professionalised knowledges of disability they produce. Difficulties with the structuralist understandings of disability in this work, particularly in the 'social model' (Oliver, 1987), are outlined. Discussion of 'intellectual disability' – or rather its absence – is located within these wider theoretical debates over the nature of disability, and dissenting voices presenting work on intellectual disability from a social constructionist perspective (e.g. Taylor, 1998; Goode, 1996) are discussed.

In the second part of the book, I turn to a series of case studies which examine both the application of psychological technologies ('interviews', 'testing', 'assessment') and the mundane management of everyday life in supported accommodation for adults described as intellectually disabled. In each of these case studies the matter in hand is the interactional production of incompetence.

Chapter 3 presents an analysis of the professional literatures which construct persons described as intellectually disabled as irretrievably interactionally incompetent. A large psychological literature is concerned to demonstrate that, by virtue of a dispositional tendency to 'response biases' in general, and 'acquiescence bias' in particular, people with an intellectual disability are incompetent to report on their own subjectivity. This chapter firstly examines the professional disenfranchisement of people with intellectual disability in the literature. Secondly, again drawing on conversation analytic studies, the chapter examines 'acquiescence bias' as a local and contingent product of professional psychological practices.

Chapter 4 examines the ascription of moral disreputability/accountability to persons diagnosed as 'intellectually disabled' by the construction of attention to 'doing being ordinary' (Sacks, 1992) as 'passing' or 'denial of disability' in the psychological, sociological and ethnographic literatures. The chapter then draws on conversation analytic methods to explicate the interactional management of 'normality' and 'intellectual disability' as contested social identities in professional encounters between psychologists, researchers and 'persons with an intellectual disability'. Attention is also paid to the ascription of disreputability via the professionally constructed 'demonstration' of intellectually disabled persons' accountable ignorance of their social status in these encounters.

Chapter 5 begins the turning of the tables, by close attention to the mundane management of everyday interaction in supported housing. Here we see clear instances of supposedly interactionally incompetent persons not only deftly managing their care staff interlocutors, but also demonstrating mastery of a range of normative cultural practices that should, according to conventional psychological wisdom, be well beyond their grasp. The flip side of this analysis is, once again, the (identity) management work that staff set out to accomplish: via sustained interactional practices that produce persons as equivalent in social and moral status to dogs and infants, it becomes clear that supported housing represents a site of contested agency. Through a close inspection of mundane interaction it also becomes clear that the resistance of people with an intellectual disability to infantilisation and control is both subtle and, even where ineffective, exquisitely attentive both to normative rules of conversational sequencing and such matters as cultural rules for the use of kinship misidentifications as insults.

In a single case analysis, chapter 6 offers a deviant case. Here we see another example of the turning of the tables and again, it is the wit, artfulness and cultural sophistication of the supposedly intellectually disabled interlocutor that is the focus of attention. In what amounts to a naturally occurring breach experiment, we see an empirical confirmation of Sacks's (1992) conjecture about the existence of omni-relevant devices for conversation, in and through the careful management by a man described as 'having' a 'moderate' intellectual disability of a testing encounter (in both senses of the term) with a psychologist. This chapter then offers an empirical recapitulation of the theoretical discussion of identity and identity management as situated interactional accomplishment in chapter 1.

Finally, in chapter 7, I offer some limited and tentative conclusions. This final chapter offers a synthesis of the preceding case studies and discussion. The chapter draws together analysis of the professionalised psy-complex discourse of individualised, accountable, incompetence in a respecification of the construction of the social identity 'intellectually disabled person'. The social consequences of the current hegemony of professional discourses of otherness for people 'with' intellectual disability are discussed; alternative ways of knowing 'intellectual disability' are offered and some thoughts about the reconstruction of psy-complex practices and ways of theorising disability are offered.

1 A discursive psychological approach

> The conduct of persons becomes remarkable and intelligible when, as it were, displayed upon a psychological screen, reality becomes ordered according to a psychological taxonomy, abilities, personalities, attitudes and the like become central to the deliberations and calculations of social authorities and psychological theorists alike.
>
> (Rose, 1999a: np)

> Reality enters into human practices by way of the categories and descriptions that are part of those practices.
>
> (Potter, 1996: 98)

Introduction

Intellectual disability is constructed in both 'official' discourses and every-day commonsense as an irretrievable 'disorder' of competence afflicting individual subjects, requiring professional diagnosis, treatment and management. This book deconstructs and critiques the social construction of intellectual disability through a detailed analysis of (i) a range of 'official' texts and (ii) the enactment of professional psychological practices. Primarily based in analysis of the talk-in-interaction of psychologists and people described as intellectually disabled, the book offers a contrasting view of these 'incompetent' social identities as *the product of* technological professional practices and knowledges.[1] A secondary focus of the book is on the interplay and reproduction (intertextuality) of discourses of difference, deviance and incompetence in human/social policy rhetoric and

---

[1] The great majority of the interactions analysed in this book are between people described as intellectually disabled and psychologists, researchers or care staff: that is, people occupying positions of power relative to their disabled interlocutors. While part of the purpose of the book is to demonstrate (rather than to assume) that power asymmetry, the absence of interactions between people with intellectual disabilities and their disabled peers could be seen as an omission. However, if what we see shows people with impairments being competent, making sense of interactions, and dealing successfully with others' presumptions and expectations, in the face of asymmetric power, then the case has been made. I am grateful to an anonymous reviewer for this point.

in the (re)production of knowledge about intellectual disability in the psychological professions.

I argue throughout that the operation of power/knowledge (Foucault, 1977) is visible at multiple levels of analysis and that, although either discounted in the professional psychological literature (or, in the instance of such self-serving professional constructions as 'dual diagnosis', pathologised) so too is *resistance* to the exercise of professional power from persons described as 'intellectually disabled'. That is, in this book I adopt a discursive psychological approach. This chapter outlines my reading of discursive psychology.

Discursive psychology

Discursive psychology has, over the last ten to fifteen years, matured into a substantial alternative approach to mainstream psychology: it is a programme which seeks to reconfigure psychology as a 'post-cognitivist' discipline (Potter, 2000). The project is, perhaps, best described as a theoretical and methodological *inversion* of contemporarily dominant forms of psychological thought. Edwards and Potter (2002: 12) describe discursive psychology (DP) as:

The application of discourse analytic principles to psychological topics. In psychology's dominant 'cognitivist' paradigm, individuals build mental representations of the world on the basis of innate mental structures and perceptual experience and talk on that basis. The categories and content of discourse are considered to be a reflection, refracted through various kinds of error and distortion, of how the world is perceived to be. In contrast, DP *begins with* discourse (talk and text), both theoretically and empirically. Discourse is approached, not as the outcome of mental states and cognitive processes, but as a domain of action in its own right . . . Both 'reality' and 'mind' are constructed by people, conceptually, in language, in the course of their performance of practical tasks.

What this, canonical, version of discursive psychology seeks to do, then, is to call into question the very taken-for-grantedness of the way in which we go about (as either academics or as 'lay people') talking and writing about ourselves as psychological subjects.[2] Discursive psychology thus asks us to suspend our habitual understandings of ourselves and other persons as correctly describable in what professional psychology (and

[2] The version of discursive psychology with which I work is sometimes, disparagingly, referred to as 'Loughborough Relativism' (cf. McLennan, 2001. See Edwards, Ashmore, and Potter (1995)) as distinct from other variants, often associated with the work of Ian Parker (e.g. Parker, 1990; 1992; Parker and Burman, 1993) and colleagues which adopt 'critical realism'.

everyday 'lay' or 'folk psychology') tells us are neutral, objective and scientifically derived terms. Rather, discursive psychology points to an alternative view of talk and text as *actively constitutive* of those very 'truths' that constitute our mundane vocabulary of the 'mental' (McHoul and Rapley, 2003). As such, a discursive psychological view draws on the ethnomethodological work of Harvey Sacks (1992) and Harold Garfinkel (1967), studies in the sociology of scientific knowledge (for example, Gilbert and Mulkay, 1984) and employs the analytic tools of both conceptual (cf. Coulter, 1979; 1990; Wittgenstein, 1958) and conversation analysis, to explicate the manner in which 'reality', 'society', 'culture' and the nature of persons in the world is constructed in and through talk and texts. While acknowledging the importance of post-structuralist perspectives on the so-called 'turn to language' in social psychology, key figures in discursive psychology differ perhaps most clearly in the level of their emphasis on, and explicit use of, the work of Foucault, Derrida, Laclau and Mouffe and other writers in this tradition. As Wetherell (1998: 388) points out: 'it has become commonplace in social psychology in recent years to distinguish between two or more styles of discourse analysis . . . typically boundary lines are drawn between styles of work which affiliate with ethnomethodological and conversation analytic traditions and analyses which follow post-structuralist lines.' With Wetherell, I take the view not only that 'a stance which reads one in terms of the other continues to provide the most productive basis for discourse work in social psychology' (1998: 388), but also that EM/CA-informed analyses can, as Schegloff (1998) concedes, show the operation, in operation, of a range of otherwise 'grand theoretical' constructs such as power/knowledge.

What all workers in the 'Loughborough' variant of discursive psychology would accept, however, is that there is, from the discursive psychological perspective, no 'reality' to 'mind', or 'culture' or 'society' or 'persons' that is independent of descriptions of them. Discursive psychological social constructionism is, thus, *epistemic* rather than *ontological*. As Edwards (1997: 48) suggests: 'if texts constructively describe their objects, then so do the texts that say so . . . Mind and reality are treated analytically as discourse's topics and business, the stuff the talk is about, and the analytic task is to examine how participants *descriptively* construct them . . . culture should not be treated merely as a causal variable. But the same principle is extended to not treating "mind" as a dependent one.' Discursive psychological work thus also draws explicitly and extensively on the work of Wittgenstein, particularly in relation to the issue of what it is that we can, sensibly, talk of ('this running against the walls of our cage', Wittgenstein, 1926), and – crucially – for both 'mainstream psychology' (and its everyday variant) refuses to privilege the claims to scientificity of cognitivist, professional, psychological discourse.[3] That is discursive psychology accepts the proposition that:

All testing, all confirmation and disconfirmation of a hypothesis [e.g. the hypothesis that *this* is the correct way to go on in following a rule] takes place already within a system. And this system is not a more or less arbitrary and doubtful point of departure for all our arguments: no, it belongs to the essence of what we call an argument. The system is not so much the point of departure, as the element in which arguments have their life. (Wittgenstein, 1969: 105)

In this respect then, what Wittgenstein describes as a 'system' may be read as analogous to (a) 'discourse', or the notion of an 'interpretative repertoire' (Potter and Wetherell, 1987; Wetherell and Potter, 1992), in that a system of thought provides the element within which persuasion of the veridicality or otherwise of a set of propositions may be made. Where discursive psychology offers its most radical challenge to how we have conventionally come to think ourselves (and such objects in the world as 'people with an intellectual disability') is in its insistence, *contra* the usual proclivity in psychology (and everyday commonsense) not to deliberate upon fundamental systemic propositions, that these be subject to scrutiny and analysis. As Flathman (2000) points out, Wittgenstein (1969: 88) noted the possibility that 'all enquiry on our part is set so as to exempt certain propositions from doubt, if they are ever formulated' and that such unformulated propositions, by virtue of no longer being disputed 'for unthinkable ages', belong to the 'scaffolding of our thoughts' (1969: 212). It is here that my variant of discursive psychology diverges somewhat from the canonical Edwards and Potter form, in that I believe it is essential that we *foreground* the historic adventitiousness (Sacks, 1992; McHoul and Rapley, 2001) of our contemporary psychological 'truths', make explicit the historical construction of the 'scaffolding of our thought' and contextualise any analysis of contemporary forms of life with an appreciation of their provenance. As such what I attempt in this book is an examination of how it has come to be that there exist in the world such sayable things as 'persons with an intellectual disability' in all the solidity and taken-for-grantedness with which the term is nowadays invested – to present, in Foucault's and Rose's terms, a critical history of the present – and also to lay out how it is that people, in talk and texts, become fixed-as-such in and through interactions with those

---

[3] See Edwards (1997) for a detailed analysis of the shortcomings of 'scientific' cognitive psychology and Potter (1996) for a rigorous overview of the discursive psychological project *tout court*.

authorised to name them as such.[4] In this respect then, in company with Wetherell, I take the view that Foucauldian scholarship, particularly that of Nikolas Rose on the development of governmentality, offers a *deepening* of discursive psychological analysis rather than a *necessarily* competing account of the way that things stand with being human, as is assumed by proponents of 'Bolton Realism' and, further, avoids fruitless debates about whether conceptual analysis should or should not point out to users of the language whether their usages are grammatical (cf. Coulter, 1999; McHoul and Rapley, 2003) by virtue of a demonstration of the very social and historical contingency of what it is and is not possible to say.[5]

That is to say, it is perhaps as (if not more) unsettling to habitual forms of thought to *show* them to be, simply, habitual, un-deliberated, conventions than it is to *tell* it thus. It is, further, by the incorporation of Foucauldian thinking into ethnomethodologically informed discursive psychological analyses, possible to show the doing of power/knowledge (and, in principle, any other such putative social-structural phenomenon such as 'racism', 'class', 'gender', and so on) as and where it is a members matter, in and through the detailed examination of interactional practices, rather than taking such social scientific things to be, and to have been, for unthinkable ages, simply givens.[6] Accordingly, a brief detour into Rose's account of the development of psychology as a profession and as a discipline is in order prior to a return to a more detailed explication of key precepts of a discursive psychological approach.

Nikolas Rose and the history of psychology

Rose's work offers a critical analysis of the manner in which a series of propositions about what it means to be human at all are now absolutely sedimented into 'western' discourse. That is he shows how ideas of a personal, individualised subjectivity, of the 'ghost in the machine' (Ryle, 1949), a department of internal affairs, have come to be the

---

[4] Rose points out that: 'legitimacy is claimed by our contemporary "engineers of the human soul" on the basis that they can deal truthfully with the real problems of human existence in the light of a knowledge of the individuals who make it up' (Rose, 1999b: xxii).

[5] Little work in the Bolton realist tradition seems to offer much in the way of, for example, the analysis of the conditions of possibility of contemporary psychological thought, preferring instead to enumerate 'discourses', as if train spotting were actually a form of transport analysis.

[6] See the extensive debates on the compatibility (or otherwise) of conversation analysis, (critical) discourse analysis, and post-structuralist thought between Margaret Wetherell and Emmanuel Schegloff, and between Emmanuel Schegloff and Mick Billig in *Discourse and Society* (Billig, 1999a; b; Schegloff, 1997; 1999a; b; Wetherell, 1998). Yates, Taylor, and Wetherell (2001) and Wetherell (2002) offer a helpful overview of this debate.

unspoken screen on which contemporary action-in-the-world is made intelligible as such. As we have seen, he argues that, within this system of thought, 'reality becomes ordered according to a psychological taxonomy, abilities, personalities, attitudes and the like become central to the deliberations and calculations of social authorities and psychological theorists alike' (1999a: np), and, such is the familiarity of the propositions that the psy-complex advances, they 'are often unsusceptible to deliberation because accepting them is a condition of thinking and acting within the systems of which they are a part' (Flathman, 2000: 9). Psychology then, has come to offer both the ubiquitous vocabulary of our present (Hansen, McHoul and Rapley, 2003) and a series of techniques whereby we make ourselves over into self-governing subjects. It is the very ubiquity of these techniques and the taken-for-grantedness of the terminology within which they are framed which renders them routinely unavailable for questioning or deliberation. Thus it is that notions like 'attitudes' or 'mental illness' have (supposedly) formal, technical senses and (according to mainstream psy-discourse at least) inaccurate, lay ones; that technological innovations such as the formalised IQ or personality test and their popular offspring (ranging from TV programmes to DIY personality quizzes in 'women's magazines') are unremarkable, and that 'helping' professionals and counsellors of every stripe proliferate exponentially alongside ever expanding lists of forms of conduct which are held to be 'symptoms' of one mental disorder or another. There is no reason to suppose that 'intellectual disability' is not, and has not been, similarly constituted. Yet despite the current overwhelming dominance of such systems of thought, and associated technologies, this manner of thinking ourselves is, historically, extremely recent and indeed at least for present purposes can be traced to the latter half of the nineteenth century.[7]

Contemporary psychology relies – as it has, explicitly, from at least 1904 – for its 'positivity' (Foucault, 1978) upon a specific truth claim, that it employs the methods of *science* to describe, factually, things-in-the-world. Indeed, the Editorial introducing the very first issue of the *British Journal of Psychology* in 1904 stated unequivocally that: 'psychology . . . has now at length achieved the position of a positive science . . . "Ideas" in the philosophical sense do not fall within its scope; its enquiries are restricted entirely to *facts*' (BPS, 1904: 1; my emphasis). Rose (1999a) points out that this truth claim is buttressed (much to the dismay of newly enrolled undergraduate psychology students) by two linked 'truth

---

[7] See Foucault (1967) for an archaeology of the development of systems of thinking madness.

techniques', newly invented and solidified in the human sciences during the nineteenth and twentieth centuries. He writes:

The two truth techniques that were pre-eminent here were 'statistics' and 'the experiment'. Both exemplify not merely the alliances formed by psychology with other scientific disciplines, but also the reciprocal interplay between the theoretical and the technical . . . [I]n the course of the nineteenth century, the earlier assumption that statistical laws were merely the expression of underlying deterministic events gave way to the view that statistical laws . . . were laws in their own right that could be extended to natural phenomena. A conceptual rationale was constructed for the claim that statistical regularity underlay the apparently disorderly variability of phenomena.

Here Rose draws attention to the manner in which professional practices work, actively, to constitute their objects of study, and the interplay whereby, to paraphrase Edwards, Ashmore and Potter (1995), we see that 'method is theory in disguise'. What Rose also clearly identifies is the transformation of the public and political *legitimacy* of possible ways of knowing about human experience via the incorporation of the procedures, techniques and assumptions about the nature of the world of the physical sciences: the decline of individual introspection and the rise of the experiment. Nowadays it is absolutely taken for granted – and yet repeatedly asserted in introductory texts on the discipline as a whole, and on 'methods' in particular – that psychology is an experimental, scientific, discipline which uncovers orderly phenomena by virtue of carefully controlled, methodologically rigorous, and statistically robust tests of hypotheses about tightly defined variables, quanta of which are measured in representative samples. And, it is claimed, this is absolutely essential if we are to arrive at truth, by virtue of the 'apparently disorderly variability of phenomena' (Rose, 1999a: np) that psychology wishes to know. But this story is not quite as unproblematic as it may appear.[8] Rose (1999a) goes on to point out that theory and method cannot be so simply divorced, and neither can the development of 'psychological reality' over the course of the last hundred years be in any way divorced from the politics of knowledge.

In the first thirty years or so of psychology's disciplinary project, from the 1870s to the early years of this century, programmes for the stabilisation of psychological

---

[8] The model of science usually proclaimed by psychology as that to which it adheres is, as work in the sociology of scientific knowledge makes clear (Gilbert and Mulkay, 1984), not one that many physicists, geologists or chemists would recognise as descriptive of their practices (Boyle, 2002). With regard to the borrowing of the methods of the 'natural sciences' by the 'social sciences', Ian Hacking (1992; 1995) helpfully reminds us that 'human kinds' and 'natural kinds' are not *of a kind*. See also Mehan and Wood (1975, esp. chapter 3) and Schütz (1962).

truths went hand in hand with the construction of the technical devices necessary to demonstrate that truth . . . from the notion of a 'normal distribution' to the devices for calculating correlations, the relation between the theoretical and the statistical was an internal one . . . By the 1920s, statistical laws appeared to have an autonomous existence which was merely accessed by statistical devices. Statistical tests appeared merely a neutral means for the demonstration of truth deriving from a universe of numerical phenomena which, because untainted by social and human affairs, can be utilised to adjudicate between different accounts of such affairs . . . From this point forward, the means of justification come to shape that which can be justified in certain fundamental ways: statistical norms and values become incorporated within the very texture of conceptions of what is today's psychological reality.

It is of course no accident that the period of the stabilisation of psychological truths is more or less coterminous with the development of universal compulsory education, the development of child heath surveillance, the end of 'idiocy' as an undifferentiated private matter and, via the collection of 'idiots' into asylums from the 1840s on, its translation into a problem of social hygiene (Rose, 1999b; Simpson, 2000b), and the development and refinement of psychometric tests of 'intelligence'. It is also clear that the widespread acceptance of these new forms of knowledge was neither immediate nor uncontested. Danforth (2002: 52) argues that 'it took decades to convince the public and the politicians to embrace the belief that these professions had a scientific knowledge base that was superior to commonsense, religious convictions, and cultural traditions of nonprofessionals' and that, but for the adoption by psychology of the language of the medical and engineering professions (in much the same manner that mad doctors had successfully appropriated the language of medicine to re-describe the insane (Scull, 1979; 1977)) such persuasion may have been much delayed.[9] And while psychology as a discipline may have laid claim to the 'neutral' mantle of scientific methods, it was abundantly clear (not least of course through the Eugenics movement, e.g. Hooton, 1937) that the purposes of this new science were, at base, of the management and the control of 'moral defectives' or 'moral imbeciles', the production across the 'lower orders' of 'docile and capable bodies' (Foucault, 1977: 294; Howe, 1848; Bateman, 1897; Tredgold, 1908) and a general improvement in social order, social 'efficiency' and racial fitness (Brown, 1992; Burt, 1955).

---

[9] Ryan and Thomas (1998) note that Daniel Defoe's (1697) call for the establishment of a 'public fool house' on the grounds of natural justice was unsuccessful. Not until the language of medicine became available was the start of the asylum movement possible: Ryan and Thomas (1998: 92) cite Edouard Seguin (1846) as remarking that: 'while waiting for the medicine to cure idiots, I have undertaken to see that they participate in the benefit of education'.

Central to the success of the professionalisation of the discipline was, along with statistics and the experiment, the development of the intelligence test. Indeed Danforth (2002: 53) describes the intelligence test as 'the primary vehicle of the rise of the psychological profession' as it allowed the impression that the discipline had access to a *scientific instrument* capable of the objective 'diagnosis' of a real, though invisible, interior defect. He observes that:

Goddard, Cattell, Terman, and other leading early psychologists frequently described intelligence tests as diagnostic instruments that would allow them to discern mental health from mental deficiency. In both professional and popular writing, early psychologists repeatedly compared the new intelligence tests to the standard diagnostic instruments used by physicians: thermometers, sphygmomanometers, even x-rays. Subnormal IQs were described as objective indicators of a mental disease . . . they developed mental tests and measurements as instruments imitating and enacting the mathematical precision of engineers, claiming to measure the mental realm just as engineers measured the physical realm. (Danforth, 2002: 53)

And, of course, measurement, testing, statistics and the experiment are very much still with us. Such practices are not only the historically rooted conditions of possibility for the successful emergence of the *profession* of psychology, but remain, today, definitive of it. The public, political, legitimacy of the discipline inheres precisely in this supposed technological substrate to the discipline's claims to scientificity. As we will see, these technologies and the standardised psychometric test – the means of access to the neutral truth of the statistic; the exact position of the person on 'that bell-shaped curve' (Jenkins, 1999); and the 'amount' of whatever capacity persons 'possess' – continue to form the dominant modes of production not only of the intelligence of the person, but also 'in' the newly-minted 'intellectually disabled person', the 'true' representation of everything from their 'quality of life' to their propensity to 'acquiescence bias'. That is the psy-disciplines demonstrate, as part of their positivist, aggregationist, inheritance, what Smith and Mitchell (2001) describe as a propensity to typological thinking:

[T]he belief that complex individual variations can be reduced to underlying human types or essences . . . [D]efinitions of mental retardation, regardless of their particulars, are grounded in typological thought. The core of mental retardation as a field is the assumption that somehow there is a 'mental retardation essence' that eclipses all of the differences that characterize people described by the term. (Smith and Mitchell, 2001: 145–6)

The notion then that there is an 'essence' (or varieties of essences) to persons is visible across the psychological project. Classification of persons into 'types', 'sorts', or 'kinds' (personality types; Type As and Type Bs; the myriad 'types' of 'mental illness') is again one of the early borrowings from the natural sciences of the nascent psy-disciplines in the nineteenth century. In what again can be understood as a concerted effort at the acquisition of legitimacy by an aping of botany, for example, psy-professionals began a fractionating of the undifferentiated mass of lunatics, idiots and other indigents. So began a concerted effort to define 'selves' according to their (newly) interiorised essentials and defects (Boyle, 2002a; Simpson, 2000b; Rose, 1996). That is, a project began (and of which we are still a part) which, over the course of the nineteenth and twentieth centuries, transformed human beings from: 'the moral subject of habit, to that of the normal subject of character and constitution in the second half of the nineteenth century, to the social subject of solidarity and citizenship rights in the first half of the twentieth century, to the autonomous subject of choice and self-realization as the twentieth century drew to a close'(Rose, 1999b: xix).

It is here, in the recognition of 'selves' not as an essence, an immutable piece of personal property, but rather as essentially mutable and contingent discursive formations that the commonalities across Rose's Foucauldian work and the precepts of discursive psychology can be particularly clearly seen. Both share in a fundamental stance towards psychologised notions of 'the self' or 'the person' as a being with a list of interiorised attributes of various quanta (McHoul and Rapley, 2002). Rose (1999a: np) puts the position clearly when he states that:

The human being is not the eternal basis of human history and human culture but an historical and cultural artifact . . . [Under] our modern western conception of the person . . . the self is construed as a naturally unique and discrete entity, the boundaries of the body enclosing, as if by definition, an inner life of the psyche, in which are inscribed the experiences of an individual biography. But modern western societies are unusual in construing the self as such a natural locus of beliefs and desires, with inherent capacities, as the self-evident origin of actions and decisions, as a stable phenomenon exhibiting consistency across different contexts and times. (Rose, 1999a: np)

The discursive psychological project then is to examine the manner in which such selves, with their array of capacities, and supposedly interior psychological attributes, are produced. In this version of the discursive psychological project, analysis engages with the discursive production of such selves both historically and via the examination of the situated practices made possible through that history, and which in their enactment confirm or challenge, refine and reproduce, not the stable phenomenon of the psychological project, but rather these contingent, fluid, selves.

Rather than accept the contingency and fluidity of social phenomena, and 'psychological' phenomena as, essentially, *social*, Margie Wetherell (1999) points out that many, if not most, of the 'big' theoretical debates in psychology are not only *binary* but also resolutely *determinist* (nurture vs. nature; individual vs. social; 'mind' vs. 'reality'). So too are the characterisations of *persons* offered by the discipline (sane/mad; normal/defective; Type A/Type B). The difficulty that this either/or conceptualisation of the questions of the discipline engenders, especially when added to the modernist quest for unambiguous answers, preferably expressed as statistical 'laws' about 'stable phenomena', is that the discipline thus loses the ability to: 'focus on the unceasing human activity of making meanings (the horizon of discourse) from which social agents and objects, social institutions and social structures emerge configured in ever-changing patterns of relations' (Wetherell, 1999: 401).[10] And it is not only within psychology that the walls of the regime of truth built by psychology constrain the possibility of alternative ways of knowing. Thus, Young writes of the 'social model' of disability that:

While the social model of disability destabilises the assumption that the 'problem' with some people has to do with attributes of their bodies and functions, it nevertheless continues to presume a certain *fixity* to these bodies, and thereby understands many of the experiences and self-conceptions of persons positioned as disabled as grounded in such bodily facts. (Young, 2002: xiii, my emphasis)

If, however, a Foucauldian/post-structuralist focus is adopted, it then not only allows a 'way out of this constraining logic of the individual vs. the social' but also for 'investigation [to be] focussed instead on modes or practices of subjectification, the rituals and routines which produce human natures' (Wetherell, 1999: 402). And clearly, as Edwards and Potter (2002) also argue, following ethnomethodology, the most pervasive site for the production of 'human natures' is in interaction. What such studies can produce then 'is an account of the ways in which this modern "regime of the self" emerges, not as the outcome of any gradual process of enlightenment, in which humans aided by the endeavours of science, come at last to recognize their true nature, but out of a number of contingent and altogether less refined and dignified practices and processes' (Rose, 1996: 129). In short, discursive psychology might be said to be precisely the study of those practices and processes by which we produce our selves, as our 'selves'.

---

[10] Thus it is that beliefs about persons as stable phenomena that require them to show 'consistency across different contexts and times' become translated into such notions (and problematics) as test-retest reliability.

Self as category membership

Recent work in discursive psychology has suggested, following Sacks (1992), that 'selves' or 'identities' can be understood as *category memberships*; not as immutable properties of persons, but rather as achieved social statuses, entitlement to which requires both negotiation and maintenance (Edwards and Potter, 1992; Potter and Wetherell, 1987; Potter, 1996; Antaki, Condor and Levine, 1996). As Potter (1996: 137) points out 'category entitlement is not a fact of nature'. Similarly, Antaki, Condor and Levine (1996); Widdicombe and Wooffitt (1995); Rapley, Kiernan and Antaki (1998); and Rapley (1998) demonstrate that self-categorisations may be dynamic and fluid within the course of a single interaction, being locally crafted, or worked up, in an occasioned manner, to meet the moment-by-moment exigencies of conversational interaction, research interview or political performance. In other words entitlement to membership of social categories (such as 'recently qualified-but-cynical-medical student'; 'a Goth' or 'a punk'; 'just an ordinary Australian' – or even 'an intellectually disabled person') is not automatically to be assumed in conversation, but must be worked up, indeed worked at (Potter, 1996). Social identity – indeed self identity – is, thus, not a fixed attribute of pervasive relevance, as is suggested by the cognitivist psychological tradition, but rather a 'flexible resource' (Antaki, Condor and Levine, 1996) which may be deployed in talk to a speaker's argumentative, or rhetorical, advantage.[11]

That is to say, then, as Antaki and Widdicombe put it, talk of 'identity' under EM/CA informed discursive psychological analyses can be characterised as respecting five general principles:

- for a person to 'have an identity' – whether he or she is the person speaking, being spoken to, or being spoken about – is to be cast into a *category with associated characteristics or features*;
- such casting is *indexical and occasioned*;
- it *makes relevant* the identity to the interactional business going on;
- the force of 'having an identity' is in its *consequentiality* in the interaction; and
- all this is visible in people's exploitation of the *structures of conversation*.

(Antaki and Widdicombe, 1998a: 3, emphasis in the original)

This understanding of 'identity' *qua* 'category membership' offers an antidote to essentialist thinking about the varieties, types or classifications of persons that is propounded by mainstream psy understandings

[11] See Will Coleman (1990) and Derek Edwards (1998) on the *impossibility* of universal (supra-local) *categories*. Coleman advances the argument that it cannot be universally relevant that a particular person is categorizable as 'British' or as 'a man'. Edwards argues similarly with respect to the categories 'Irish', 'girl' and 'married woman'.

of being human. It dissolves the notion of the 'fixity' of both bodies and the various ghosts in the machine, and centres the production and management of identity (or rather its avowal and disavowal) not in the heads or bodies of speakers, but in 'interactional business', and it forces us to confront the fact that the 'supra-local relevance' (Coleman, 1990) of professionally ascribed identities like 'schizophrenic', 'manic depressive' or 'intellectually disabled person' is not an expression of some underlying law of the universe revealed by statistics or the experiment, but rather, as Rose (1999) puts it, a truth claim 'enthroned by violence'.

Instead of accepting these professionally ascribed identities as 'truth', the perspective adopted here suggests that if we wish to discover where and when, how and why, identities such as these are *relevant to persons themselves*, then we must look at the doing of interactional business, and be prepared to encounter both *collaborative* identity production and also struggles, in interaction, over the relevance – or otherwise – of the candidate identities that psy professionals proffer to their interlocutors.[12]

Discursive psychology: fundamental precepts

We can see then that in its rejection of mainstream psychological orthodoxy, the idea of the self as the individuated 'locus of beliefs and desires, with inherent capacities, as the self-evident origin of actions and decisions, as a stable phenomenon', discursive psychology represents a rather different conception of both being human, and the conduct of social life, to existing psychological approaches. Discursive psychology postulates a series of basic precepts which can be said to start from the premise of *non-separation* of 'the individual' and 'society' or 'culture'. Two observations made by Harvey Sacks (1992) are crucial to this understanding: firstly Sacks's insight that, if we are to understand a culture (and being in, and productive of 'the culture', our 'selves') it may be assumed that cultures show *order at all points*. Secondly, descriptions of persons and their actions may be 'correct' in an indefinite number of ways – such that 'correctness' *per se* cannot be the basis for the use of any given description on any specific occasion.

In his introduction to Sacks's lectures, Schegloff (1992) explicates the Sacksian position on the issue of 'order', and makes clear the startling

---

[12] The discursive psychological approach to identity can produce some very unsettling results. See Paoletti (1998) in the edited collection by Antaki and Widdicombe (1998b) for an analysis of the way in which 'being senile' – a medical fact, surely – is *co-produced* in interaction. See Widdicombe (1998) for an overview of the upshot of this perspective for mainstream psychology and sociology. For a more standard, linguistic, account of such activities see Hamilton (1996) on the co-construction of identity-as-Alzheimer's-patient.

contrast that this view of the nature of sociality offers to taken-for-
granted mainstream psychological assumptions about 'methods', where
the canonical position is, very clearly, that 'valid' results can be arrived
at *only* by properly sampling, aggregating and statistically interrogating a
multiplicity of instances of a cultural phenomenon:

> Sacks points out that [sampling] depends on the sort of order one takes it that the
> social world exhibits. An alternative to the possibility that order manifests itself at
> an aggregate level and is statistical in character is what he terms the 'order at all
> points' view. This view . . . understands order not to be present only at aggregate
> levels and therefore subject to an overall differential distribution, but to be present
> in detail on a case by case, environment by environment basis. A culture is not
> then to be found only by aggregating all of its venues; it is substantially present
> in each of its venues. (Schegloff in Sacks, 1992: xlvi)

The importance of this is that so-called 'positivistic' methods in
psychology – based as they are upon a borrowing of the aggregationist model of the natural sciences – must *always* miss the essential cultural
(and therefore non-aggregationable) grounds of human action.[13] That
is cultural-moral phenomena are visible, in regular ways, if a sufficiently
careful inspection is conducted – and regardless of sampling, distribution, aggregation, statistical manipulation and so on. In short: a close
enough look at 'molecular' instances of a moral–cultural universe will
reveal important properties of its whole.

The second foundational observation that Sacks makes, again in contrast to the 'correspondence theory' of categorisation adopted by psychology, is in pointing out that there can be indefinitely many 'correct
identifications' of persons and their conduct in the world. The 'correctness' of any given identification is, of course, crucial to the technical
procedures and classificatory efforts of the psy-disciplines: as Mehan and
Wood (1975) and Coulter (1979) among others have shown us it is,
often, by failing to provide identifications that are 'correct' in the lights
of psychology that persons can come to be describable as 'mad', requiring 'remedial education' or 'intellectually disabled'. For Sacks and discursive psychology though, the 'correctness' of any given identification
is not the point. The critical point is that particularly selected correct

---

[13] In the *Philosophical Investigations*, Ludwig Wittgenstein (1958: 232) remarks of psychology that: 'the confusion and barrenness of psychology is not to be explained by calling
it a "young science"; its state is not comparable with that of physics, for instance, in
its beginnings. (Rather with that of certain branches of mathematics. Set Theory.) For
in psychology there are experimental methods and *conceptual confusion*. (As in the other
case conceptual confusion and methods of proof.) The existence of the experimental
method makes us think we have the means of solving the problems which trouble us;
though problem and method pass one another by.'

identifications can do, among many other things, explanatory, rhetorical and – essentially – moral work. Sacks suggests that:

We can start out by noticing that the problem of selecting identifications is by no means a simple one. It is *in principle* never the case that persons are simply faced with applying a correct identification. And the procedures whereby they then go about selecting identifications in systematic ways, are a major problem for us. Now one whole range of ways that identifications get picked turns on category-bound activities. (Sacks 1992: 588, my emphasis)

By 'category-bound activities', Sacks means kinds of actions routinely associated with particular categories of persons; and such that if the category is known, then the activity can be inferred – and vice versa. Of course 'activities' here must be widely understood: the category-bound predicates of any category may be broad. Thus it is routinely to be expected that the predicates of 'teenage boy' may include 'activities' such as (what parents may view as obsessive) grooming, playing the stereo (too) loud and associating with unsuitable friends. It is *also* the case that predicates may routinely include other characteristics that are less immediately thought of as 'activities': thus it would not be unreasonable to suggest that predicates of the category 'teenage boy' may also include ways-of-being-in-the-world like surliness, self-absorption and social clumsiness. Likewise, to employ Antaki and Widdicombe's (1998a) example, if a group of persons is collected together under the category 'cabin crew' one might reasonably expect category-bound predicates such as politeness, being well-travelled and having extensive knowledge about aircraft safety. But, and crucially,

If you cast *the very same people* [into the category] 'white collar union members', you dissolve any such job-specific implications and *replace* them with what is conventionally knowable about people who have joined a staff association; if you cast them as 'British', you allow them to pass through British immigration checks, without caring about whether they are in a union or not, and so on . . . If you look and act a certain way, you might get taken to be a flight attendant . . . (Antaki and Widdicombe, 1998a, emphasis added)

Sacks's point is that if some action is known to have occurred (a shopping centre was bombed; an immigration check was passed) then, if there is a category of person for whom that action is 'category-bound', it can be a *routine assumption* that that category of person ('terrorists', 'British citizens') was responsible for the action. Then, if such an actor was in fact responsible, that categorisation ('It was a terrorist group', 'she was British') can be used as an *explanation* of the event:

In the first instance, a way that you go about selecting an identificatory category – given, say, that some action is going on, done by some person – is to determine if there is a category-bound activity of that sort, and if that person is a member of that category, then use that category to identify them. Now these kinds of things are not just 'correct descriptions', they're correct descriptions in quite powerful ways . . . Whereas lots of category-and-activity combinations will pose problems like 'Why in the world did that happen?', 'Gee, isn't that unusual', in the specific cases where you've got a category-bound activity and the category for that is applied to some scene, why the thing happened is not a question. *That it happened is explained by the very characterization.* (Sacks, 1992: 588–89, my emphasis)

As Sacks (1992) notes it is this widely shared knowledge of Membership Categorisation Devices (MCDs) and their predicates that permits the use of category memberships and their predicates for 'subversion' ('If you look and act a certain way, you might get taken to be a flight attendant' – it is not necessary to *be* a flight attendant, as such) and which, to anticipate a later argument, seems to concern so much of the sociological and psychological literatures on the 'identity' of people described by psy-professionals as 'intellectually disabled' – that they are, subversively and disreputably, 'putting on a flight attendant's uniform' that they have no 'right' to, that they are trying to get taken to be 'normal'. But subversion, and category work more generally, need not be so unsubtle. Edwards (1997) illustrates the finely powerful accountability work that seemingly simple and innocuous identifications, or characterisations, can do, via their making relevant of the *category of person* that is, normatively, to be associated with a particular characteristic. He reproduces a fragment from a couple counselling session where a contentious evening in the local pub was the focus of the session.

Extract 1: From Edwards, 1997: 158

```
1    JIMMY   Connie had a short skirt on I don't know. (1.)
2            And I knew this- (0.6) uh ah- maybe I had met him.
3            (1.) Ye:h (.) I musta met Da:ve before. (0.8)
4            But I'd heard he was a bit of a la:d ( ).
5            He didn't care (1.0) who he chatted up
6            (. . .)
7            So Connie stood up (0.8) pulled her skirt right
8            up her side (0.6) and she was looking straight
9            at Dave (.) >°like that°< (0.6) and then turned
10           and looked at me (1.2) and then she said w- (.)
11           turned and then (.) back to Dave and said (.)
12           by the way that wasn't for you.
```
                            (DE–JF: C2:S1:10)

While it may appear that here the characterisation of Dave (notably via psychologised, typological, attributes – he is 'a bit of a lad') is a major matter in hand ('I'd heard he was a bit of a la:d ( ) He didn't care (1.0) who he chatted up'), Edwards points out that it is also the case that Jimmy's identification of a characteristic not of an *actor*, but rather a predicate of that actor, the shortness of a skirt, which does as much work here in producing Connie (Jimmy's wife) as accountably flirtatious, and *her* character as well as Dave's as disreputable. Edwards also notes that the 'I don't know' in Jimmy's first utterance, making relevant the character-inferential properties of mini skirts, also attends to establishing a version of his character – in this case as other than an obsessive and jealous husband. Discursive psychology thus follows Sacks's lead in assuming that, in the examination of fragments of a culture (from couple counselling sessions to newspaper articles, from interviews between psychologists and 'people with an intellectual disability' to academic articles; and from policy documents to political speeches), what operates across a culture as a whole will come clearly into view. It is also the case that an analysis of such 'holographic' fragments reveals much more than mere 'names' and 'events' – as is assumed by conventional cognitivist psychology. If Sacks is right, we will also find logically implied explanations, evaluations, and rhetorical positionings (Billig, 1991; 1996) in the obvious-but-unstated connections between 'identifications' (ways of referring to persons) and 'activities' (ways of referring to what they do or did). As Edwards (1997: 259) puts it: 'categories are not just available sense-making devices that get triggered by events; that kind of theory grossly underspecifies situated talk'. And *all* talk is situated: in the case of talk-in-interaction it is readily apparent that talk is situated, occasioned, and rhetorically organised (though the prevailing view in social psychology and sociology would appear to have some difficulty with recognising this), but it also the case that, with talk understood as discourse in Rose's sense, this 'talk' *too* is situated in the sense both that it is attentive to its rhetorical function (Billig, 1991) and also that it is situated within a regime of truth: to the sustenance and reproduction of which it is an essential part.

In brief, then, discursive psychology focuses analytic attention on three features of discourse. Firstly discourse is understood as *situated*, both in being occasioned, or attentive both to its immediate sequential position and its more distal setting events (cf. Leudar and Nekvapil's (2000) concept of dialogically distributed conversation). That is, as Edwards and Potter (2002: 13) suggest: 'talk and texts are embedded in sequences of interaction, and in various kinds of mundane and institutional activity. This is not a mechanical contextual determinism; talk is *oriented* to, but not *determined by*, its sequential position and settings.' Talk and texts are situationally organised, secondly, in that they are 'pervasively rhetorical' (Edwards and Potter, 2002; Billig, 1999b; 1991), being attentive to the production of accounts which attend to potential alternative versions, to disqualification via the imputation of stake or interest, and to their own defeasibility. Such situated discourse, as Billig argues strongly, is thus constructed in order to counter potential counter-arguments.

Secondly discourse is understood as *active*, or 'action-oriented'. Discursive psychology flatly rejects the prevailing 'telementational' model (Taylor and Cameron, 1987) of talk in mainstream psychology and respecifies talk *as* action. That is to say, talk and texts *do things*, they enact and accomplish practices in the world: talk does not, in some uncomplicated manner, hold up a mirror either to the world or to the supposedly 'interior' contents of persons' heads. What this means is that a fundamental principle of discursive psychology is that: 'activity is treated as primary, and reality and cognition are secondary . . . in ethnomethodological terms mind and reality, and their interplay, are DP's topic rather than resource' (Edwards and Potter, 2002: 15). The upshot of this position is, of course, that the mentalistic vocabulary that we employ in talk about our 'own' or others' 'beliefs', 'emotions', 'thoughts', 'attitudes', 'intelligence' and the rest becomes an analytic topic in its own right, rather than being viewed as either a messily approximate 'folk psychology' *or* as a professionally established inventory of cognitive entities or processes. Instead claims – in talk or texts – to the possession of such things, their imputation to others, or their 'measurement', come to be seen as *part of* discourse practices, employed and deployed in the prosecution of such practices. Thus it is that 'attitudes' can be respecified as 'evaluations' and their local production in and through social psychological research methods can be studied (Puchta and Potter, 1999; 2002; Houtkoop-Steenstra, 2000; Wetherell and Potter, 1992); 'not knowing' can be viewed as a technique for interactional management, of accountability perhaps, rather than a specification or reflection of the contents of one's long-term memory (Lynch and Bogen, 1996; 1997; Beach and Metzger, 1997; Edwards and Potter, 1992) and 'anger', 'jealousy' and 'unhappiness' may be respecified as resources available for use in constructing sequences of apportioning blame, holding to account or excusing forms of conduct in the world, rather then being understood as interiorised mental processes (Edwards, 1997; 1999).

Thirdly discourse is *constructed*. Discursive psychology views discourse as both socially construc*ted* (it is assembled, on-the-spot, pervasively in social interaction) and socially construc*tive* (in that discourse – be it talk or text – constructs *versions* of events, actors and their attributes, in order to accomplish social actions). Discursive psychology then asks: 'how [do] people categorise and formulate the world, establishing certain particulars as relevant, characterising its moral flavour, and it asks how people at the same time formulate a relevant "inner" world of beliefs, values, emotions and dispositions, that make their actions accountable' (Edwards and Potter, 2002:15). Clearly, for present purposes, it is precisely the issue of *how* the psy professions construct 'certain particulars' of 'intelligence' or 'competence' as relevant, and the manner in which 'dispositions' are cemented as belonging to an 'inner world' of persons, that is central to understanding the social construction of intellectual disability.

If this approach to matters of identity, to issues of capacity, competence and categorisation, to the question of what it is that discourse accomplishes is adopted, then we will proceed rather differently to the manner customary in social scientific work. While he discusses the use of a particular conversational object (a 'counterfactual') Charles Antaki's account may as readily be read as referring to the analysis of the use of *any* utterance:

> We get up out of the armchair to try and find out what the counterfactual is doing here, in its actual usage; what features it has, what functions it fulfils, what it is made of. We leave off the sort of speculation that makes us invent elaborate lab conditions that imperfectly simulate something which may not ever happen anyway. It's an analysis that assumes as little as possible, and tries to make its claims sensible by grounding them in what actually happened, somewhere, at some time, to some real people who were involved in something they seemed to care about and which would have had material consequences. Maybe from there we could work back to the 'cause' of the explainer's use of counterfactual, maybe not; but we would at least have something solid in our hands (or as solid as social scientists are liable to get). (Antaki, 2000: 329)

That is, in conjunction with Sacks's reconceptualisation of the notion of order – as being visible at all points – we will examine the way in which discourse (in talk and texts) is used, in practical ways, to accomplish things-in-the-world, where they matter to 'some real people who were involved in something they seemed to care about and which would have had material consequences'.

The scope of the project

The project of discursive psychology is then to afford a respecification of the ways in which such matters as mind and mentality are brought off in interaction, the analysis of the work that such activities do, and the methods by which members produce an orderly social world. This does not, as Potter and Edwards take pains to point out (cf. Coulter, 1999) commit the project to an ontological constructionism, which sees 'mind' and its various putative (in)capacities as 'real', and in some fashion 'made' in and through talk.[14] The important point that discursive psychology makes is that, like 'discourses', such 'things' may most profitably be understood not as *a priori* social scientific objects, but as resources which are available to members, as repertoires for the production of locally relevant meanings – and, particularly, for the avowal and ascription of moral character. A concise summary statement of the project is offered by Edwards and Potter:

> The focus of discursive psychology is the action orientation of talk and writing. For both participants and analysts, the primary issue is the social actions, or interactional work, being done in the discourse. [T]he major concern . . . is epistemological. It is with the nature of knowledge, cognition and reality: with how events are described and explained, how factual reports are constructed, how cognitive states are attributed . . . And rather than seeing such discursive constructions as expressions of speakers' underlying cognitive states, they are examined in the context of their occurrence as situated and occasioned constructions whose precise nature makes sense, to participants and analysts alike, in terms of the social actions those descriptions accomplish. (Edwards and Potter, 1992: 2)

The critical historical analysis of psychology-as-discipline, and its means of production are central, in my view, to that project. This is to say that an appreciation of the recency of the coinage of what are now sedimented 'identities' assists in the project of destabilising them; and an appreciation of the historical contingency of the success of psychology in setting bounds for itself reinforces the demand that psychology cannot be allowed to delimit itself; to delegitimate those who would question its pretensions on the grounds that they do not use its methods; nor to claim some master truth status. As Antaki (2000); Edwards (1997); and Potter (1996) have argued, it is no longer possible for the discipline to sustain an archaic conception of itself, or of science more broadly, as insulated from its social, historical and intellectual circumstances.

> Psychology . . . cannot be regarded as a given domain, separate from something called 'society' – the processes by which its truths are produced are constitutively 'social'. And, further, the object of psychology cannot be regarded as something given, independent, that pre-exists knowledge and which is merely 'discovered'. Psychology constitutes its object in the process of knowing it. In this sense . . . the 'subject' of psychology is 'socially constructed' both in the sense of the construction of the discipline and in the sense of the construction of its thought object – the human subject. (Rose, 1999a: np)

---

[14] In an unpublished manuscript Edwards and Potter (nd) clearly note that: 'we do not take our *study of* the practice of describing, avowing, or attributing mental entities as committing us to *the endorsement* (or, in itself, of the denial) of such things'. I am grateful to Derek Edwards and Jonathan Potter for this paper.

In his analysis of the participation of 'Alvin', described as a commisuro-tomised man with 'challenged and suspect linguistic capacities', in a for-mal language assessment, Schegloff argues that in order fully to under-stand the effects of commisurotomy:

We need empirically grounded accounts of what such persons *can* do – *do* do – in circumstances embodying ordinary contingencies of interaction, and not just how they perform in testing situations which, far from neutralizing interactional contexts, themselves can constitute distinctive speech-exchange systems which confront participants with quite distinctive, and potentially complicating, inter-actional exigencies. (Schegloff, 1999: 419)

Equally, if we are to fully understand just what it is that people described as 'intellectually disabled' can do or be, it is also essential that we exam-ine 'what such persons . . . *do* do' – rather than continuing to rely upon experimental or other artificial encounters and the statistical manipula-tion of arbitrarily selected 'variables' in the name of 'science'. And yet this is, despite nearly thirty years of work since the so-called 'crisis' in social psychology, the way in which the discipline still conceives of itself. As Antaki (2000: 328) puts it '[T]hey take it implicitly that paper condi-tions in one place and time translate adequately to non-paper conditions in all other places and times because it triggers this taken for granted universal thing inside us, part of the human condition.' As will become clear in the rest of this book much, if not most, of what is taken-for-granted as everyday technical knowledge of 'intellectual disability' in the professional literatures is precisely a product of the modes and means of production of that 'knowledge', or 'regime of truth', and nothing more.

If, for example, it is insisted that *only* the use of standardised question-naires with fixed-format responses can allow us to enquire into people's happiness, then it is inevitable that the fault-finding imperative in psy-chology will produce 'messy' results as a diagnostic indicator of the inade-quacy of the individual respondent (cf. Goode, 1983). If one's capacity to act successfully in the world is arbitrarily defined as reflected by, among other things, one's capacity to respond correctly to questions like 'Who wrote Hamlet' (cf. Wechsler, 1981) then (despite widely known profes-sional failure to even agree a consensual definition of 'intelligence', to develop a coherent statement of what IQ tests actually 'measure', and to account for the observed anomalies in the population distribution of scores: cf. AAMR, 2002; Richardson, 2002) it is unsurprising that pro-fessional accounts of persons' competence shaped by these truth regimes can have little other than negative or pessimistic things to say about the capacities of persons.[15] If one's 'reliability' as a reporter on one's own life is to be determined by the asking of bizarre, unoccasioned, questions in artificial encounters with professionals, then it is perhaps not surprising that the disqualification of people with intellectual disabilities as human agents is so readily accomplished. That is, as Rose (1999a: np) has it:

Contemporary scientific reality – and this goes for a science like psychology as much as any other – is the outcome of the categories we use to think it, the techniques and procedures we use to evidence it, the statistical tools and modes of proof we use to justify it. But this does not amount to a de-legitimation of its scientific pretensions. It is merely the basis from which we become able to pose questions concerning the means of construction of these new domains of objectivity and their consequences.

The task of the analyst then, is not 'spotting', nor the provision of a tally of 'discourses' identified (cf. Antaki *et al.* 2003), but rather the explication of the way in which social life – what is to count as 'true', what is to be allowable as 'rational' or 'competent', what may be understood as (and to be) an aspect of the (defective) mental states and capacities of oneself and others – is produced, in and for the moment, by and through the use of language, the local crafting of discursive repertoires and the flexible (and sometimes resistive) deployment of rhetorical devices. What such an approach promises is 'a respect and a sensitivity to what people are saying, and what they are doing, in their own terms and in their own lives' (Antaki, 2000: 330).

The remainder of this book attempts to do just that.

---

[15] It seems that this problem (often described as 'ecological validity') is not restricted to assessment of people with intellectual disabilities. In a study of the assessment of linguistic competence of second language speakers, Jacoby and McNamara (1999) note that the relationship between formal assessment scores of overseas doctors on the widely used Australian instrument, the Occupational English Test (McNamara, 1990) and the perceptions of their linguistic competence by co-workers in employment settings were 'mismatched'. They note that: 'whatever the doctors were complaining about was *not* being captured by the OET' (1999: 223), despite the fact that, like the measures which we will encounter later, the OET has acceptable levels of (psychometric) reliability and 'validity'.

2 Intellectual disability as diagnostic and social category

> [U]nder the best conditions only a very small proportion even of the higher grade cases become desirable members of the community. They need protection and care and the family and community should be protected from their certain tendency to drift into pauperism, prostitution and crime.
>
> (Fernald, 1903: np)

> [T]he definition of a person is to be found in the relationship between the definer and the defined, not determined either by personal characteristics or the abstract meanings attached to the group of which the person is a part.
>
> (Bogdan and Taylor, 1989: 136)

Preamble

It is not my intention here to provide a full-scale history of intellectual disability as a psychological concept. There are several such histories which offer either excellent overviews or detailed analyses of specific periods and places: it would serve little purpose to attempt to reproduce that work here.[1] However, as I argued in chapter 1, it is important that the analyses which follow are grounded in an appreciation of not only the recency of the concept of intellectual disability as an attribute of persons, but also of the inextricable linkage between the ascription of the category and explicit, and more recently, implicit evaluations of moral conduct. Accordingly this chapter provides a thumbnail sketch of the provenance of 'intellectual disability' as a diagnostic and social category, and attempts

---

[1] Wright and Digby (1996) provide a collection of essays on the history of intellectual disability in the UK. See Simpson's (2000a) Bibliography of the History of Idiocy (www.personal.dundee.ac.uk/~mksimpso/histories.htm) and Taylor and Harris's (1997) Selected annotated bibliography: disability studies and mental retardation for useful guides to this literature. Ryan and Thomas (1998, chapter 5) offers an excellent and highly accessible condensed history. The websites 'Classics in the History of Psychology' (http://psychclassics.yorku.ca/index.htm) and 'The Disability Museum' (www.disabilitymuseum.org) contain reproductions of many specific historical texts.

to begin a reconceptualisation of 'intellectual disability' via a critical analysis of current professional texts and their assumptions; a consideration of the 'social model of disability' (Oliver, 1990); and an overview of problems with totalising understandings of 'competence' as an attribute of persons.[2] The chapter concludes with a consideration of some data that place into an interactional context the way in which 'competence' may be accomplished.

'Intellectual disability' as a diagnostic category

It has come to be the case that intellectual disability is understood as an historically continuous, clinico-medical, thing-in-the world that can be 'diagnosed' or even differentially diagnosed, by 'type'. Thus Edgerton, Lloyd and Cole (1979: 4) write that: 'it is practicable to refer to two basic types: clinical and sociocultural . . . Clinical retardation can usually be shown to have concomitant organic deficits of a neurological, metabolic, or physiological sort . . . In Sociocultural retardation . . . such children are most likely to have been born to parents who are economically, socially, and educationally disadvantaged.' Likewise, according to Barlow (1978: 1–2):

Mental retardation is a symptom complex, the chief features of which consist of (1) intellectual subnormality associated with (2) maladaptive behavior. The term implies onset during childhood or before. The symptomatic diagnosis is based on analysis of behavior, and the cardinal features of the symptom complex vary quantitatively in different individuals. There is general agreement with these rather obvious statements . . . I should like to exclude a numerically large group of individuals from the current discussion. Here I refer to the people who test in the borderline (IQ 70 to 84) or upper range of mild retardation (IQ 55 to 69), but who should *probably* be regarded as biologically normal. In general, such individuals are reasonably well adapted, and the behavioral aspect of the definition of mental retardation does not apply. (my emphasis)

This conception of intellectual disability, Heber (1961: 3) suggests, 'incorporates all of the meanings that have been ascribed historically to such concepts as amantia, feeblemindedness, mental deficiency, mental subnormality, idiocy, imbecility and minority, etc.' Indeed the definition provided by Heber ('mental retardation refers to subaverage intellectual functioning which originates during the developmental period and is associated with impairment in adaptive behavior' (1961: 3)) is essentially

---

[2] See the edited collections by Kovarsky, Duchan and Maxwell (1999); Langness and Levine (1986); and Jenkins (1999) for further contributions to a relational understanding of competence.

identical. Edgerton, Lloyd and Cole concur on the historicity of the condition, noting that:

> *In the past* an idiot *was* someone with an IQ of less than 30, an imbecile *had* an IQ of 30 to 50, and a moron an IQ of 50 to 70. These terms have been replaced throughout much of the English-speaking world by the AAMD system in which there are these categories: mild retardation (IQ 55–69), moderate retardation (IQ 40–54), severe retardation (IQ 25–39), and profound retardation (IQ less than 25). (Edgerton, Lloyd and Cole, 1979: 3, my emphasis)

Historic continuity is cemented here not only by the assertion that new terms have, with wide support, simply replaced old ones, but by the use of the past tense: '*in the past* an idiot *was* someone with an IQ of less than 30 an imbecile *had* an IQ of 30 to 50'. Such a grammatical construction obscures the fact that 'idiots' and 'imbeciles' were widely spoken of centuries before the invention of IQ tests and, hence, it can only be said with accuracy that 'since 1905 it has become customary for people who score below 30 on an IQ test to be referred to as "idiots" and for people who are scored in the range 30–50 to be described as "imbeciles"'. As Jenkins notes:

> The statistical plotting of a normal curve of distribution for measured intelligence has probably been the single most influential factor in the definition and creation of a category of persons known as the 'mildly mentally retarded'. Before the advent of the bell-shaped curve, the category simply did not exist. (Jenkins, 1999: 17)

As such a brief foray into etymology can be of value. It is evident (and, in the case of 'idiot', amusingly ironic) that the terms which practitioners have wished to invest with professional skill are, in mundane English, usages that have entered the language from the Middle Ages on. *Contra* the claim of the AAMR that 'idiocy' and 'imbecility' are terms 'coined in 1877 to describe different levels of intellectual functioning based on decreasing language and speech abilities' (AAMR, 2002: 25), the term 'idiot' has, in English, from the early fourteenth century connoted a lack of education, but certainly does not constitute a historically continuous term of identification for the persons described today as 'intellectually disabled'.[3] Indeed, historically, given the elite nature of education and learning, 'ordinary person' or 'layman' is sufficiently non-specific as to suggest a broad *generality* of persons. It also seems to be the case, *contra* many suggestions in the literature about the *necessarily* devastating

---

[3] The earliest usage recorded in the OED (1989: 625) dates from 1300: Cursor M. 10456 (Cott) you sais to me als til a sott, Haldes you me for an idiot [Gott. a fole]? Possibly the first usage that bears a resemblance to contemporay usages is in Swinburne's (1590: ii, 39) *Testaments*: 'An Idiote, or a naturall foole is he, who notwithstanding he bee of lawfull age, yet he is so witlesse, that hee can not number to twentie, nor can tell what age he is of, nor knoweth who is his father, or mother, nor is able to answer any such easie question.'

stigmatic or toxic nature of the appellation, that while since at least the fourteenth century a 'term of reprobation', usages such as 'idiot box' call this notion into question.

idiot [a. F. *idiot* (13th c. in Hatz.–Darm.) = It., Sp., Pg. *idiota*, ad L. *idiota* uneducated, ignorant person, ad. Gr.

ιδιωτης – private person, common man, plebeian, one without professional knowledge, 'layman'; and so, ignorant, ill-informed person, f. ιδιος – private . . . peculiar.

1.a. A person without learning; an ignorant, uneducated man; a simple man; a clown.

1.b. A layman.

1.c. One not professionally learned or skilled; also, a private (as opposed to a public) man.

2.a. A person so deficient in mental or intellectual faculty as to be incapable of ordinary acts of reasoning or rational conduct. Applied to one permanently so afflicted, as distinguished from one who is temporarily insane, or 'out of his wits', and who either has lucid intervals, or may be expected to recover his reason.

2.b. A term of reprobation for one who speaks or acts in what the speaker considers to be an irrational way, or with extreme stupidity or folly; a blockhead, an utter fool.

2.c. A man of weak intellect maintained to afford amusement to others; a household or court fool; a professional fool or jester.

[. . .]

4. *Comb.*, as idiot-born . . . idiot asylum, a term formerly used for a hospital for the mentally ill; . . . idiot box *colloq.*, a television set.

Likewise, for 'imbecile' or imbecility'. Here again we do not, as we are assured by Edgerton *et al.* (1979), have a long history of our diagnostic terms, used by uneducated (possibly idiotic?) laypersons until superseded by more up-to-date diagnostics.[4] Rather the first usages of 'imbecile' are *adjectival* rather than *nominal*, and specify clearly that imbecility is a generic term indexing anyone's incapacity or incompetence with respect to specific actions – which usage is first recorded in 1767.

imbecility –[a. F. *imbécillité* (14th c. in Littre). ad. L. *imbecillitatem*, n. of quality f.*imbecillus*, *-is* IMBECILE . . . The condition or quality of being imbecile.

1. Weakness, feebleness, debility, impotence.

1.b. Incompetency or incapacity (*to do* something).

1.c. with *an* and *pl.* An instance of weakness, infirmity or debility.

2. Mental or intellectual weakness, esp. as characterizing action; hence, silliness, absurdity, folly; a specimen or example of this.

---

[4] The OED (1989: 672) notes that 'the history of this word can scarcely be disentangled from that of EMBEZZLE *v.* The latter (in 15–16th c. *embesil* (*l, imbesill*)) was evidently thought to be derived from the L. *imbecill-us*, *-is*, or F. imbécille, weak; thence arose a series of spellings and senses connecting it with this supposed derivation, the ultimate result of both being imbecile (l in the sense to impair, weaken)'.

Indeed, the OED suggests that far from being the historic form, the modern usage of imbecile is 'a nonce-use from the adj., having no historical relation to the 16–17th c. word' (1989: 672). The first recognisable use of the nonce form is dated to 1862 where it appears, not in some specialist medical text, but rather in *The Times*. The nonce use did not, as the AAMR suggest, then simply supplant idiotic (lay) usages, but continued to be accompanied by them for a considerable period: thus Inglis's *Tent Life in Tigerland* contains the wonderful dismissal of 'the sneers and stupid imbecilities of the untravelled . . . sceptic' (1888: 4). It would, thus, appear that it is not merely the 'mildly mentally retarded' who had no discursive existence as such prior to the advent of the 'bell-shaped curve'. It is important in this context also to recognise that, despite a thriving discussion in secondary sources about mediæval recognition of 'idiots' as 'changelings', that in their analysis of the 'changeling myth', Goodey and Stainton find: 'it is false to think that the essentially modern distinction between physical and mental disability has always been made, and therefore that some positive entity known as "intellectual disability" might have been isolated as a topic of discussion in the pre-modern era and attached to these children' (2001: 225). Equally it would seem to be over-egging the pudding to suggest that what are now archaic professional terms (themselves, as we have seen, borrowings from everyday English, via Middle French and Latin) always have been, in some lay or pre-professional sense, diagnostic categories of 'intellectually disabled' people (as for example does Wickham (2001: 141) who writes of 'idiocy, the historical antecedent of mental retardation' in Puritan New England) (cf. McHoul and Rapley, 2002). Indeed, as Wickham later notes, in the pre-Modern era it is: 'likely that idiocy in the Puritan New England colonies was interpreted in a *variety* of ways. For practical purposes colonists defined idiocy in terms of incompetence' but idiocy also had 'scientific and medical dimensions . . . Furthermore, idiocy carried a *metaphoric* message, with *moral* and spiritual implications' (Wickham, 2001: 150, my emphases).

But, as we can see, not only can careful historical accounts easily slip into what may be taken for apparent historicist fallacy, but also that less careful descriptions of the 'condition' may actively confect an historic continuity of the proposed *identity* between IQ test scores and the category of personhood ascribed on their basis. Thus for Edgerton, Lloyd and Cole (1979) idiots and imbeciles are defined, as such, by their scores as *things* that they 'were', like being tall, or 'had' like arms and legs. This account also obscures the formerly widespread practices of ascribing 'imbecility' *solely* on the grounds of unwanted moral (frequently sexual) conduct *whether or not* the persons so diagnosed displayed any difficulties with everyday living or showed any signs of being 'mentally deficient' in the sense of poor IQ test performance (cf. Walmsley, 2000).

A little later, again we are offered an account that stresses the historical continuity in understandings of the condition. All that has changed, it would appear, are the terms used to describe it. Thus Zigler, Balla and Hodapp (1984: 223) provide a table titled 'Past and present terms to describe retarded persons'. Under the heading 'Organic' are listed Organically involved; Organismically impaired; Moderate, severe and profound; Endogenous Imbecile; Idiot; Trainable and subtrainable. Listed under 'Familial' we find Cultural-familial retarded due to psychosocial disadvantage; Nonorganically involved; Lower portion of the polygenic curve of intelligence; Mild, Exogenous; Garden variety; Feeble minded; Moron; Educable. Similarly, in his 1977 discussion of the then newly minted AAMR terminology, Grossman suggested that:

Mild retardation is roughly equivalent to the educational term 'educable;' moderate retardation includes those individuals who are likely to fall into the educational category of 'trainable;' the severe group includes individuals sometimes known as 'dependent retarded;' individuals in the profound retardation level are among those sometimes called 'life support' level. (1977: 19)[5]

Like the definitional efforts of Edgerton et al. (1979) and Zigler et al. (1984) above, what this serves to do, rhetorically, is to appeal to the solidity and inevitability of this knowledge – phrases such as 'individuals who are likely to fall into the educational category of "trainable"' of course produces the category 'moderate retardation' as a straightforward thing-in-the-world, like a hole, into which some individuals will, naturally, 'fall'. Simultaneously, in these definitions, progress, newness and modernity are appealed to as a warrant for today's way of talking about intellectual disability – why else would archaic terms 'have been replaced throughout much of the English-speaking world' (Edgerton et al. 1979) were it not for their greater suitedness to the present? – and to sweep into a *new* and simplified classificatory scheme, the huge heterogeneity of previously diagnostic terms which are held, at the same time, to have always already been referents for the same group of people.[6]

It appears then that this literature (of which the above is a brief, but representative, sample) can be seen to concur on a number of matters, namely that what is termed intellectual disability or mental retardation

---

[5] See AAMR (2002), Mercer (1994) and Dybwad (1996) for historical accounts of the changing nomenclatures of the AAMR.

[6] Gelb (2002) points out that, etymologically, 'mental retardation' is, to all intents and purposes, merely a translation of 'feeble minded' or 'psycho asthenic', terms current as descriptors of the 'group' at the turn of the twentieth century. 'Imbecile' is, itself, as we have seen merely a nonce borrowing of to weaken or to impair.

today is the same thing as was, previously, described as say, 'imbecility', 'garden variety' or 'subtrainable'; that intellectual disability is a thing which is both biological and non-biological, a 'symptom complex' that may be 'diagnosed'; that it entails a varying degree of proficiency in the management of everyday life and, equally, a varying degree of demonstrated proficiency at tests of 'intelligence'. Authorities vary in their emphasis on matters of 'intelligence' and the apparently interchangeable social 'competence', 'adaptive behaviour' or 'social function'. Thus Jensen (1998: 336), quoting Spitz, suggests that:

Mental retardation is, rather, a thinking disability, and intelligence is synonymous with thinking. Although it is possible to educate mentally retarded persons and to train them to perform many tasks, up to a point, we do not yet have the means of raising their general level of intelligence. We have no prescription that will change their capacity to think and to reason at the level of persons of average intelligence, to solve novel problems and real-life challenges of some complexity, and to respond effectively to an infinite variety of circumstances, but just to those used in training.

Jensen, it would seem, regards intellectual disability as essentially a cognitive matter, it is a 'thinking disability'. Whilst brute performance may be trainable, 'reason' is unsusceptible to professional 'prescription'. Alternatively, Sattler (1992) lays more emphasis on social performance and specifically suggests that the term 'mental retardation' is one which does not point to a single unambiguous condition, but rather that it encompasses heterogeneity.

The term mental retardation describes a heterogeneous group of conditions characterized by low or very low intelligence and deficits in adaptive behavior . . . Adaptive behavior refers to the effectiveness with which individuals meet the standards of personal independence and social responsibility expected of individuals of their age and cultural group . . . During late adolescence and adult life, adaptive behavior centers on vocational and social responsibilities and performances.

In much the same way then that 'madness' can be 'the absence of work' (Foucault, 1965), it appears that people who will not, or can not, meet societal expectations about self-sufficiency, employment and normative expectations about the discharge of social responsibilities – of proper conduct – can, potentially, be diagnosable as intellectually disabled. Such criteria do indeed have an historical continuity – for example, as we shall see, with those offered by early authorities such as Howe (1848); Seguin (1846); and Binet (1905) – but arguably it is not so much that this continuity represents an ever closer scientific approximation to the 'truth' of intellectual disability, as changes in professional nomenclature, the elaboration and refinement of diagnostic criteria, or the identification of gene sequences may suggest, but that 'definitions of intellectual disability' in the present share with those of the mid-nineteenth and early twentieth century a continuity of the deprecation of certain forms of moral conduct that is, in the present, pronounced in a different language, and in what may appear (at least to twenty-first century sensibilities) a kinder form (Trent, 1994).

Indeed the response of some authorities to work questioning of the 'real' existence of persons described as 'mildly' intellectually disabled (the inheritors of the former category 'feeble-mindedness') suggests such a continuity. Jacobson (2001), for example, provides a scathing attack on what is termed 'environmental postmodernism' in which it is suggested that constructionist 'ideological slogans' have led to the misuse of 'objective' tests of adaptive functioning, particularly by gullible teachers. In a paper which presupposes the real existence of something called 'mild mental retardation', that Jacobson (2001) seeks to restore to its proper place in the diagnostic pantheon, two other works on the difficulties of 'objective measurement' are cited to shore up the argument that misclassification is occurring as a consequence of the pernicious influence of 'postmodern' thought. McMillan *et al.* (1996a, b) are thus quoted as follows:

Children with mild mental retardation have intellectual limitations that manifest in inefficient learning of academic material and subtle social learning problems that do not carry over into the domains tapped by extant adaptive behavior scales. (McMillan *et al.* 1996a: 357)

The rather capricious categorization of children as MMR or LD attests to the similarities between children with MMR and those with LD. They have certain context-specific behavioral symptoms that have proven difficult to capture in terms of reliable classification. (McMillan *et al.* 1996b: 367)

Quite aside from assuming that which it sets out to demonstrate, this is simply a condemnation of unwanted conduct dressed up as objective behavioural science. We know that these children are mentally retarded because they behave in ways ('have certain context-specific behavioral symptoms') that displease us. That we cannot actually specify exactly what these forms of conduct are with any consistency ('symptoms . . . have proven difficult to capture in terms of reliable classification') and that we are unable to clarify or measure precisely what these 'symptoms' might be ('subtle social learning problems that do not carry over into the domains tapped by extant adaptive behavior scales') is thus not really a problem of conceptualisation, but to do with the 'subtlety' of the problems that these children 'have', and a matter amenable to a technical fix – if 'extant' scales cannot capture these problems, new ones might. The overlap between the categories 'LD' and 'MMR' is not a result of poorly defined operational criteria, or the invalidity of the constructs, but rather a consequence of 'capricious categorization'.

The conclusions Jacobson (2001) draws are simple. Children with 'MMR' exist. Their intellectual impairment is a given, and because of it they behave in morally troublesome ways (for instance they do not 'efficiently' learn 'academic material', and they display 'subtle' 'behavioral symptoms'). And the problem is not that current measurement is invalid, or classification unreliable, but that workers on the ground, gulled by 'postmodernism', do not recognise this truth. In effect we are being told that certain children behave in ways that professional psychologists regard as problematic and unwanted and that, on account of this, they are to be held to be 'symptomatic', and diagnosable as being 'disordered', as 'mentally retarded'.[7]

Schroeder, Gerry, Gertz and Velasquez (2002: 3) conducted a comprehensive survey of the literatures on 'mental retardation' in the lead up to the debate by the American Association on Mental Retardation (AAMR) about whether it should officially change its name.[8] Having surveyed the work of an array of professional bodies (the AAMR, the American Psychiatric Association, the World Health Organization and the American Psychological Association) as well as pedagogic and testing materials, scholarly journals, and monographs they concluded as follows:

There are many definitions of mental retardation but four are the most prevalent, i.e. the AAMR 1992 definition, the DSM IV 1994 definition, The ICD 10 1994 definition, and the APA 1996 definition. Of these, the AAMR definition is the most used in the US and the ICD 10 definition is the most used outside the US Textbooks and research articles on the topic of mental retardation are quite consistent, while other related textbooks and test manuals are not consistent in their use of an accepted definition of mental retardation. In the US

---

[7] Intriguingly, in calling for 'more modern and more informed classification' Jacobson (2001: 224) also cites Bruininks et al. (1988: 270, my emphasis) as follows: 'in the context of mild mental retardation the most salient finding about the structure of adaptive behavior is that ". . . adaptive behavior factor analytic research does not appear to show *any difference* in the structure as a function of degree of retardation or presence or absence of retardation"'. In the light of this one would have imagined that what was needed was not 'more modern ways' of classifying unicorns (Sarbin and Mancuso, 1980), but rather the abandonment of what is clearly an invalid hypothetical construct: indeed McMillan et al. (1997) go on to ask whether Mild Mental Retardation is 'a concept that may have lived out its usefulness'. That 'more modern classification' is, then, still called for can only be motivated by what Jacobson deplores in 'postmodernists', namely an ideological commitment to an idea in the absence of evidence for it. See also Boyle (2002) for an analysis of this form of thought in relation to 'schizophrenia'.

[8] See the official symposium 'What's in a name' published in the Association's journal *Mental Retardation* for substantive contributions to this debate.

the AAMR 1992 definition has increased in usage over the past decade. Nearly all efforts at definition have been directed toward diagnosis rather than toward prognosis.

Goodey and Stainton (2001: 223) make the important point that 'the multiplicity of labels for the concept suggests its problematic character', but if, for a moment we put this aside and, following Schroeder *et al.* (2002), open any introductory psychology textbook, we will find a section on 'abnormal' psychology. Alternatively, we might consult a specialist textbook devoted to the subject of abnormal psychology in its entirety. In either, it is highly likely that a definitive, diagnostic, statement such as this will be found:

Mental retardation is a disorder evident in childhood as significantly below-average intellectual and adaptive functioning (Luckasson *et al.* 1992). People with mental retardation experience difficulties with day-to-day activities, to an extent that reflects both the severity of their cognitive deficits and the type and amount of assistance they receive. (Barlow and Durand, 2002: 472)

If the official statements of the professional bodies concerned with the regulation of 'normality' are consulted the definitions are little different: the American Psychological Association (1996) suggests that 'Mental Retardation refers to (a) significant limitations in general intellectual functioning; (b) significant limitations in adaptive functioning, which exist concurrently'; the World Health Organization and the American Psychiatric Association both state that the 'diagnostic criteria' for the 'condition' are: '(A). Significantly subaverage intellectual functioning: (B). Concurrent deficits or impairments in present adaptive functioning: (C). Onset is before age 18 years.'

The most recent AAMR (2002) 'operational definition' reads:

Mental retardation is a disability characterized by significant limitations both in intellectual functioning and in adaptive behaviour as expressed in conceptual, social, and practical adaptive skills. This disability originates before age 18.

The following five assumptions are essential to the application of this definition:
1. Limitations in present functioning must be considered within the context of community environments typical of the individuals' age peers and culture.
2. Valid assessment considers cultural and linguistic diversity as well as differences in communication, sensory, motor and behavioral factors.
3. Within an individual, limitations often coexist with strengths.
4. An important purpose of describing limitations is to develop a profile of needed supports.
5. With appropriate personalized supports over a sustained period, the life functioning of the person with mental retardation generally will improve.

(American Association on Mental Retardation, 2002: 13)

Here we have straightforward, factual, accounts of the way things stand in the world.[9] The 'problem' is one that is identified by 'limitations', 'impairments' and 'deficits', and has 'diagnostic criteria', 'referents', or just '*is*'. Thus if we look at the Barlow and Durand (2002) account – designed as it is for the most general of audiences rather than specifically for professionals – we can see that, accompanied by the citation of the next most up-to-date 'official' AAMR definition (Luckasson, 1992), 'mental retardation' '*is* a disorder evident in childhood' in much the same way that we might say 'measles *is* a disorder evident in childhood' or 'congenital syphilis *is* a disorder evident in childhood'. This 'disorder' is 'evidenced' '*as* significantly below-average intellectual and adaptive functioning'. It is clearly an odd 'disorder' then, in that it, and its 'symptoms', are in a relationship of *identity*.[10]

This is to say that, aside from the strange notion that 'conceptual skills' should be considered under the rubric of 'adaptive behaviour' (are 'conceptual skills' not also definitive of the supposedly separable 'multidimensional construct, "intelligence"' – what else are IQ tests said to measure if not cognitive or conceptual abilities?), even the most recent AAMR definition elides that which is termed characteristic of the 'disability' with the 'disability' itself.[11] 'Diabetes', for example, may be 'evident as' or 'characterised by' excessive thirst and the presence of sweet urine, but one cannot sensibly say that 'diabetes' *is* sweet urine and excessive thirst – despite the shorthand linguistic habits of medical professionals who refer to the correspondence rules (the characteristics that must be observed) for the hypothetical construct 'diabetes' as if 'diabetes' were a thing

---

[9] See Appendix 2 for these definitions and Appendix 3 for the AAMR fact sheet on 'mental retardation'.

[10] See Boyle (1999; 2002a, b) for an extended critical analysis of the misuse, and consequent intellectual incoherence, of the use in the psy professions of medical terminology such as 'diagnosis' and the habits of thought entrained by it.

[11] It is also of note that in discussion of the two key 'characteristics' or 'symptoms' of the 'disability', intelligence and adaptive behaviour (AAMR, 2002: chapters 4 and 5), the AAMR concedes that both literatures are still incapable of unambiguously defining, let alone validly and accurately measuring, these constructs. Perhaps for this reason chapter 6 (pp. 93–6) enters a plea for the necessity of 'clinical judgment . . . expertise and experience' in 'diagnosis' (AAMR, 2002: 96). The parallels with appeals by the mad doctors to 'clinical judgement' in the early nineteenth century are intriguing. Scull (1979: 237–8) cites Mayo who claimed in 1817 that while there is 'great unanimity among experienced observers as to the presence of certain mental states, characterised by certain generally accepted names, which states, at the same time, it would be very difficult to describe in any form of words, insomuch that the indefined name, in the use of which all experienced men are agreed respecting these states, will convey to all a more clear and distinct impression than any attempt at definition or even description'. In 1817, as now, then, 'I can't actually describe it accurately, but – as an expert – I know it when I see it.'

(cf. Boyle, 1999; 2002b). Not only this, but the 'disorder' appears not, like, say measles or syphilis, to actually be inferred from a bodily lesion, the presence of a pathogen, or some other physical perturbation, but identified with and via the ease (or otherwise) with which day-to-day activities are carried out. 'People with mental retardation', then, are simultaneously 'symptomatic' and 'disordered' by virtue of receiving assistance and 'having' 'cognitive deficits' that amount to 'significantly below-average intellectual functioning'.

The AAMR then proceeds to summarise its definitional endeavours by offering a resume of the definition which reads something like a riddle. It is stated that:

In summary, mental retardation is not something you have, like blue eyes or a bad heart. Nor is it something you are, like being short or thin. It is not a medical disorder, although it may be coded in a medical classification of diseases; nor is it a mental disorder, although it may be coded in a classification of psychiatric disorders. *Mental retardation* refers to a particular state of functioning that begins in childhood, is multidimensional and is affected positively by individualized supports. (AAMR, 2002: 48)

It is an intriguing approach to definition to summarise by stating what not-something is. To suggest that 'it' is 'a particular state of functioning that begins in childhood, is multidimensional and is affected positively by individualized supports' is also to reduce the official definition of the term 'mental retardation' to nothing other than its everyday, vernacular, meaning (stupid, dumb, country simple, daft, not very bright, a cabbage, a mong, a retard, etc etc. cf. Goodey and Stainton, 2001). Under this definition 'being a woman'; 'adopting a minority religion'; 'voting Green'; 'being a sensitive new age guy'; being 'black' or 'gay' all are possible referents of the criterion. Perhaps it is just as well that, on the very next page, Part 2 – Diagnosis, begins. Not-It is, it would seem, something which may still, despite the vagueness of the summary definition of this 'particular state of functioning', be recuperated to reassuringly 'expert' practices of 'diagnosis'.

Like 'diabetes' then, we are dealing not with what is presented to us, simply, as a factual matter about a 'real' disorder or 'disability' that *is* in the world (like syphilis or measles) but rather, like 'schizophrenia', 'multiple sclerosis' or 'diabetes', an *hypothetical construct*. Immediately then we might suspect that, in the same way that past hypothetical constructs like phlogiston, drapetomania and dementia præcox were coined at specific times for specific purposes, and were abandoned when their usefulness expired, so too what Barlow and Durand (2002) (and the professional associations) present to us might, rather than being a 'thing' like the measles virus, be an idea, or a historically contingent *way of talking* about people who appear to be in need of assistance and who are not very good at IQ tests.

That is, rather than asking 'what is mental retardation', which immediately reifies the construct, Simpson (2000b: np) suggests that we might, sensibly, ask something rather different:

'What is an intellectually disabled person?' Self-evidently it is a person, but it is a person in the way that a 'prisoner' is a person, or a 'social worker' is a person. Their subjectivity as 'intellectually disabled' is the outcome of certain social processes; it is mediated by certain specific bodies of knowledge which make it possible to know who is and who is not intellectually disabled and to know what it is to be either.

This question clearly effects a relationship between intellectual disability and the person that is not immediately implicative, or constructive, of identity – in both senses of the term.[12] (And, following Rose, this is not to suggest that the notion of 'the person' is any less historically contingent than the notion of 'intellectual disability'.) Rather what Simpson makes clear is that which is implicit, and which Barlow and Durand's 'definition' conceals and even the AAMR's obscures, namely that being identified as 'intellectually disabled' is not to possess a singular entity, discovered as the outcome of some pathognomic, objective, physicochemical test, but rather a social judgement consequent upon the enactment 'of certain social processes mediated by certain specific bodies of knowledge'. It is the analysis of these processes and practices, and the bodies of knowledge that underpin them, that may lead us out of the circularity of current 'diagnostic definitions' which cannot *but* produce the following: How do you know that someone is intellectually disabled? Because they are incompetent and stupid, according to our psychometric tests. Why are they incompetent and stupid, according to our psychometric tests? Because they are intellectually disabled. And of course, given the circularity observed, it is hardly surprising that 'nearly all efforts at definition have been directed toward diagnosis rather than toward prognosis' (Schroeder *et al.* 2002). It is difficult to imagine how, on this effort, such a definitional endeavour could do other than leave the objects of its construction trapped with a fixed, 'diagnosed', 'disorder' (Gillman, Heyman and Swain, 2000).

---

[12] See also the alternative definitions by Gold (1980) and Greenspan (1997) in Appendix 1.

The invention of 'intellectual disability' as a 'diagnosable disorder'

If it is the case that 'nearly all efforts at definition have been directed toward diagnosis' (Schroeder *et al.* 2002), and there is no reason to question this evaluation, it immediately raises the question about why this might be. 'Diagnosis' is, in medicine, a process of pattern matching mediated by a series of correspondence rules which allow for a specific disease to be identified, or an hypothetical construct – like 'diabetes' – to be inferred on the basis of the presence of symptoms (multiple, grossly overdetermined and frequently subjective phenomena, such as 'excessive thirst'), signs (fewer, objectively establishable phenomena such as pathological tissue changes or the presence of independently verifiable anomaly, such as glucose in the urine), or, unusually, source indicators (rare, independently observable phenomena, which unambiguously indicate their antecedent) (Boyle, 1999). Boyle (1999; 2002a, b), following Scull (1979) and Rose (1999) argues that it has been by the appropriation of the language of medicine (with all of the supposed scientificity that goes with it: cf. Danforth, 2002) to talk of unwanted conduct that the psy professions have assumed authority over the management and control of those who, in one way or another, trouble the social order. The psy disciplines, as she elegantly shows, of course do not use terms such as 'diagnosis', 'symptom', 'sign', 'disorder', 'syndrome' and the like in the same way that they are used in medicine, but rather trade on the fact that, to a naïve general public, this will not be apparent. That is, the everyday psy (as opposed to medical) use of the term 'symptom' is roughly synonymous with the medical term 'sign' or, for example, in the 'definitions' of 'intellectual disability/mental retardation' above, even 'source indicator'.

That is 'symptom', in everyday English, is immediately hearable as an unequivocal indication of the presence of disease, not to mention the fact that 'diagnosis' is now so much part of the vernacular that it is what plumbers do to recalcitrant washing machines, agony aunts do for the writers of letters telling of woeful relationships, and what Feng Shui practitioners will do to your bedroom decor. Of course, in medicine, a symptom is the *weakest* possible indicator of anything, and 'making a diagnosis' does not necessarily connote the *naming* of a specific pathogen or disease: as with 'diabetes' (and, indeed, 'intelligence') saying 'you have diabetes' or 'you have a high IQ' simply means that, in translation as it were, 'what I can observe, the ways in which you act, and the experiences you report, allow me to infer the hypothetical construct x'. If, however, multiple, grossly overdetermined, and frequently subjective phenomena (such as finding the practical tasks of everyday life difficult, not knowing who wrote Hamlet, not doing very well on IQ tests) are redescribed as 'symptoms', or as 'diagnostic criteria', then the impression is furnished not that these are essentially relative, socially and interpersonally constituted judgments of the *adequacy of forms of conduct*, but rather that via the use of objective, neutral, scientific, and medical technology, specifically identifiable pathology has been found. Boyle (1999) writes that:

Most of what we think of as diagnostic labels are therefore more accurately thought of as concepts, as abstract ideas. The distinction is crucial, for two related reasons. First concepts are provisional, that is, they are always subject to abandonment or change if challenged by new observations. Second, concepts are just that: concepts, or abstractions, rather than things with a spatiotemporal location. Yet the way we talk about medical diagnosis obscures this, as when we say 'she *has* multiple sclerosis' or 'he *is* diabetic' . . . The problem with this language is that it confers on these concepts a permanence and solidity which is quite unjustified . . . suggests that they are entities that people possess . . . and obscure[s] the fact that [diagnosis] is a highly abstract and assumption laden process. (Boyle, 1999: 78–9)

Thus, in the naming of persons as 'intellectually disabled' or 'mentally retarded', the invocation of an hypothetical construct is disguised as the 'diagnosis of a disorder' or 'identification of a symptom complex' with all of the permanence and solidity that such descriptors accomplish. And behind the practice of diagnosis lies the promise of power/knowledge.[13] As Gergen, Hoffman and Anderson (1996: 3) have it: 'diagnostic systems give a sense of legitimacy, confidence and predictability, both to the professional and the client'. Or, alternatively, *if* it can be *known, then* it can be controlled, medicated, treated.

And of course, such an endeavour is, professionally, self-serving. There is, as noted, insufficient space to provide as detailed an account as is merited of the relationship between profession-building in medicine, psychiatry and allied trades over the course of the nineteenth and twentieth centuries, and the development of multiple, and competing, classification systems for the originally undifferentiated mass of 'lunatics' (a category inclusive of idiots until the accelerating fractionation of lunacy itself in the latter nineteenth century (see Boyle, 2002; Scull, 1979; 1985; Wright and Digby, 1997; Trent, 1994; Thomson, 1998; Goodey, 1999; Goodey and Stainton, 2001)). However, it is important to recognise that

---

[13] Benjamin (1937: 184) describes the way in which the hypothetical method of scientific activity proceeds by 'inventing a fictitious substance or process or idea in terms of which the experiences can be expressed. It correlates observations by adding something to them.' Clearly here we have a set of experiences (poor performance on IQ tests) being used to infer one hypothetical construct 'intelligence' which is itself then correlated with a second set of experiences (difficulty with everyday life) by superadding the hypothetical construct 'intellectual disability' to account for both.

the contemporary solidity and familiarity of the use of terms like 'diagnosis' (and all of the expertise, acumen, clinical judgment and certainty
thereby connoted) to describe the identification of idiocy or any other
unwanted conduct, is recent: a consequence of struggles for professional
jurisdiction between mad doctors, moral managers and lay proprietors of
asylums or mad-houses through this period. A struggle that, in the case
of madness, was won by those proclaiming allegiance to medicine, and in
the case of idiocy by those, like Edouard Seguin, who promulgated physiological theories of idiocy which, as Simpson (2000b: np) notes 'blurs
the distinction between the physiological body of the idiot, and his social
functioning' – a blurring that is, to all intents and purposes, retained
today. Thus Seguin (1866) writes of:

Idiocy [as] a specific infirmity of the cranio-spinal axis, produced by deficiency of
nutrition in utero and neo-nati. It incapacitates mostly the functions which give
rise to the reflex, instinctive, and conscious phenomena of life; consequently, the
idiot moves, feels, understands, wills, but imperfectly; does nothing, thinks of
nothing, cares for nothing (extreme cases), he is a minor legally irresponsible;
isolated, without associations; a soul shut up in imperfect organs, an innocent.

That is to say, over the last two hundred years, a nexus has developed
between the authorities responsible for the problem of ensuring the pro-
priety of conduct, the discharge of social responsibilities and the pro-
ductivity of citizens, and an array of psychological professions who have
claimed the ability not only to diagnose the (faulty) interiority of potentially troublesome social actors (be it a 'specific infirmity of the cranio-
spinal axis' or the contemporary 'cognitive deficit'), but also to effect the
management, treatment and cure of those persons. This understanding
was *not*, as is suggested or implied by current professional literatures, a
consequence of progressive developments and refinements of science and
medicine, in a straight line from Willis's (1672) account of stupidity in *De
Anima Brutorum*, but rather a recuperation into a psychologised network
of understandings of political, legal, literary and theological thought from
the mid-seventeenth century on (Goodey and Stainton, 2001).[14] Indeed
Goodey and Stainton note that even then, for example in Locke's work
(Locke, 1690/1975), while the term 'idiot' was available as a category,
Locke's use also made it clear that 'idiocy' was not a separate kind, but
rather 'shades into the intellectual shortcomings of the general population, for example, the labouring poor' (Goodey and Stainton, 2001:
237). As Rose suggests then, the mid-nineteenth century 'pioneers' of

---

[14] For instance, in a factsheet about 'mental retardation', the AAMR (2003) states that it
has 'updated the definition of mental retardation ten times since 1908, based on new
information, changes in clinical practice, or breakthroughs in scientific research'.

'intellectual disability', Howe *et al.* whose work is now enrolled by the professional literatures as the first 'scientific descriptions' of intellectual disability, *per se*, are workers in a simultaneous, and also rather different project, that of the:

Enrolling of agents into a 'psychologized' network . . . Establishing the linkage between the nature, character and causes of problems facing various individuals and groups – producers and shopkeepers, doctors and patients – and forming a relation between the problems of one and those of another, such that the two seem intrinsically linked in their basis and their solution. (Rose, 1999a).

The construction of our contemporary 'psychologised network' is then the product of the psychological professions successfully claiming that they do, indeed, have the knowledge and associated technologies not only to truthfully specify the 'nature, character and causes of problems facing various individuals' (even if, *pace* Jacobson, 2001) they are 'subtle', difficult to capture, and unamenable to reliable measurement and classification), but that also, and in and through that knowledge, they possess the power to solve the problems so identified. And social problems in the contemporaneous eras of the stabilisation of industrial capitalism and of psychological truths were manifold. Barnes (1997: ms 16) notes that:

The nineteenth century is synonymous with the emergence of 'disability' in its present form. This includes the systematic individualisation and medicalisation of the body and the mind (Armstrong, 1983; Foucault, 1975), the exclusion of people with apparent impairments from the mainstream of community life into all manner of institutional settings (Scull, 1984) and, with the emergence of 'Social Darwinism', the 'Eugenics Movement', and, later, 'social hygiene' 'scientific' reification of the age old myth that, in one way or another, people with any form of physical and or intellectual imperfections pose a serious threat to western society. The 'logical' outcome of this was the proliferation of Eugenic ideals throughout the western world during the first half of the twentieth century.

This suggests then, as Rose and Foucault have argued, that it is difficult to separate out 'psychological' truths, and the available understandings of both human subjects and the most appropriate ways to deal with them, from the eras in which they are developed.[15] And the promise of the psychological professions in the nineteenth century was little different to that which they make today: if society still has to wait for a medicine to cure idiots, as did Seguin, we are assured that, in the meantime, the psy professions have the positive knowledge to identify such persons and the

---

[15] See also Danziger (1990) for an extended discussion of the manner in which psychological languages have shaped those they appear merely to describe over the last hundred or so years.

protocols for their improvement. It remains the case, however, that as the nineteenth century progressed, authorities remarked on the exponential growth of numbers of both lunatics and idiots in the expanding asylum archipelago (Simpson, 2000b). For example, in England and Wales estimates of prevalence of 'insanity' (a category inclusive of 'idiocy' and 'lunacy') rose from one in 802 in 1844, to one in 432 in 1868, and to a staggering one in 266 by the outbreak of World War I in 1914 (Hare, 1983). (See Boyle, 2002a, chapter 2, for a discussion of the competing accounts of the origins of this phenomenon.) It does not appear that there is an absolutely compelling case to be made that 'insanity' really was 'on the increase' (Hare, 1983) but, as Jenkins (1999: 11) suggests, it certainly is the case that:

The size of the category of intellectually disabled persons has been variable over time . . . At different times, more or less people, and different kinds of people, have fallen under the purview – the gaze – of the institutional and bureaucratic systems that have been developed to address the problem of incompetence. This is partly a consequence of differing levels of concern about the threat that their incompetence was believed to pose, and partly due to changing methods for identifying incompetence and variations in their use. (Jenkins, 1999: 10–11)

Making sense of variation such as this is a problem if we are not prepared to accept a relativist, constructionist, perspective. As Jenkins points out, it is certainly the case that technologies of identification have been partly responsible, but it is insufficient to appeal *simply* to changes in technology (the development of IQ tests, better measures of adaptive behaviour, improper technical administration of existing measures; the refinement of definitions) and also insufficient (if not also anachronistic) to claim simply that what was once called amantia, idiocy, feeble-mindedness and the rest is now, properly, described under our current classificatory regime. The precise constitution of, say, moral imbecility has no parallel in current nosology. And while it also seems to be clear that the level and nature of the 'threat that . . . incompetence was believed to pose' is also historically and culturally situated, many of the earlier concerns about the breeding potential of the feeble-minded (Saunders, 1988; Jackson, 2000) resurface in the late twentieth century in concerns about the 'fitness' (a term with unfortunate Eugenic overtones) – or competence – of people with intellectual disabilities to act as parents (e.g. Booth and Booth, 1998). That is, as Trent points out, 'intellectual disability' is a 'construction whose changing meaning is shaped both by individuals who initiate and administer policies, programs and practices, and by the social context to which these individuals are responding' (1994: 2).

Competence, and the 'abilities' of intellectually disabled people

The prevailing, psychologised, view of intellectual disability draws both on notions of individuals showing defective 'intelligence' and an impoverishment of 'competence'. Such conceptualisations frequently employ one of this pair of characterisations as warrant for the existence of the other, thus defective 'intelligence' may be inferred from 'incompetence', and 'incompetence' is taken as an indicator of possibly suspect intellectual capacities (the possibility, however, of asymmetry in this reading off is raised by Greenspan (1994) to suggest that IQ remains a dominant, if silent, partner in the 'diagnosis' of intellectual disability). This tautology is clearly visible, as is the debt to Kantian thought (cf. McHoul and Rapley, 2001), in the definition of mental retardation offered by Das and colleagues (1994).

The definition of mental retardation typically used . . . stems from four possible combinations of IQ and adaptive behavior. There are certain characteristics that describe the level of adaptive functioning of a child or a retarded individual, such as social skills and good work habits, but adaptive behavior itself is a combination of a person's competence and adjustment. Competence is another name for cognitive functioning or ability, and adjustment is part of personality . . . [B]oth cognitive functioning and personality lead to an important component of adaptive behavior, judgement. (Das, Naglieri and Kirby, 1994: 143–4)

Here then, 'competence' (as may be evidenced by the inescapably moral-evaluative criterion 'good work habits') is but a 'component' of the highest order achivement of Enlightenment thought, ratiocination, or 'judgement': recall that Jensen regards mental retardation as a 'thinking disorder', under which persons are incapable of reason. And in the explicit moral evaluation of such conduct, the debt to Locke is also evident. And, like 'personality' this characteristic of 'retarded individual[s]' is inherent in them, as individuals. That is such definitions of both competence and intellectual disability (reading one in terms of the other) rely on the Chomskyan (1968) distinction between linguistic competence and performance. *Contra* Chomsky, ethnomethodological and discursive psychological work sees competence not as an inherent feature of specific individuals, an internalised, abstract knowledge, but rather *as* an intersubjectively accomplished, practical performance. Furthermore such situated performances may take place under circumstances where one party to the encounter is formally ratified to make *evaluations* of the quality of the performance of the other, be that in circumstances of IQ or ability testing, or in less structured assessment encounters. Thus it is that evaluations of competence enacted in and as social performance by and through the negotiation of a series of professional practices comes to *stand for* the presumed totality of the capacity of persons in any and all situations. Such problems, as the professional literatures tend to acknowledge – and then to ignore – can lead to not only the constitution of people as 'intellectually disabled', but also to some serious misapprehensions about the nature of competence.

For example, in a series of studies which should have passed into the common stock of applied psychological knowledge, Cicourel *et al.* (1974), MacKay (1974) and Mehan (1973) examined the sense made, by children, of the intelligence, reading and language development tests employed by southern Californian elementary schools to identify children with intellectual or developmental difficulties. Mehan and Wood (1975) summarise and describe these studies, the results of which suggest that unilateral, professional, specifications of competence may seriously underestimate the cultural, that is normative, social, competence of persons. Mehan and Wood (1975: 39–40) suggest that:

To see the child as a 'more or less competent adult' is to distort the reality of the child. The distortion thereby obscures the very phenomenon – the child's competence – that the test hopes to measure. These tests measure only adult competence, the reality in which the world of play fantasy, television and work are rigorously separated. These tests do not capture the intricate and subtle ways children use language or concepts within their own realities.

In order to understand the way in which the tests Mehan and Wood (1975) discuss 'distort the child's reality' it is necessary to quote at some length, but it is important that while Mehan and Wood's work relates to children, such phenomena are not peculiar to this age group. Indeed current measures of adaptive behaviour and intelligence may be said to measure persons, as more or less competent, against an idealised subject in the shape of the entirely mythical statistical abstraction, the 'normal person', who just happens to bear a striking similarity to an upper middle class psy professional. They write that:

In the California reading tests, word, sentences, or paragraphs, contained in an arrow, appear along the left side of the page. The arrow points to a series of three pictures arrayed along the right side of the page. The child is told to mark the picture that 'goes best' with the words in the arrow. One question has the word 'fly' in the arrow pointing to pictures of an elephant, a bird and a dog. The correct answer to this question is the bird. The answer sheets of many of the first grade children showed that they had chosen the elephant alone or along with the bird as a response to that question. When Mehan asked them why they chose that answer they replied 'That's Dumbo.' Dumbo, of course, is Walt Disney's flying elephant, well known to children who watch television and read children's books as an animal that flies . . . When the child applies the word 'fly' to an elephant . . . this is evidence to the tester that the child cannot abstract similar features of objects. According to this criterion, the child who does not answer such questions properly has been found to be an inadequate adult, a nonresident of the tester and teacher reality. But to therefore conclude that the child's reading and conceptual abilities are 'impoverished' is to deny the actual complexity and richness of the child's day-to-day life . . . MacKay (1974: 240) concludes: . . . the complexity of what the child knows is not recoverable from the test results. (Mehan and Wood, 1975: 38–43)[16]

That is to say, whatever the *psychometric* validity and reliability (or otherwise) of measures of 'competence' such as these, it remains the case that they offer a distorted and distorting account of what the person knows (see Antaki and Rapley, 1996a, b; Hatton, 1998 for an analysis of the way in which a *psychometrically* reliable and valid measure of quality of life produces, in actual use, a distortion of the responses offered by respondents). In assuming that competence is a quantifiable attribute that persons carry around with them in some fashion, measures such as these cannot but traduce the 'complexity of what the child knows', and whatever it is that *is* recoverable from the test results, it is not an adequate description of the capacities or competences of persons.[17]

The existing sociological and psychological literatures on the social and linguistic competence of people with intellectual disabilities are, with few exceptions, still based in the assumptions that underpin the testing materials analysed by Mehan and Wood (1975). Although some recent work has begun to adopt qualitative rather than quantitative approaches, it remains the case that a substantial body of this work too is informed by essentialist, intra-individual assumptions about the location of 'competence', and much of it prosecuted on the basis of assessments of linguistic capacity employing measures of interactional competence or adaptive behaviour which, based as they are in researcher and staff assessor reality,

---

[16] Similar discounting of displays of cultural competence is readily seen in the intelligence testing of adults with intellectual disabilities. In a practical administration of the Wechsler Adult Intelligence Test, as one of my students prepared the Block Design subtest by placing the red and white coloured blocks on the table, his 'intellectually disabled' interlocutor said 'It's the Swans'. Only later did the student realise that the strip of the Australian Rules Football Team, the Sydney Swans, is red and white. Thus what was dismissable as an irrelevant intrusion into formal testing (and *was* dismissed as such) is *also* seeable as a display of cultural competence. Of course, under standing psychological protocols, such a display of cultural membership cannot be 'counted' towards an estimation of the 'competence' of the speaker.

[17] The cultural and historical relativity of the assessment of competence is neatly illustrated by Peter Mittler (1979). He notes that study of the former 'Special Reports and Certificates' issued under the Mental Deficiency Act 1913 reveals assessment gems such as 'He cannot tell the difference between a bloater, a kipper and a herring' (Mittler, 1979: 19).

are not attentive to the actual complexity of language and language use.[18]

It is thus axiomatic in definitions of intellectual disability in the present that language problems are diagnostic of the condition. According to Luckasson *et al.*'s statement for the AAMR, for example, 'communication' is itemised as the first 'limitation' in 'skill areas' viz. 'Mental retardation refers to substantial limitations in present functioning. It is characterized by significantly subaverage intellectual functioning, existing concurrently with related limitations in two or more of the following applicable adaptive skill areas: communication, self-care, home living...' (1992: 1). Further, if the AAMR's 'factsheet' on mental retardation ('Frequently asked questions about mental retardation and the AAMR definition' (AAMR, 2003)) is consulted, following a definition of adaptive behaviour ('the conceptual, social, and practical skills that people have learned to be able to function in their everyday lives . . . Limitations in adaptive behavior can be determined by using standardised tests') we are presented with the question 'What are some examples of adaptive behavior skills?' The first area of limitation identified, determinable via 'standardised tests', is 'Conceptual skills: Receptive and expressive language' (AAMR, 2003: www.aamr.org/).

The literature is thus replete with studies of the social competence/ social impairment of persons which start from the premise of deficit or incompetence, and rate this incompetence using pre-given coding schemes. A recent example of this practice can be seen in the following extract from a major study of the 'effects' of 'deinstitutionalization' on 'social impairment' published in *Research in Developmental Disabilities*.

The Quality of Social Interaction question from the Schedule of Handicaps, Behaviours and Skills (HBS, Wing and Gould, 1978, 1979) was used at Time 4 to collect data on social impairment (see Appendix A). The second author and her co-interviewer interviewed each participant and their carers and rated the quality of participants' social interaction using the relevant question from the HBS. This allowed the researchers to classify each person as aloof, passive, active but odd or sociable. (Beadle-Brown and Forrester-Jones, 2003: 35)

Appendix 1 makes it clear that this question from the HBS is a 'measure' of the 'person's *usual* quality of interaction' (Beadle-Brown and Forrester-Jones, 2003: 42 original emphasis). That is, global judgements of an inescapably moral flavour – such as 'active but odd' – are made on the basis of a single 'question' answered by an interview of unspecified

---

[18] For a brief overview of these procedures aimed at trainee psy-professionals see Cullen and Dickens (1990).

duration between a researcher and 'participants and carers'. A second set of 'variables' from the SBI supplement this global judgment ('conversation and social mixing; initiation of conversation and social interaction; non-verbal communication; length of conversation; odd gestures or mannerisms; consideration (with regard to noise and feelings of others); inappropriate interpersonal manners'). Of this collection, apparently conversation and social mixing, initiation of conversation and social interaction, length of conversation and inappropriate interpersonal manners are said to be 'predictive of social impairment on HBS at $p < .05$' (Beadle-Brown and Forrester-Jones, 2003: 36). This tells us little more than that those who were thought to be, for example, 'aloof' or 'active but odd' by these particular researchers, were thought to be so on the basis of what are essentially judgments of etiquette. Is there a universally 'right' quantum of 'social mixing'? Do we have 'norms' for 'length of conversation'? What scientific body of knowledge determines the appropriateness or otherwise of 'interpersonal manners'?

Similarly, in work examined in more detail in chapter 3, most research in the sociological and psychological literatures fails to provide adequate examples of what people with intellectual disabilities – or their interviewers – actually *say* during the encounters which apparently furnish statistically significant characterisations of persons as 'active but odd' or, globally, 'socially impaired' or 'socially incompetent'. This is typical of the intellectual disability literature (and the psychological sciences) in general. Some workers, for example Flynn (1986; 1988); Flynn and Saleem (1986); Atkinson (1988); Cattermole, Jahoda and Marková (1988); Domingo, Barrow and Amato (1998) have reported snippets of speech, but in such a manner as to strip away all detail of intonation, pitch, speed of delivery and, usually, the interviewer's contribution, despite the fact that since at least the late 1980s a stream of studies in EM/CA have reported that people with learning disabilities routinely use the kind of conversational structures and devices CA has identified in 'normal' talk such as normative turn-taking, responses to openings, and the competent management of adjacency pairing (Brewer and Yearley, 1989; Yearley and Brewer, 1989; Abbeduto, 1984; Abbeduto and Rosenberg, 1980) (see also Wootton's (1990) analysis of talk with young children with Down's Syndrome; and Leudar and Fraser's (1985) pragmatic analysis of 'withdrawal strategies'). If the talk of people with learning disabilities *is* reported, it is – if not analysed on the unsustainable basis that meaning is inherent in semantics – still most usually represented in meta-categories (such as, in the Beadle-Brown and Forrester-Jones (2003) paper, whether or not it can be rated as displaying 'consideration (with regard to noise and feelings of others)' – whatever that may actually *be* in interaction, we are not told), or in terms of the number of utterances that have been put into pre-conceived categories. The hugely influential study of 'acquiescence bias' by Sigelman *et al.* (1981a) is a good example of this. People's 'responsiveness' to questions about participation in chores, friends and other domestic details was measured by scoring utterances as 'no response', 'unintelligible', 'irrelevant', 'do not know', 'inadequate (vague)', 'request for clarification', 'refusal to answer', 'minimally appropriate . . . one bit of information', and 'expanded'. The paper offers no reporting of speech, either to amplify what might count as an 'irrelevant' utterance for example, or what it meant to be 'unresponsive'. One notes, in passing, that there are, in this scheme, at least five, and possibly seven, categories that reflect the 'inadequacy' of the speaker, one the 'minimal appropriateness' of their utterance and only one that reflects a positive assessment of the intellectually disabled person's speech.

Thus we also see studies assessing the 'complexity of staff communication and reported level of understanding skills in adults with intellectual disability' (Bradshaw, 2001) which offer no examples of speech at all, complex or otherwise; studies which offer to assist in 'canvassing the views of people with a mental handicap' (Lowe and de Paiva, 1988) which do not actually provide the 'views' of the respondents except in tabulated numerical form; analyses of 'subjective judgments of quality of life: a comparison . . . between people with intellectual disability and those without disability' which provide not examples of 'subjective judgments' made by people in talk, but rather impressive tables of f values (Hensel, Rose, Stenfert Kroese and Banks-Smith, 2002); or investigations of 'factors associated with expressed satisfaction' among people with intellectual disability receiving residential supports (Gregory, Robertson, Kessissoglou, Emerson and Hatton, 2001), which represent the satisfaction people expressed in terms of a three and a half page table of correlation coefficients between entirely decontextualised 'grabs' of speech (e.g. for the factor 'Risks', 'we all say we're lucky living here (VC)' is, apparently, correlated at $r = 0.258$, $p < 0.05$ with the 'associated variable' 'being a woman', p. 287). Similarly, analyses of 'tangential speech' in people with Fragile X Syndrome (Sudhalter and Belser, 2001), while basing analysis on transcribed videotapes of contrived conversations between participants and researchers, do not offer interactional data to show the sequential circumstances under which 'tangential language' occurs, but rather provide MANOVA results.

In the literature that has focused specifically on linguistic competence, language and language use, the deficit tradition is well represented in studies where 'the most pervasive problem among . . . mentally retarded persons is disorders of communication' (Sisson and Barrett, 1983: 98).[19] Domingo *et al.* (1998) note that Linder (1978) summarises the linguistic incapacities of people with an intellectual disability as including restricted vocabulary, age inappropriate syntax, shorter sentence length, idiosyncratic meanings of conventional words and a paucity of propositional abstractions; Sabsay and Kernan (1983: 283) suggest pragmatic failures of 'communicative design', neglect of Gricean maxims (Grice, 1975) and non-recognition of social and interpersonal as well as linguistic aspects of speech episodes; Kernan and Sabsay (1984) note failures of intersubjectivity, inadequate referential usage; Sabsay and Platt (1985) identify unmarked topic shifts; Edgerton (1967) points to other-dependent interaction management; Miller (1980) to poor articulation and lack of motivation to communicate; Scudder and Tremain (1992) to failures of repair in protracted troubles sequences.

Despite this comprehensive listing of problems, Hatton's (1998) review of the literature on pragmatics and intellectual disability suggests two important conclusions, namely that:

First, people with intellectual disabilities can and do acquire basic pragmatic language skills, although more subtle aspects of conversational competence are less commonly displayed. Second, the communicative environments of children and adults with intellectual disabilities appear to inhibit the acquisition and display of pragmatic language skills. (Hatton, 1998: np)

Critical to the non-display of conversational competence may be the 'communicative environments' (Leudar, 1989) that people with an intellectual disability find themselves in. That is to say, whereas much of the literature has been concerned to document deficits in the linguistic competence of the intellectually disabled speaker, less work has attended to the interaction context itself as a potential source of interactional trouble. Marková however suggests that if 'many people with learning difficulties suffer from a language and communication deficiency . . . the non-handicapped on their part rarely have sufficient skills and sensitivity to communicate with people whose speech is impaired, who need a longer time to respond or who try to communicate non-verbally' (1991: 221). A range of studies have also suggested that in interactions between care staff and intellectually disabled people, competence is actively constrained by the structure of interaction, with staff initiated interaction most frequently focused on instructions or orders (Marková, 1990; 1991; Prior *et al.* 1979; Kuder and Bryen, 1993) with little evidence of 'interest in people with learning difficulties *qua* personal and social beings rather than as

---

[19] See Beveridge *et al.* (1989) for a useful edited collection on the topic.

patients to be kept alive' (Marková, 1991: 222), which may contribute to the development of active strategies to avoid communication (Leudar, 1989; Leudar, Fraser and Jeeves, 1981; Leudar and Fraser, 1985; Yearley and Brewer, 1989). 'Communicative withdrawal' may, then, be demonstrated by a reluctance to engage in conversations or by terminating interaction abruptly, or by displaying an appearance of co-operation, but producing informationally-impoverished speech. While such tactics may also be seen in arguments between spouses, in the context of 'staff/client' interaction, Leudar *et al.* suggest that not only are these interactional styles understandable as *strategic*, and directed at face-preservation, but that they may commonly be viewed by non-disabled interlocutors as evidence of hostility or as behaviour problems.

Conversely, studies of people with an intellectual disability interacting with people other than care staff, or other figures of authority, suggest that in these situations 'dominant' or 'high status' interactional strategies are visible (Price-Williams and Sabsay, 1979; Abbeduto and Rosenberg, 1980; Ryave, 1973; Ryave and Rodriguez, 1989). In this respect, Hatton argues that, although these studies are limited by being grounded in field notes as opposed to transcripts of interaction, and also of being undertaken in large institutional settings in many cases:

> The conversational strategies employed by people without disability to minimise conversational trouble operate on the assumption that the recipient is incompetent, passive and insensitive to the demands of the speaker, and that the speaker has the responsibility (and power) to unilaterally attempt to hide this fact. The overall effect, as Sabsay and Platt (1985) put it, is one of 'well-intentioned condescension' (p. 30) . . . [T]he communicative environments of adults with intellectual disabilities may also act to inhibit the expression of such conversational skills, particularly in conversations with people without disability perceived as high-status, powerful or dominant. (Hatton, 1998: np)[20]

What this literature would seem to suggest, then, is that there may indeed be a range of difficulties that can, specifically, be attributed to individuals, but that to leave an analysis of the competence, particularly the pragmatic competence, of people with an intellectual disability there is to tell less than half the story. Inasmuch as 'well-intentioned condescension' is only possible as a *joint* production, so too conversational or interactional competence is not a unidimensional, once and for all, all or nothing, property of individual subjects, but rather is only visible *in situ*, in interaction – hence findings such as that reported by Bradshaw (2001) and Purcell,

---

[20] Hatton notes that: 'studies consistently demonstrate that people in community-based services have greater pragmatic language skills than people in institutions, even when matched for general cognitive skills or formal language skills' (e.g. Brinton and Fujiki, 1991; 1994).

Morris and McConkey (1999) suggesting mismatches between staff pencil and paper ratings of communicative ability and actual communication practices.[21] This would seem to suggest that, *contra* the traditional approach in psychology and sociology, we should not attempt to locate competence *within* individuals, but rather recognise that competence is made available for inspection, as it were, in social relations. Writing of the idea that it is possible that individuals may be judged to be differentially competent, or 'fit', to be a parent, Booth and Booth suggest that:

Competence may more properly be seen as a distributed feature of parents' social network rather than as an individual attribute. The notion of what might be termed 'distributed competence' attests to the fact that parenting is mostly a shared activity and acknowledges the interdependencies that comprise the parenting task. (Booth and Booth, 1998; 206)

Such a social, or ethnomethodological, conceptualisation of the notion of competence allows for a situational and indexical stance in relation to assumptions – not only about parenting (in)competence – but also towards the notion of (dis)ability, and, hence, impairment more broadly. Fitness for, or competence in, parenting (or anything else) is not, of necessity, an individualised quality but a product of social and relational networks. Rather than adopt such a perspective, however, and recapitulating Wetherell's (2000) observations on psychology, that the discipline tends to deal in binaries, Reindal (1999) has also argued that, in the disability studies literature, theorising tends to emphasise the dichotomies of competence–incompetence or independence–dependence.[22] That is both literatures share in a realist commitment which places truth and

---

[21] In this context it is of note that Houtkoop-Steenstra and Antaki (1998) note that, in quality of life interviews with intellectually disabled people, interviewers routinely project the relevance of positive assessments of life circumstances by reformulating three part list options into 'yes–no' questions. Such an interactional management strategy cannot but patronise: 'happy', but 'incompetent', people are so produced.

[22] As I hope is evident from the above, claims in the psychological literature over the last thirty years that progress has been made towards: 'the rejection of handicap as being simply a property of a disabled individual [and] disability [being] increasingly viewed as the outcome of an interaction between a person and the environment in which he or she lives' (Hogg and Raynes, 1987: 3) are called into question by contemporary diagnostic and professional practice manuals which seek to diagnose not 'person–environment interactions' but 'persons'. It is also the case that Hogg and Raynes's chapter containing this assertion is entitled 'assessing people with mental handicap', which seems to leave the environment somewhat out of the analysis. Similarly, while the AAMR (Luckasson *et al.* 1992) suggested that their then newly minted definition of mental retardation was a 'paradigm shift' to an interactional account of intellectual disability, with a focus on needs rather than deficits, the definition then, and the revised 2002 version, suggests that 'substantial limitations in present functioning' of *individuals* are definitive of the condition. This is, in truth, not much of an advance on Seguin's characterisation of such people as 'a soul shut up in imperfect organs'.

value at one pole and not the other: as Edwards (1997) has noted, and Goodey and Stainton observe, this variety of thinking both sustains modern psychology and 'predisposes us to assume a sharp antithesis between popular mythological explanations for intellectual disability . . . and the current explanations supplied by biology' (2001: 224). In contrast, and as an alternative to this dominant form of thought, Goodley and Rapley (2001) suggest that:

> This is based on a modernist view of the human being that emphasises the voluntary and rational components of the human condition. Yet . . . there is a need to situate the self in relational understandings. If we maintain the independence–dependence dichotomy, independence remains an individualized quality, with related essentialist views of the subject being kept in place. (Goodley and Rapley, 2001: 230–1)

It is precisely 'essentialist views of the subject' that current respecifications of 'intellectual disability' promulgated by the professional associations seek, at least in rhetoric, to undermine. And yet all such definitions – and the practices which flow from them – continue to rely on the identification of deficient capacities (be they intellectual or 'adaptive behavioural') in individuals. What such essentialist, individualising, thought thus proposes – disclaimers notwithstanding – is that there is a thing, called mental retardation, which if it is not 'possessed' by the individual, possesses them – that it is definitive of their subjectivity, it is the essence of their social and personal identity. Indeed, as the AAMR (2002: 12) notes, it is the facility with which 'diagnosis' effects the making over of persons into bureaucratised, 'entitled', objects of knowledge that remains one of the key justifications, in their view, of these practices of objectification.[23] But there is another effect that the essentialisation and individualisation of (in)competence, (un)reason and (dis)ability has had, and that is to impose, in return for 'eligibility', an obligation to 'own' one's 'true' identity, to confess one's status as a psychologically constituted object of knowledge (cf. Foucault, 1977; Hansen, McHoul and Rapley, 2003). As Rose observes:

> Western man . . . has become a confessing animal. The truthful rendering into speech of who one is, to one's parents, one's teachers, one's doctor, one's lover, and oneself, is installed at the heart of contemporary procedures of individualization. In confessing, one is subjectified by another, for one confesses in the actual

---

[23] In their 'Framework for Assessment of Mental Retardation' the AAMR notes that the purposes of diagnosis are 'establishing eligibility for services, benefits and legal protections' while the purposes of classification are identified as 'grouping for service reimbursement or funding, research, services and communication about selected characteristics' (AAMR, 2002: 12).

or imagined presence of a figure who prescribes the form of the confession, the words and rituals through which it should be made, who appreciates, judges, consoles or understands. But in confessing, one also constitutes oneself. In the act of speaking, through the obligation to produce words that are true to an inner reality . . . one becomes a subject for oneself. (Rose, 1999a: 244)

This is, of course, an essentially ethical (Foucault, 1986), or moral, requirement.

Intellectual disability as moral category

The forms of life now called intellectual disability have, from the start of psychological investigation, been linked to morality: if not directly to criminality, deviance and hereditary vice, then to unseemly or improper conduct of one variant or another. Such a juxtaposition clearly implies a strong link between evaluations of the *moral* self and *scientific* judgments of 'deficiency'. As Rose argues of the liberal democratic polities of Europe, the United States and Australia:

The conduct of the self and its powers have been linked to ethics and morality, to politics and administration, and to truth and knowledge . . . such societies have been constituted, in part, through an array of plans and procedures for the shaping, regulation, administration of the self, that, over the last two centuries, has been inescapably bound to knowledges of the self. And psychology – indeed all the 'psy' knowledges – have played a very significant role in the re-organization and expansion of these practices and techniques which have linked authority to subjectivity. (Rose, 1999a: np)

While Eugenic accounts dealt in extreme, and biologically-determined, depravity – for instance suggesting that 'criminals as a group represent an aggregate of sociologically and biologically inferior individuals' (Hooton, 1939: 304), and were despairing of the prospects for 'reform' ('let us cease trying to make the world safe for morons, and endeavor rather to save it from them', Hooton, 1940: 230), the originators of what we can call the psychological project (even those most optimistic about the possibility of education) were still concerned with forms of life that offended against polite sensibilities. In Howe's (1848) *On the Causes of Idiocy*, a report to the Commonwealth of Massachusetts on a commission of inquiry 'into the condition of the idiots' it is clearly established that the presence of idiots is a threat to the commonwealth, not least via their 'idle and often mischievous' conduct. He notes that:

There are at least a thousand persons of this class who not only contribute nothing to the common stock, but who are ravenous consumers; who are idle and often mischievous, and who are dead weights upon the materiality of the state. But this is not all; they are even worse than useless; they generally require a good deal of watching to prevent their doing mischief, and they occupy considerable part of the time of more industrious and valuable persons. (Howe, 1848: np.)

The clear link between the social costs of such forms of conduct and the moral weighting of persons is explicit. Idiots are not only worse than useless, they waste 'the time of more industrious and valuable persons'. Industriousness, contributing to the state, eschewing mischievousness are then morally highly valued, whereas those persons not displaying such conduct – those of the class of idiots – are not. Mischievous, turbulent, or rebellious conduct was also of concern to Alfred Binet (1905) who, in 'New methods for the diagnosis of the intellectual level of subnormals', writes that:

Most subnormal children, especially those in the schools, are habitually grouped in two categories, those of backward intelligence, and those who are unstable. This latter class, which certain alienists call moral imbeciles, do not necessarily manifest inferiority of intelligence; they are turbulent, vicious, rebellious to all discipline; they lack sequence of ideas, and probably power of attention. It is a matter of great delicacy to make the distinction between children who are unstable, and those who have rebellious dispositions.

This is not, however, to be the only limitation of our subject because backward states of intelligence present several different types. There is the insane type – or the type of intellectual decay – which consists in a progressive loss of former acquired intelligence. Many epileptics, who suffer from frequent attacks, progress toward insanity. It would be possible and probably very important, to be able to make the distinction between those with decaying intelligence on the one hand, and those of inferior intelligence on the other. But as we have determined to limit on this side also, the domain of our study, we shall rigorously exclude all forms of insanity and decay.

Here, as in the current 'diagnostic' definitions of the notion of intellectual disability we saw earlier, Binet blends notions of social performance, impaired capacities that are today conceived as aspects of 'intelligence', and unwanted conduct, all the while leaving open the possibility that 'moral imbeciles' may also be 'inferior in intelligence'. He notes that those 'which certain alienists call moral imbeciles, do not necessarily manifest inferiority of intelligence; they are turbulent, vicious, rebellious to all discipline; they lack sequence of ideas, and probably power of attention'.[24] Conducting oneself in a manner that is 'turbulent, vicious, rebellious to all discipline' or even merely 'mischievous', is clearly to present oneself

---

[24] No doubt those with a penchant for presentist disorder spotting will claim that here Binet actually offers an early identification of 'what we now call' ADHD.

to those in authority to make distinctions 'of great delicacy' in a morally disreputable fashion.

The links between vicious, disgusting and degrading conduct, and proper supervision (or its absence) preoccupied early modern writers on defectiveness. In a paper, the authorship of which is unclear (Simpson, 2000a), published in the *American Journal of Insanity* in 1847, it is stressed that the moral conduct of idiots is, at least in part, a function of the adequacy of the intelligence and expertise of those in charge of them.

In some towns, we found the idiots, who were under the charge of kind-hearted, but ignorant persons, to be entirely idle, given over to disgusting and degrading habits, and presenting the sad and demoralizing spectacle of men, made in God's image, whom neither their own reason, nor the reason of others, lifted up above the level of brutes. In other towns, idiots, who, to all appearance, had no more capacity than those just mentioned, were under the charge of more intelligent persons, and they presented a different spectacle – they were healthy, cleanly and industrious. We found some, of a very low grade of intellect, at work in the fields, under the direction of attendants; and they seemed not only to be free from depraving habits, but to be happy and useful. (*American Journal of Insanity*, 1847: 76–9)

Here then we again see the linkage of 'the charge of more intelligent persons' with the production of healthy, clean, industrious, happy and useful idiots, a group which, left to its own devices, or under the care and control of well-meaning, good-hearted but uninformed laypersons, would display brute-like, non-human, conduct rightly attracting opprobrium and disapprobation. Likewise, early twentieth-century definitions of mental deficiency drew attention to ethical-moral failures, but increasingly framed them within a vague, but technical sounding, medical lexicon. Tredgold, for example, writes of mental deficiency as:

A state of mental defect from birth, or from an early age, due to incomplete cerebral development, in consequence of which the person affected is unable to perform his duties as a member of society in the position of life to which he is born. (1908: 2)

And, thirty-five years later, he describes mental deficiency as:

A state of incomplete mental development of such a kind and degree that the individual is incapable of adapting himself to the normal environment of his fellows in such a way to maintain existence independently of supervision, control or external support. (Tredgold, 1937: 4)

As in McDonagh's (2000) analysis of literary representations of 'learning disability' in early- and mid-nineteenth century Britain, in his review of Thomson's (1998) *The Problem of Mental Deficiency: Eugenics, Democracy and Social Policy in Britain, c. 1870–1959*, Barham notes that what were construed as forms of immoral conduct were central to the identity of the 'defective' throughout this era:

> Through to the 1920s, the proffered images of the wayward defective were generally quite distinct and gender specific, and provided a pivotal focus of moral concern. She was sizzling hot, a regular randy Mandy, ready to tumble with all comers; he was unmanly and ineffectual, a social non-starter, incapable of attracting either an employer or a marital partner . . . The obsession with wayward female sexuality, in particular, not infrequently overwhelmed the evaluative frame and resulted in the certification of women who were occupationally perfectly competent, and promptly found themselves jobs again when they were finally released in 1959. (Barham, 1999: 113)

Returning to the early twenty-first century, the ethical–moral dimension of intellectual disability central to accounts dating back to the 1840s remains in place. Thus, for example, in asking 'Why is the term mental retardation offensive?' Schroeder *et al.* (2002: 90) immediately illuminate the survival of moral judgement inherent in the contemporary diagnosis of the 'condition'. Like a diagnosis of AIDS, perhaps, being diagnosed as 'mentally retarded' immediately performs a socially constitutive assessment of moral character and conduct. We would not, that is to say, be able sensibly to ask 'Why is the term "measles" offensive?' Schroeder *et al.* answer their question by reference, again, to the social, moral, work that such characterisations do: they suggest that: 'to be labeled intelligent is regarded as "flattering"'. Undoubtedly, 'individuals would prefer to be viewed in those terms rather than as "slow", "stupid" – an especially denigrating epithet – as "retarded"' (Schroeder *et al.* 2002: 90). Again we might ask: can it sensibly be said that to be diagnosed with the flu is 'flattering', or that a diagnosis of diabetes is 'insulting'? What this demonstrates is that intellectual disability is *also*, unlike many – if not most – other, properly, medical conditions, still a moral categorisation, and as such very clearly to be located in the social–moral world.

That is, it would seem that despite the scientificity of talk of diagnostic criteria, objective assessment, disorders and symptoms, there remains something inherently social and moral about the evaluation of persons' being-in-the-world as describable as 'intellectually disabled' or 'retarded'. While Simpson (2000b) argues that, historically, in the production of 'idiocy as a regime of truth' the 'sayability' of the 'condition' was defined by its conceptual parameters rather than a 'core' or 'essence', it seems, to the contrary, to be the case that there is clear evidence of essentialist thought in contemporary professional discussions of 'it', and its associated 'indicators', poor IQ performance, and 'impoverished' social functioning. And, in the era of the confessional, the individualisation of intellectual disability as a professionally identifiable attribute of persons carries with it – perhaps as a substitute for the failure that Tredgold (1908) noted of the 'perform[ance of] his duties as a member of society in the position of life to which he is born' – the moral requirement of 'the truthful rendering into speech of who one is' (Rose, 1999b: 244). That is to say it is a requisite corollary of the professional identification of one as 'retarded' that one should acknowledge oneself as such. And – if this requirement of ethical conduct is not complied with – this may, in and of itself, be held both as grounds for the ascription of irretrievable incompetence, and hence the correctness of the initial identification, and also as warrant for moral censure. Indeed, the conceptualisation of disability as a political–ethical–moral social status is central to the arguments of the theorists of the 'social model of disability'.

The social model of disability

Developing from the work of UPIAS (1976) the social model of disability as a formal statement of social scientific theory is usually held to originate in the work of Mike Oliver (1981; 1983; 1985; 1986; 1990). Although described as an 'outdated ideology', Shakespeare and Watson claim that it has 'now become the ideological litmus test of disability politics in Britain, used by the disabled people's movement to distinguish between organisations, policies, laws and ideas which are progressive, and those which are inadequate' (Shakespeare and Watson, 2002: 3). As we have seen, the fractioning of a monolithic 'Disability' into notions of a (physical or mental) *impairment*, with concomitant *disability* caused by societal barriers is central to this understanding. As Oliver (1996: 30) has it, a binary division is established between the biological and the social. In criticising medical, sociological and psychological models of disability Oliver suggests that the social model:

Does not deny the problem of disability but locates it squarely within society. It is not individual limitations, of whatever kind, which are the cause of the problem but society's failure to provide appropriate services and adequately ensure the needs of disabled people are fully taken into account in its social organisation. (Oliver, 1996: 32)

Writing of recent developments in the work of the originators of the social model, Bury (1996) suggests that:

Perhaps the sharpest challenge to existing ideas about disability is the argument that disability should be seen as a form of 'social oppression' (Oliver, 1990; 1992). In contrast to existing notions of disability, which, it is argued, portray it as a characteristic of individuals, 'disability' is seen, instead, as a wholly social phenomenon . . . that 'disability as a category can only be understood within a framework, which suggests that it is culturally produced and socially constructed' (Oliver, 1990, p. 22). 'Disability' is seen to be a function of those practices and perceptions linked to certain bodily mental or behavioural states which are so designated . . . disability is not the resulting limitations caused by chronic illness, impairment or trauma, but the way such matters are responded to and categorised by the wider society.

While such a statement – with the suggestion that 'disability' is a 'wholly social phenomenon' – may be taken to be congruent with a relativist, social constructionist, position, this possibility is ruled out by other foundational writers in the tradition. Thus Finkelstein offers an essentialist, realist, account in what he terms a 'general hypothesis on disability', namely that:

Disabled people have been abstracted from society and as an abstraction we embody the essence of social relationships at a particular point in historical time (Finkelstein, 1997). In this sense, then, I believe that we cannot understand or deal with disability without dealing with the essential nature of society itself. To do this disabled people must find ways of engaging in the class struggle where the historical direction of society is fought, won or lost. It is in this arena that the boundaries of knowledge that have put disabled people aside from the 'normal' can and have to be openly questioned. (Finkelstein, 2001: 5)

Oliver (1999: 2) also continues to argue for a Marxist understanding of the oppression of people with disabilities (intellectual or otherwise) and suggests that a social model, in his view, must be based in 'a materialist view of society':

To say that the category disability is produced by capitalist society in a particular form implies a particular world view. Within this world view, the production of the category disability is no different from the production of motor cars or hamburgers. Each has an industry, whether it be the car, fast food or human service industry. Each industry has a workforce which has a vested interest in producing their product in particular ways and in exerting as much control over the process of production as possible.

The crucial importance of structural economic factors is also emphasised by American workers such as by Albrecht (1992). Complementing Oliver's (1999) view, it is argued that that, like cars or hamburgers, 'disability' is commodified and transformed into a 'good' – the key product of 'the disability business', along with a series of techniques for its treatment, management and rehabilitation. Associated with this materialist world view of disability as product, Barnes (1991) and Barnes and Oliver (1993) argue that the underlying 'ideological' conception of disabled people in capitalist societies – the 'personal tragedy theory' of individualised disablement and its consequences – is crucial to the success of the 'industry'. They argue that 'the continued ideological hegemony of "personal tragedy theory"' is a consequence of 'its professional expediency, both at the individual and at the structural levels'. Individualising disability as inherent in the person thus affords the possibility of victim-blaming and professional exculpation. For instance they argue that 'personal tragedy theory' allows for the failure, on the part of specific, individual, persons to live up to, engage with, or succeed in professionally determined ameliorative strategies may thus be explained by 'the disabled person's perceived inadequacy – whether it be physically or intellectually based or both. The "expert" is exonerated from responsibility, professional integrity remains intact, traditional wisdom and values are not questioned, and the existing social order remains unchallenged' (Barnes and Oliver, 1993: 5).

Barnes and Oliver also take issue with prevailing acceptance of Goffman's work on stigma. As we will see in chapter 4, the theory of stigma has been adopted, largely uncritically, across the sociological and psychological literatures as a social scientific given. In this view people with 'accredited impairments' are, simply, stigmatised. Finkelstein (1980) further suggests that Goffman's work and that which has flowed from it, 'takes as given the imposed segregation, passivity and inferior status of stigmatised individuals and groups including disabled people without seriously addressing questions of causality'.

From the perspective of 'first wave' writers on the 'social model', existing sociological and psychological theories of disability can then be criticised not only for being an apologia for industrial capitalism, for functioning as ideological supports for a 'disablist society' (Bury, 1996), and for having 'accepted almost without question the legitimacy of the individualistic, biomedical approach to disability', but also on three other counts. Barnes and Oliver (1993: 1) contend that contemporary analyses of disability are, firstly:

Essentially determinist; behaviour is only viewed positively if it is commensurate with professionals' perceptions of reality. Second, they ignore extraneous economic, political and social factors. Third, they undermine and deny subjective interpretations of impairment from the perspective of the person concerned. In sum, they are the product of the 'psychological imagination' constructed upon a bed-rock of 'non-disabled' assumptions of what it is like to experience impairment.

A second wave

However, as Barnes (1997) also notes, whether they be influenced by American functionalism and deviance theory, or the Marxist materialist analysis of history 'both approaches have been criticised for their neglect of the role of culture by a "second generation" of British writers concerned primarily with the experience, rather than the production, of both impairment and disability'. This is, in fact, not necessarily an accurate characterisation of 'second wave' writing in disability theory, a considerable body of which has been precisely concerned with the *discursive* rather than the *materialist* 'production' of disability. Indeed, writers in this second wave (e.g. Chappell, 1998; Corker and Shakespeare, 2002a, b; Thomas and Corker, 2002; Goodley *et al.* 2000; Goodley, 2001; 1997) have been much more receptive to post-structuralist thought and recognise that 'disability' is (from a Foucauldian perspective) the product of an array of discursive practices – which as we have seen – arose and proliferated over the course of the nineteenth and twentieth centuries, being widely taken up in judicial, educational and social welfare fields subsequent to their promulgation by the medical and ur-psychological professions. That is to say, writers such as Corker and Shakespeare suggest that while '"disabled people" did not exist before this classification . . . impairment and impairment-related practices certainly did' (2002a: 8).

Barnes (1997) objects strongly to the sort of analysis that Shakespeare (1994) offers on two counts: that by 'endorsing [a] largely phenomenological approach . . . he implies that all cultures respond to impairment in essentially negative terms'. Quite how a phenomenological approach is able to accomplish this implication is opaque, and it is well accepted by 'second wave' disability theorists that not only is what is to count as 'impairment' culturally relative but so are responses to 'it'. Barnes's second objection is that a post-structuralist approach is said to 'reduce[s] explanations for cultural perceptions of people with perceived impairments as abnormal to the level of metaphysics or thought processes. Besides successfully attracting attention away from economic and social conditions this analysis also implies that the marginalisation of those perceived in this way is somehow unavoidable – regardless of what we do.' Again, and this is a recurrent criticism made by second wave theorists of their predecessors, this is not only to do 'strong social model' rhetoric (Shakespeare and Watson, 2002) but also grossly to oversimplify in dichotomous terms. 'Marginalisation' may well be theorised as a question of 'economic and social conditions' but that need not necessarily *exclude* consideration of the ways in which 'disability' is also already a cultural, moral, discursive formation. That is this too surely is to fall victim to the 'psychological imagination' constructed upon an uncomfortable bed-rock of both 'dialectical materialist' *and* 'psychologised' assumptions about a binary separation of mind/body; individual/society; economy/culture.

Problems with the social model

Second wave writers have identified a number of difficulties with the social model as it has been described by workers such as Oliver, Barnes and Finkelstein. Corker and Shakespeare (2002a: 15) note that: 'both the medical model and the social model seek to explain disability universally, and end up creating totalizing, meta-historical narratives that exclude important dimensions of disabled people's lives and of their knowledge. The global experience of disabled people is too complex to be rendered within one unitary model.' As Bury (1996) has noted the social model/social oppression (Abberley, 1987) approach to disability is open to the criticism of reductionism. Under the social model (first wave) 'causality' is treated according to billiard ball theory, as structural, linear and ineluctable. Such an account simply cannot accommodate either the historical, or the local, fluidity, contingency and situatedness of the making, and making relevant, of 'impairment' or 'disability' as such. Rather, impairment and disability are, paradoxically for a self-titled 'social model', reified as structurally given things. Disability and impairment are, as in the medical model, retained as experiences or characteristics of the individual, who is positioned as the victim of grand theoretical constructs such as history, capitalism or industrialisation. The fixed, singular, subject is counterposed to the monolithic 'social forces' of capitalism: thus not only is 'disabled' constructed as an attribute of persons of pervasive and permanent relevance, but also – despite the regularity of statements like 'the problem is society' – 'the disabled' or 'the impaired' can, if they take issue with this account, via the first wave social model's theoretical adherence to Marxism, be further delegitimated by the attribution to them of a 'false consciousness' (itself a product of the 'psychological imagination' *par excellence*). However, as Shakespeare and Watson (2002) point out in their criticism of the 'crude determinism' of the social model, 'impairment is not a pre-social or pre-cultural biological substrate (Thomas, 1999, 124) . . . the words we use and the discourses we deploy to represent impairment are socially and culturally determined. There is no pure or natural body, existing outside of discourse. Impairment is only ever viewed through the lens of disabling social relations.'

But there still remain at least two difficulties with this rewriting of the social model. We see the residue of a theoretical assumption of determinism. That is, Shakespeare and Watson (2002) suggest that 'discourses . . . are socially and culturally determined'. This is both to misrepresent by overstatement a Foucauldian position (which might, in a more measured fashion, talk about conditions of possibility) and to fail to acknowledge that 'discourses', under both an ordinary language philosophy and a discursive psychological reading, are better understood as available resources and that social interaction is rule-*oriented*, not rule-*governed* (Edwards, 1997). Further, in what appears to be a shaking out of the term 'discourses', 'disabling social relations' are assumed to, in some fashion that is not specified with clarity, determine how impairment is 'viewed', presumably implying that the 'viewing' is somehow deterministic of the production of 'impairment'. Hence, again, the psychological imagination is smuggled in by the back door: this is simple cognitive determinism. Despite their optimistic recognition that 'impairment and disability are not dichotomous . . . [and that] It is difficult to determine where impairment ends and disability starts . . . Disability is a complex dialectic of biological, psychological, cultural and socio-political factors, which cannot be extricated except with imprecision' (Shakespeare and Watson, 2002) this account also at least holds open the possibility that it *may* be possible to 'determine where impairment ends and disability starts, even if this is accomplished "with imprecision"'.

Secondly, we see here, if not a failure to accommodate the issue, certainly a presumption of the reality of 'intellectual impairment' (presumably professionally defined) and a tendency in the retheorising of disability to 'tag it on as an afterthought' (Chappell, Goodley and Lawthom, 2001: 46). Thus although much of what Shakespeare and Watson (2002) suggest is eminently sensible, the limits of the imagination of even key second wave writers become evident in their use of questions such as 'If someone has a significant intellectual limitation, how can society be altered to make this irrelevant to employment opportunities, for example?' as an effort to deflate the 'fairy tale' of a barrier free utopia they suggest that Finkelstein (1981) proffers. That is, 'significant intellectual limitation' remains – even under this analysis – a static, *a priori* given: significant intellectual limitation thus remains outside the remit of a re-made, postmodern, social model, despite the fact that, inasmuch as the way that 'employment opportunities' are just as much a socially structured 'barrier' to people with an intellectual disability as a flight of steps is to a wheelchair user, so too may they be socially re-made.

That is, despite claims to the contrary, it appears that some 'impairments' – specifically intellectual impairment – are immune to understanding as relative, socially constructed category memberships, and are taken as natural kinds: as Goodley (2001: 211) has suggested, the new social model still tends to see intellectual impairment as 'an excluded category, marked the biological we cannot sociologise'. Although Shakespeare's position has clearly changed since the 1990s, it remains the case that many in the social model tradition would not resile from his earlier position that in attacking 'psychologism', 'it is vital to start by distinguishing between impairment and disability, and to remove the causal reductionism of which both psychologists . . . and biomedical clinicians are guilty' (Shakespeare and Watson, 1997, ms 5). Likewise French suggests that 'some of the most profound problems experienced by people with certain impairments are difficult, if not impossible, to solve by social manipulation' (French, 1993: 17). To the contrary: if we are to provide a thoroughgoing rethinking of intellectual disability and impairment it is essential that nothing is defined, *a priori*, as off limits.

Intellectual disability as social-moral category

Social scientists have become familiar not only with thinking of 'intellectual disability' as a 'real' attribute of persons that may be diagnosed, but also as a form of life, or personhood, in its own right. Not only this, but as we have seen above, to 'have a disability' is widely understood as also to entail 'having' a 'stigmatised' identity (Goffman, 1963). It is important to be clear here about the strength of the commitment to the 'reality' of the notions both of stigma and of identity in this literature: in Goffman's (1963: 12) terms such social identities are 'actual', Szivos and Griffiths (1990) write of 'a mentally retarded identity' as something, like cancer, heart disease or a bereavement, that persons so diagnosed have to 'come to terms with'. Davies and Jenkins (1997) state, quite unequivocally, that 'people with learning difficulties often appear to experience significant incongruence between their categorical identity as someone with learning difficulties and their self-identity' (Davies and Jenkins, 1997: 95) a formulation which simultaneously psychologises and reifies categorical-identities and self-identities as internal componentry, and naturalises 'learning difficulty' as something which is essential to the person. This essentialist understanding is taken to its realist limit when it is noted that 'people with learning difficulties carry a label and an associated social identity which is a major determinant of their material prospects and the character of their social relationships' (Davies and Jenkins, 1997: 95). Thus it is also that Edgerton (1967: 205–7) states very clearly that to 'find oneself as a mental retardate is a shattering stigma . . . the ultimate horror' and, later, that such is the supposed social toxicity of the identity, that 'never is mental retardation admitted' (Edgerton, 1967: 207).[25] Such accounts would, it seems, lend weight to the views of Schroeder *et al.* (2001) which we have already encountered, that 'mentally retarded'

[25] The construction 'to find oneself as a mental retardate' is fascinating. Simultaneously the existence of 'mental retardates' in the world is naturalised, as is the possibility that one might 'find oneself' as such, all by oneself – by introspection possibly? The fact that people do not 'find themselves', but rather are *found to be* 'mental retardates' by an array of professional practices vanishes.

is a stigmatising term, an offensive appellation, an 'especially denigrating epithet'. As noted, social model theorists raise strong objections to the manner in which this form of thinking naturalises, individualises and reifies what they view as a social process. That is, rather ironically, they suggest that *this* contribution to structuralist thought does not help us to understand what it means for a person with a disability to manage, and perhaps to contest, such an identity in a social world.

However, in a neat symmetry with the notions of Finkelstein, Oliver and other social model theorists – that many physically disabled people may be afflicted by a 'false consciousness' – a number of researchers following Goffman (1963) and Edgerton (1967; 1993) have suggested that many people with intellectual disabilities may not only be chronically stigmatised and, hence, psychologically 'damaged', but may, if they have not 'come to terms with a mentally retarded identity' (Szivos and Griffiths, 1990) also be 'invisible to themselves' (Davies and Jenkins, 1997; Finlay and Lyons, 1998; 2000; Jahoda, Marková and Cattermole, 1988; Sinason, 1992; Todd and Shearn, 1995; 1997) or unknowing victims of parental 'fictional identity building' (Todd and Shearn, 1997: 362).

Studies in this genre then seek to show people with intellectual disabilities demonstrably failing to understand the 'real nature' of their disability, or as lacking an understanding of the enduring 'realities' of the categorical identity they 'carry'. Thus it is reported that:

The meanings of having a learning disability were imprecise among the small number of people . . . we spoke to . . . the people we spoke to held very limited knowledge of their disability and its consequences . . . meanings focussed upon specific impairments . . . People . . . also seemed unaware of its social significance or the impact it would have on their careers. (Todd and Shearn, 1995: 19–20)

It may be worth recalling that, as Rose (1999a: np) puts it: 'in confessing, one is subjectified by another, for one confesses in the actual or imagined presence of a figure who prescribes the form of the confession, the words and rituals through which it should be made, who appreciates, judges . . .' In this context then Todd and Shearn (1995) go on to suggest that peoples' lack of awareness may be judged by them 'denying' their disability, or at least demonstrating in interaction with researchers, that they do not 'know' that they are disabled.[26] This trope is also clearly

---

[26] The very use of the term 'denial' accomplishes two linked rhetorical projects: it recruits commonsensical psychologised (or more precisely, psychodynamic) vernacular understandings of people 'being in denial', that is people not wanting to know the awful truth about their cancer or whatever; and simultaneously recruits the discourse of crime, in which 'to deny' a charge is also to acknowledge that a real offence has been committed, while disavowing responsibility for it. Either way, the term cements the 'reality' of that to which people are invited to 'confess'.

visible in the work reported by Davies and Jenkins (1997: 96) who suggest that 'at the simplest level this becomes a question of whether people with learning difficulties "understand" what is meant by that label . . . and, further, whether they apply such a label to themselves'. Describing the participants in their study they suggest that:

Their responses may be divided into a number of categories . . . which reflect their attempts to provide definitions for these terms and the ways in which their self-identities appeared to be involved in their understandings. The largest category (42%) included those who responded to questions about the meaning of mental handicap *with apparent complete incomprehension*. Answers were mostly very brief: 'No', 'Don't know', 'You tell me'. (Davies and Jenkins, 1997: 98, my emphasis)

As we will see shortly, it is not unreasonable to expect someone invited to confess to an offence, to morally disreputable or otherwise sanctionable conduct, by a figure in authority, to dissimulate or to issue a denial. Thus it might be a piece of everyday television police drama for an officer to ask similar 'social/categorical identity' questions. 'Are you the man seen running along the High Street after the post office robbery?', and for a 'suspect' to answer 'No', 'Don't know' or 'You tell me'. We immediately hear such utterances *not* as 'apparent complete incomprehension', but rather as its *opposite*. Another way of understanding this, of course, is that in these studies people with an intellectual disability may be being held accountable (and liable to moral disqualification) by virtue of their failing the moral requirement of 'the truthful rendering into speech of who one is' (Rose, 1999b: 244).

While chapter 4 examines this issue in greater detail, as we saw in chapter 1, briefly a discursive psychological approach respecifies 'having' a social or categorical identity as the avowal – or otherwise – of that identity (intellectually disabled or not) as a matter of local interactional business. The fundamental point at issue here is that identity claims are not just 'confessions' or 'denials' of category membership, although this might be one of the things they can be described as, but rather are claims made in and for specific interactional contexts to do local, situated, work in the management of 'self'. As Edwards points out:

Everyday descriptions and psychological attributions, viewed in the context of their occurrence as discourse, perform normative, reality-defining, intersubjectively oriented work. That work includes the invocation of a range of psychological categories whose status is not so much definitive of the persons described, nor even of the person-perceptions of the describers, but, rather constitutive of the interpersonal actions performed using them. (Edwards, 1997: 66)

Whether or not people 'know' or 'deny' that they 'have' an intellectual disability has then become the focus of a considerable body of work. While chapter 4 will look at this issue in more detail, it is important to trail the matter here. In brief the main difficulty with this literature is that it misses the point that categories are available for use, by members, and that it is the way that members use them (rather than an inspection of the 'correctness' of their use in 'our' terms) that should be the focus of analysis. For example, in his discussion of police interrogations of (intellectually 'normal') murder suspects Rod Watson (1983) makes the simple but telling point that:

The most immediate observation that we can make . . . is that the identifications 'victim' and 'offender' are rarely used *per se* in the interrogations. Instead, in the account of the offence or the 'lead up' to that account, we get a variety of 'other' descriptions of the offender, the victim and indeed for third parties. (ms 3)

Now it would seem to be reasonable to suspect that the social categories 'victim' and 'offender' are, given the context of a police interrogation, likely to be highly salient. Yet, as Watson observes, they are rarely used. Instead what we see is the widespread deployment of a range of other categories ('tough guy', 'member of a gang' and 'independent' for 'offenders' and 'faggots', 'niggers' and 'fags' for 'victims'). The point here is that such membership categorisations are employed to do the moral work of accomplishing accountability, blame, and motive rather than to display the contents of people's heads, whether or not suspects 'really' 'know' that they are 'offenders' who have 'victims'. Indeed, to ask whether those being interrogated 'know' that they are candidate members of the category 'offender' seems ludicrous. And yet, we have a literature which repeatedly asks people described as intellectually disabled whether they 'know' that they are members of this category (and in so doing holds up to critical scrutiny their status as fully human). Why might this be? Why do we not see a literature which speculates about the 'self-identity' of murder suspects as 'offenders' when clearly that identity is, to the onlooking analyst, patently salient? In the very asking of the question, we see the construction of the category 'intellectual disability' as one which is self-constituting by virtue of its professionally ascribed incumbents' accountable 'failing' to meet the requirements of researchers that they admit to, or as Rose would have it 'confess to', membership. Or, as Garfinkel (1967) would have it, perhaps we have another instance of the social sciences treating their objects of study as 'cultural dopes'.

This body of work also overlooks the fact that matters of identity management can be accomplished in a multiplicity of ways, and brought off by a range of conversational devices, which do not in any sense resemble straightforward avowal or disavowal, confession or denial, of categorial incumbency. Establishing membership in the category 'competent member' is not accomplished simply by making a claim to membership in a research interview. As shown by Sacks's work, by a substantial corpus of work in MCA since, and in the couple counselling extract in chapter 1, categorial identities may be managed as effectively by, for example, laying claims to the predicates associated with a particular category as by a bald claim. For example, in his analysis of a set of police interviews, Derek Edwards (2002) points out that the claim by the suspect West that 'I wouldn't do that to an old lady' is hearable not only as a claim about the actuality or otherwise of the suggestion that an elderly shopkeeper had been assaulted during the course of a robbery, but also works to make a claim about the category of offender – or type of person – that West *actually is* by virtue of the sorts of actions conventionally to be associated with particular categories of people. That is to say West lays claim to membership in the category 'petty offender', or to a social identity describable as 'a thief', rather than in the altogether more serious category 'robber' not by simply saying 'I am a thief' – or indeed, 'I am not a robber' – but rather by calling upon the shared knowledge that he and his interrogators have of the predicates of the category 'thief' – which do not include the use of violence in the course of an offence.

Further, identity is established *in and by* the successful construction of intersubjectivity: that is to say interlocutors can establish a shared status as members of a common cultural order by the use of a range of devices that constitute the architecture of intersubjectivity. In their study of joint productions in conversations between an aphasic – and demonstrably neurologically impaired – man, Ed, and his wife, Mary, Oelschlager and Damico (1998) discuss what they describe as 'motivations for joint productions' in talk-in-interaction.[27] Of course, one need not take 'motivation' here in the commonsensical psychologistic sense as meaning 'the reason for . . .', but rather take the 'motivations' identified as specifying the work that is accomplished in and through the use of joint constructions. Joint productions, to use Oelschlager and Damico's (1998) term then, are described as:

The initiation of a turn by one speaker and the syntactically and semantically coherent extension or completion of that initiation by another speaker . . . unlike interruptions that constitute an intrusion of talk occurring quite independently and without regard to the syntactic or semantic output of the other speaker

---

[27] Joint productions are also known as joint productions and utterance completions (Sacks, 1992); anticipatory turn constructions/completions or compound turn constructional units (Lerner, 1991; 1996).

(Ferrara, 1992), joint productions serve to advance both the flow of the conversation and the content that makes up the interaction. (ms 6–7)

Lerner (1996) describes the manner in which anticipatory turn completion can accomplish a number of other functions in everyday interaction between unimpaired interlocutors, including demonstrations of understanding, the production of collaborative agreement, managing repair and correction – the doing of 'face work' (Goffman, 1967). In extract 2 below Josh's anticipatory completion works to demonstrate understanding and Marty's agreement token confirms that understanding:

Extract 2: CDHQ:II:3, from Lerner, 1996: 308

```
1   MARTY   Now most machines
2           don't record that
3           slow. So I'd wanna-
4           when I make a tape,
5   JOSH    be able tuh speed
6           it up.
7   MARTY   Yeah.
```

As Lerner points out, examples of joint productions are also to be found in Sacks's (1992) Group Therapy Session data, where their structure demonstrates the manner in which initial utterances both foreshadow their completion, and the way in which competent speakers are able to identify the trajectory of a turn from its initial delivery. Lerner (1996: 307) cites a classic example of anticipatory turn completion as subversion in the doing of humour (or 'wisecracking'). Here Roger, a therapy group member, completes the therapist's (Dan's) turn having identified the 'when x, then y' device in its initial projection.

Extract 3: (2) GTS, reproduced in Lerner, 1996: 308

```
1   DAN     When the group
2           reconvenes in
3           two weeks =
4   ROGER   = they're gunna
5           issue straitjackets.
```

Turning then to interactions between speakers where one has experienced a stroke, Oelschlager and Damico (1998) offer a number of similar examples of such joint productions (both with and without active word searches and extended 'guess' sequences) as shown in extracts 4 and 5.[28]

---

[28] Oelschlager and Damico (2003) suggest that the extended 'guess' sequences – whereby the non-impaired interlocutor provides a series of semantically coherent suggestions for the 'missing' word – by their production as 'guesses' attend to the maintenance of the competence of the impaired speaker.

Extract 4: From Oelschlager and Damico 1998: ms 7

1	Ed	Yeah. About uh, Brooklyn, Brooklyn Bridge?
2	MG	Uh huh
3	Ed	That's me. On the, the =
4	MG	= other side

Extract 5: From Oelschlager and Damico 1998: ms 7

1	Ed	Yeah we got- the- tapes already but =
2	MG	= we just don't have the player
3	Ed	Er, this is what this is.

Oelschlager and Damico (1998) point to a number of features of these joint productions: one is their exquisite timing, with completions frequently latched (as in extracts 3, 4 and 5), and also the routine acknowledgement, by Ed as by Marty, of turn completion utterances which 'have the effect of indicating his acceptance of M's contribution to the co-construction and . . . enabl[ing] him to reassert his turn' (ms 16). As such joint productions can be, in Sacks's terms, 'techniques of affirmation' (1992: 147). In their discussion of the resources required for the successful interactional completion of joint productions – by either speaker – and importantly for the analysis to come, Oelschlager and Damico (1998) note that:

> The second type of resource employed in the creation of M's joint productions involve her ability as a hearer to immediately analyze Ed's initial turn component grammatically. Based on her proficiency and linguistic intuitions as a native speaker, M is able to instantaneously analyze the syntactic structure of Ed's incomplete utterance and then use that analysis to create a grammatically appropriate final completion component. (ms 26)

Four 'motivations' for the employment of joint productions in interaction are suggested by Oelschlager and Damico (1998): providing assistance; establishing affiliation; enhancing communicative effectiveness and efficiency; and establishing the perception of communicative competence. Such functions, as well as requiring speakers to possess the resources to 'instantaneously analyse the syntactic structure' of utterances in progress, are also served by deployment of other resources such as shared personal and world knowledge, which in and of themselves can act as a claim of moral/identity equivalence (and we will see in chapter 5 the deployment of expert claims as another such device). As does Lerner, Oelschlager and Damico's (1998) analysis of the functions served by joint productions suggests that matters of (relative) moral status, 'face' and interpersonal relatedness are central. They do however also suggest that while joint productions are, evidently, 'quite "doable" by ordinary speakers, this cannot be assumed in conversations with persons whose language ability is not ordinary' (ms 33).

So what of another class of persons whose language ability is held not to be 'ordinary'? In extract 6, we see a discussion of Valerie's job with Patrick, a research student. Valerie is described as 'mildly intellectually disabled' by the service that supports her and is a wheelchair user. Of note in the extract are the two anticipatory turn completions, one by each speaker. In lines 7–8, we see that Patrick completes Valerie's turn, with a downgrade of his prior assessment of the difficulty she has in going out and meeting people. That is, such activities are modulated from 'very hard' to 'pretty difficult', and the impossibility of independent movement ('like you can't go out by yourself anywhere') is finessed to the more positive 'to go out and meet new people and that sort of thing' by Patrick's latched completion of Valerie's turn at line 8. These downgrades are then accepted by Valerie with an emphatic agreement token in line 10. Such a completion is, it would seem, a clear instance of face-attentive, affiliative, work: proposed by the 'unimpaired' speaker, the joint production revises the initially proposed degree of Valerie's impairment and transforms her from a helpless, wheelchair-bound dependent into an active agent confronted by barriers to participation in a social world. The second joint production in this sequence reverses speaker positions.

Extract 6: PK/VR/1998

```
1      P   Okay (. .) I guess (. .) how do you feel about that (. . .) would you like to
2          go out on weekends (.) if you had the chance to
3      V   Sometimes (.) I did last weekend (.) my sister took me somewhere but
4          not all the time
5      P   Okay (. .) and umm (. .) the fact that you're in a wheelchair I guess
6          makes it very hard like you can't go out by yourself anywhere
7      V   No (.) I always have to have help (.) wherever I go =
8→     P   = s'pretty difficult to go out and meet new people and that sort of
9          thing
10     V   Yeah
11     P   Would you like to if you had the chance (. .) to go out an  ⌈d
12     V                                                              ⌊If I had to
13         show people around I would
. . .
16     P   Okay (. .) the people you work with here (1 sec) do you think of them
17         as your friends
18     V   Yes they are my friends
19     P   They are your friends
20     V   Yes
21     P   And do you get a chance to see those people outside of working hours
22     V   No
```

```
23:   P   Would you like to if you could
24    V   °If I could yeah°
25    P   I guess it's =
26→   V   = a bit hard at the moment
27    P   It's a bit hard because you (. .) if I get in my car I guess (.) I can drive
28        out and see someone (.) it's a bit hard for you
29    V   Yeah my disability (.) I keep on telling people that
```

In lines 25–6 Valerie recapitulates the joint assessment of the difficulties she faces arrived at earlier in lines 7–8. We see here that this time it is Valerie who completes Patrick's turn with a perfectly syntactically and semantically complete utterance, which looks back to the previous exchange.

Extract 6 (detail)

```
24    V   °If I could yeah°
25    P   I guess it's =
26→   V   = a bit hard at the moment
27    P   It's a bit hard because you (. .) if I get in my car I guess (.) I can drive
28        out and see someone (.) it's a bit hard for you
29    V   Yeah my disability (.) I keep on telling people that
```

Again, the proposed joint production is accepted by Patrick with a tentative recycle incorporating elements of both prior turns and micropauses which, hearably, represent checks of his entitlement to hold the floor and continue his turn. Valerie's affirmative response to this understanding check is straightforward: 'Yeah my disability (.) I keep on telling people that'.

In summary

What I have sought to do in these two opening chapters is to establish the contingency – both historical and local – of ascriptions of identity, or category membership, as 'intellectually disabled' and to suggest the fundamentally moral work that this achieves and displays. I have also tried to demonstrate that 'intellectual disability' is, rather than being a diagnostic term indexing some real entity – as talk of symptoms, diagnosis and disorder implies – an hypothetical construct of recent coinage in its current form and, as with its historical predecessors, pervasively attentive to matters of moral conduct. Further, matters of morality and matters of competence are, still, inextricably linked, with a recent genre of studies accomplishing the moral disqualification of persons via the casting of doubt on their entitlement to co-membership in the category of the fully ethical, confessing, human subject. That is to say, characterising persons as 'active but odd', or 'in denial' is not to do 'scientific description' but rather moral condemnation. Much of this work, and that in the disability studies literature, is then also still reliant on a materialist, indeed naïve realist, appreciation of competence and approaches to its demonstration. I have tried to argue that rather than adopting this, traditional approach, (in)competence, must be approached as a matter not for analytic or professional prescription, but rather more respectfully, as a matter for members. Competence, from a discursive psychological perspective, is much more subtle a social accomplishment than can be captured by standardised testing or the ticking of boxes on adaptive behaviour checklists. That is, if a discursive approach is adopted, as Czislowski-McKenna has put it: 'the study of participation and severe intellectual impairment need no longer be an issue of understanding difference but one of understanding common experiences and the characteristics of participation as a socially created phenomenon' (Czislowski-McKenna, 2001: np).

3   The interactional production of 'dispositional' characteristics: or why saying 'yes' to one's interrogators may be smart strategy

> If a person is forced to give an absurd reply by making use of an alternative pronounced in an authoritative voice, it does not in the least prove that he is lacking in judgment.
>
> (Binet, 1905: np)

The famous social psychological phenomenon known as the 'fundamental attribution error' (Ross, 1977) suggests that humans are predisposed to attribute the actions of *others* (especially perhaps accountable, or otherwise morally disreputable actions) to characteristics of the person in question, yet tend to account for their own conduct in terms of situational constraints.[1] John did x because he's mean-spirited, I did y because I had a gun to my head. On balance it would seem that what has been described by social psychologists as a defining characteristic of humanness, may also be seen at work in the scholarly accounts offered by these workers of the conduct of people described as 'intellectually disabled'. That is, much of the psychological, and the greater proportion of the sociological literatures, can be read as an extended attempt to account for the conduct of intellectually disabled people in terms of inherent, individual, dispositional characteristics – rather than of the situations or circumstances in which the objects of their study find themselves.

The canonical texts concerning psychological practice, and the instruments designed to assess psychological functioning, construct testing as a largely unproblematic technical encounter (Fowler and Mangione, 1990; Foddy, 1993). The psychologist's task is, neutrally and objectively, to map pre-existing cognitive capacities and attributes possessed by the informant. While these texts devote some attention to cultural and social influences in test design and test performance, and while they offer technical solutions to 'procedural' difficulties, they fail adequately to acknowledge the interactional nature of test-taking and test administration (Maynard

---

[1] Of course one can accept that, perhaps, this 'phenomenon' is indeed a routine feature of everyday moral accounting, without in any way being thus committed to the cognitivist notion that such accounting is in any sense 'hardwired' into persons.

and Marlaire, 1992; Marlaire and Maynard, 1990; Suchman and Jordan, 1990). This chapter offers a critique of these assumptions and illustrates, by analysis of the administration of measures of quality of life how, rather than such measures of necessity tapping pre-given attributes of the testee, the moment-by-moment interactional management of these encounters by psychologists, the demands of canonical testing protocols, and the requirements of professionalised knowledge actively produce acquiescent 'dopes' (Garfinkel, 1967) and a 'subject' group who are 'happy' (cf. Antaki and Houtkoop-Steenstra, 1998; Antaki, 1998; Antaki, Young and Finlay, 2002) with their lot.[2]

Whereas Mehan and Wood's (1975) work (discussed in chapter 2), demonstrates the *necessarily* misleading nature of large scale, technocratic and institutionalised systems for the evaluation of the abilities of specific, individual, children, Goode (1983) provides a detailed single case analysis of the manner in which the professional perspective brought to bear on the estimation of the competence of individuals is highly likely to be actively productive of the 'truths' which it is later claimed have been 'found', 'discovered' or 'revealed' about that person. This is not just a function of the empiricist repertoire that is hegemonic in 'scientific writing', though much of the tone of the professional psychological literature may be explained by this (Gilbert and Mulkay, 1984), but rather to do with the taken-for-granted practices, procedures and instruments that are adopted in order to seek out quantitative estimates of the competence or other capacities of persons. In 'Who is Bobby? Ideology and method in the discovery of a Down's Syndrome person's competence' Goode writes that:

What most persons would call Bobby's competence (with emphasis on the possessive) is actually part of his socially produced, organizationally adequate identity. Any clinician's assessment of Bobby's competence reflects as much about the social organization of clinical work, the clinician's training, and a particular clinic's instruments and procedures as it does about Bobby *per se* . . . radically different conceptions of his competence arose from different kinds of social relations with him. In this sense it should be no surprise that Bobby's friends felt he had no language difficulties and spoke with him freely while clinicians who were

---

[2] It is important throughout this chapter not to assume that the measure under scrutiny is in some sense particularly poorly designed, or otherwise lacking: the phenomena discussed here apply, with variations dependent upon the details of the measure in question, across the psychological measurement project. That is to say, the problems identified here are as germane to intelligence testing as they are to the Present State Examination (see, for example, Brown and Drugovich, 1995). Aside from any other difficulties, such procedures are predicated on the telemention or 'conduit' metaphor of speech exchange (e.g. Duchan, 2000) and also assume, incorrectly, that all interviewer utterances are properly formed questions, and all interviewee utterances are – more or less correct – answers.

strangers to Bobby found him to have extremely marginal language skills . . . partly because they have done their professional best . . . and partly because *they believe in the validity of their tests and procedures*, many clinicians find it difficult to accept that their clinically adequate procedures fail to detect Bobby's competence in other settings. Most often they are completely unaware of the problem, believing that their procedures capture Bobby's competence *independent of any social situation*. They perceive their test results as indicating *attributes of Bobby*, and thus they fail to grasp the social relativity of their own assessments and procedures. (Goode, 1983: 252, my emphasis)

Although the focus of this chapter is on the putative 'phenomenon' of acquiescence bias in intellectually disabled people, in a very real sense the presumed widespread, indeed definitional, incompetence of people so called may be but a failure of imagination.

If in doubt say 'yes'?

Are people with intellectual disabilities, or 'individuals with limited mental ability' (Heal and Sigelman, 1995) overly disposed to agree with their interlocutors and say 'yes'? Since the appearance of a series of papers by Carol Sigelman and co-workers in the early 1980s (Sigelman *et al.* 1980; 1981; 1981a; 1982; Shaw and Budd, 1982), and subsequently recycled in a number of spin-off publications (e.g. Heal and Sigelman, 1990; 1995; 1996) the notion of a dispositional 'acquiescence bias' has become a commonplace among those who work with people with learning disabilities, and has influenced interviewers, questionnaire designers, researchers and policy makers.[3] But let us begin by placing the phenomenon into its historical context. In a path-breaking work, Binet (1905) noted of 'suggestibility' that:

Suggestibility is by no means a test of intelligence, because very many persons of superior intelligence are susceptible to suggestion, through distraction, timidity, fear of doing wrong, or some preconceived idea. Suggestion produces effects which from certain points of view closely resemble the natural manifestations of feeble-mindedness; in fact suggestion disturbs the judgment, paralyzes the critical sense, and forces us to attempt unreasonable or unfitting acts worthy of a defective. It is therefore necessary, when examining a child suspected of

---

[3] While Binet adverts to the possibility of 'suggestibility' as an 'artificial debility', and contemporary literatures canvass this possibility *en passant*, overwhelmingly the psychological literatures dismiss this as a plausible proposition (see Krosnick (1991); Perry and Felce (2002, esp. p. 454)). The notion of the changeability of opinions representing some form of internal pathology has a fine pedigree: Goodey and Stainton (2001: 235, my emphasis) note that 'Renaissance medical texts identified changeability of the will or opinions as a medical pathology (Argenterius, 1566, p. 221) . . . applied stereotypically *only to reinforce concrete and already established difference claims*.' Plus ça change, plus c'est la même chose.

retardation, not to give a suggestion unconsciously, for thus *artificial debility* is produced which might make the diagnosis deceptive. If a person is forced to give an absurd reply by making use of an alternative pronounced in an authoritative voice, it does not in the least prove that he is lacking in judgment. But this source of error being once recognized and set aside, it is none the less interesting to bring into the examination a precise attempt at suggestion, and note what happens. It is a means of testing the force of judgment of a subject and his power of resistance. (Binet, 1905: np)

It seems then, that Binet at least was aware both that situational circumstances may have a bearing on the answers provided to interrogators' questioning and also that, in so influencing interaction, such responses, may, falsely, 'closely resemble the natural manifestations of feeble-mindedness'.[4] Indeed, in suggesting that factors such as 'distraction, timidity, fear of doing wrong, or some preconceived ideas' may lead to deceptive diagnoses Binet anticipates, by nearly a century, Krosnick's (1991) summary analysis of the difficulties presented to interview respondents in terms of the 'cognitive demands of attitude measures in surveys'. We need not accept Binet's notion of 'natural manifestations' of feeble-mindedness to admire his caution, but it is important to recognise that as early as 1905 what may now, in conversation analytic studies, be conceptualised as 'asymmetry in dialogue' (cf. Marková and Foppa) was clearly recognised, as was the possibility of employing questioning as a test of moral character: while a potential indicator of both 'force of judgment' and 'powers of resistance', in 1905 – as in today's literature – the possibility of moral taint consequent upon succumbing to suggestion was present: it might, suggests Binet, 'force[s] us to attempt unreasonable or unfitting acts worthy of a defective'. So, we might ask, how good is the evidence for what has, since Binet's caution has been forgotten, become part of the folklore of applied psychology? How might we approach the issue – as did Binet – with a thoughtful account of the situated, intersubjective, complexities of language and language use?

The structure of this chapter is as follows. First, I offer a brief account of the early work on acquiescence and provide an analysis of misgivings about it for theoretical reasons. Secondly, in the body of the chapter, a close analysis of some interview interactions between psychologists and intellectually disabled people shows how, practically, test questions and answers are managed in a complicated set of ways. Out of this examination it emerges that although some responses may look 'acquiescent', they are

---

[4] Finlay and Lyons (2002: 18–19) note that 'suggestibility' and 'acquiescence' remain poorly defined and differentiated in the intellectual disability literatures. It seems clear that here Binet is referring to phenomena that would be accepted as 'acquiescent' in the 'insufficiently elaborated' literature of today.

not necessarily motivated by the (morally disreputable) submission and willingness-to-please that the term implies, nor need we, unless already predisposed to construct inconsistency as individual predisposition, necessarily assume that suggestibility is in some fashion a test of intelligence: that is, while Shaw and Budd (1982: 108) claim that 'intellectual limitations predispose people to biased responding, social desirability factors determine the type of bias', as Binet noted, even persons of 'superior intelligence' may be suggestible for all sorts of good interactional reasons, and indeed, it may be argued that it is an extraordinarily smart strategy to agree with those in power over one. This to one side, if actual interactions, rather than staged or got-up ones are examined, on close inspection apparently 'acquiescent' responses turn out in practice more to resemble a variety of conversational strategies with which the person with an intellectual disability manages threatening, situationally peculiar, or bizarre questions. There is no single thread that binds them into one speech phenomenon.

The establishment of 'acquiescence bias' in the literature

The Sigelman *et al.* work of the 1980s has become a widely cited corpus. Certainly no paper reporting interview data from people with learning disabilities is likely to omit citation of some or all of the work, or its secondary recapitulations (e.g. Heal and Sigelman, 1990; 1995; 1996). Space limitations preclude more than an outline of the evidence, but since it is all of a kind, a brief account will suffice. In effect the Sigelman *et al.* thesis is captured by the title of their 1981a paper, 'When in doubt, say yes'. The literature in the period since has taken the 'potential of acquiescence . . . to be powerful among mentally retarded people' (Sigelman *et al.* 1981a: 53) to be a certainty. But is it?

It all starts with the observation in Sigelman *et al.* (1980) that about half of their sample of 149 children and adults with intellectual disabilities would answer 'yes' to mutually contradictory questions ('Are you usually happy?' vs. 'Are you usually sad?' and 'Are you usually by yourself?' vs. 'Are you usually with other people?') placed randomly within a variable length interview schedule of between 63 and 142 questions. Sigelman *et al.* (1981a) re-interviewed a subsample of 29 'difficult-to-interview individuals' (1981a: 55) and took two further steps. Firstly the interview incorporated paired 'factual' questions (such as 'Do you live in G-10 (incorrect cottage number) right now?' vs. 'do you live in G- (client's cottage number) right now?' and asked five questions to which 'no' was the correct answer. These latter questions were: 'Are you Chinese?'; 'Does it ever snow here in the summer?'; 'Are you a school bus driver?'; 'Do you know how to fly an airplane?' and 'Right now, is it raining outside?' (or sunny outside, whichever question should be answered 'no' at the time of the interview) (Sigelman et al. 1981a: 56).

Sigelman and colleagues also document what they term 'nay-saying', or 'self-contradictory nay-saying' described as 'responding "no" to oppositely worded items' (Heal and Sigelman, 1995: 335). While it is suggested that this problem is generally not so pronounced as 'yea-saying', in the area of 'institutional taboos' rates reportedly exceed those of acquiescence. Heal and Sigelman (1995) suggest that the work of Budd, Sigelman and Sigelman (1981) shows that 43 per cent of 35 respondents replied 'no' to both, contradictory, items as follows: 'Are you allowed (is it against the rules) to: (1) hit people? (2) call people ugly names (3) leave here without asking?' It is suggested that: 'nay-saying apparently reflects a desire to present oneself in a socially desirable light by denying any associations with taboo subjects or actions' (Heal and Sigelman, 1995: 336).

In summarising, Sigelman et al. report that 'the rate of acquiescence is staggering' (1981b: 56) and that 'while acquiescence is the most serious response bias revealed in this literature, nay-saying cannot be dismissed' (Heal and Sigelman, 1995: 336). Further papers in the series (Sigelman et al. 1981a; Sigelman, Budd, Winer, Schoenrock and Martin, 1982), come to much the same conclusion, put this way: 'because mentally retarded persons asked yes or no questions tend to acquiesce, their answers are likely to be invalid' (Sigelman et al. 1981b: 57). Furthermore, it is suggested that as well as being more likely in 'low IQ respondents', 'the results hint that acquiescence functions in part as a cover for ignorance about how to answer particular questions, it may also serve, for some, as an automatically and unthinkingly applied question answering strategy' (Sigelman et al. 1981b: 57–8). Acquiescence becomes, by 1981, a phenomenon with 'ruinous effects' on the 'reliability and validity of answers given by mentally retarded children and adults in interviews' (Sigelman et al. 1981a: 348). Indeed so severe is this supposedly 'ruinous' effect of the phenomenon that Sigelman et al. ominously conclude that: 'generally the present analyses suggests that the validity of answers given by mentally retarded people can *never* be assumed: it must be demonstrated' (Sigelman et al. 1982: 518, my emphasis).

The Sigelman work has certainly been influential. Despite failures to replicate both the extent of the 'phenomenon' and the correlation with IQ (e.g. Matikka and Vesala, 1997, see also Finlay and Lyons, 2002 for a review), the Sigelman work has attained near mythic, folkloric, status. It has served to cause (or legitimate) a belief among many researchers (and possibly among carers and practitioners) that one can only with extreme difficulty 'validly' gain access to the views of people with intellectual disabilities (as a sample, see Allen, 1989; Atkinson, 1988; Flynn, 1986; Dagnan and Ruddick, 1995). In a dispute between a person with an intellectual disability and a carer or a professional then, the literature suggests that the voice to suspect is that of the person with an intellectual disability, whose 'acquiescence bias' interferes with accurate reporting (e.g. Allen, 1989; Flynn and Saleem, 1986; Flynn, 1986; Gudjonsson, 1986; Perry and Felce, 2002). So taken for granted is the putative dispositional theory of acquiescence that it has even become a 'fast fact' about intellectual disability (Missouri Developmental Disabilities Resource Center, 2003).

Some difficulties

We need to be clear about the supposed motivation for such acquiescence. Interestingly, although a proper pragmatic analysis of such motivation would seem to be essential, it occupies very little of Sigelman et al.'s original argument and is barely present in the secondary literature (although Finlay and Lyons, 2002 and Kilsby, Bennert and Beyer (in press) offer a welcome contrast). Sigelman and co-workers do not offer a clear-cut definition of the phenomenon, rather offering, across a series of papers, a number of indicators or characteristics of 'acquiescent' behaviour. For example acquiescence is described as: 'the tendency of individuals to respond *yes* to questions regardless of their content' (Sigelman et al. 1981b: 53), or 'acquiescence is the tendency to respond affirmatively regardless of a question's content' (Sigelman et al. 1982: 511); that 'acquiescence is one particular type of response bias' (Sigelman et al. 1981b: 53); it is 'contradicting oneself by responding "no" to oppositely worded question pairs' (Shaw and Budd, 1982: 108) and offering conflicting answers to those provided by parents or carers, or as phrased by Heal and Sigelman, 'disagreements between individuals with retardation and their parents or direct care staff' (Heal and Sigelman, 1996: 98). Gudjonsson (1986), not a critic of the notion of acquiescence, also comments on the absence of an explicit discussion of the conceptual and theoretical implications of the construct in his examination of suggestibility in interrogative situations.

Despite the lack of a thoroughgoing pragmatic analysis (a difficulty at least partially rectified in Finlay and Lyons' 2002 review), the existence of some dissenting empirical results (e.g. Wehmeyer, 1994; Voelker et al. 1990), and indeed the caution of Sigelman et al.'s (1982) discussion of their own findings), uncritical acceptance of the phenomenon appears to be entrenched. The notion of 'acquiescence' appears, further, to have generalised from the specific early issues of the relative merits of yes–no vs. either–or vs. open-ended question formats, to asking any intellectually disabled individual any type of question.

Thus we see discussions of acquiescence as if it were a medical condition. Chong *et al.* (2000) for instance refer to 'the prevalence' of the problem.

Among the above response biases, acquiescence is the most common in people with developmental disabilities. Although the prevalence varies (Matikka and Vesala, 1997; Stancliffe, 1995; Yu, Garinger, and Harapiak, in press), Sigelman and colleagues (1980, 1981, 1982) found that acquiescence occurred in as much as 56% of their samples and it was negatively correlated with IQ. Acquiescence poses a threat to reliability and must be assessed or controlled in quality of life interviews. (Heal and Sigelman, 1996; Schalock, 1996b)

In other contexts, so well established is the notion of acquiescence that it is not mentioned by name, but simply by an economical reference. For example in the Method section of their paper 'Social categorizations, social comparisons and stigma: presentations of self in people with learning difficulties' Finlay and Lyons (2000) simply state that:

There are a number of methodological difficulties associated with carrying out research with this population, which constrained the question types which could be used (for reviews see Atkinson, 1988; Gowans and Hulbert, 1983; Heal and Sigelman, 1995). One major limitation is that the provision of predetermined response categories and the use of more abstract concepts were inappropriate.

In general advice to (one presumes, trainee) psychiatrists, Chaplin and Flynn state of the proper conduct of 'psychiatric interview' that:

The atmosphere should be as relaxed and informal as possible. Talk with the patient while they are doing something enjoyable on the ward, for example, playing games . . . Aside from good general interviewing technique, there are some important specifics to bear in mind. Questions relating to time and frequency may not easily be understood. Acquiescence is the tendency of the interviewee to give answers that he or she thinks the interviewer wants to hear. 'Yes/No' questions are particularly likely to have this effect, generating a series of affirmative answers. (Chaplin and Flynn, 2000: 131–2)

So taken-for-granted is the phenomenon, that, like the importance of a 'relaxed atmosphere', and the desirability of 'good general interviewing technique', no academic reference is provided to substantiate the suggestion that the problem here is located, solely, within the interviewee. Again, and this time with farther-reaching implications Havercamp (2001), opens her policy document *Health Indicators 2000–2001* with the following account of the inception of the project and its remit: she writes that

In January 1997, the National Association of State Directors of Developmental Disabilities Services (NASDDDS) launched the Core Indicators Project (CIP). The project's aim was to develop nationally recognized performance and outcome indicators that would enable a state's developmental disability service authority to benchmark the performance of its service system against performance levels achieved elsewhere. This multi-state collaborative effort to jointly assess and improve performance was unprecedented.

It is clear, then, that this policy advice is designed to make a major contribution to the evaluation of the quality of service provision for adults with an intellectual disability across the USA. In the section on 'Interviewing' it is stated that:

[T]here are several difficulties in interviewing adults with developmental disabilities that must be considered. For example, individuals with developmental disabilities have a tendency to try to hide their disability by pretending to understand questions when they actually do not. This tendency has been termed 'cloak of competence' (Edgerton, 1967). In addition, there has been noted a strong desire to please the interviewer; they may respond to a question in a certain manner because they think it is the 'right' answer. This desire can contribute to 'acquiescence', or the tendency to answer 'yes' to questions.

Once more, we see acquiescence unproblematically pressed into service as an out-there-in-the-world phenomenon. Like the so-called 'cloak of competence' phenomenon, but lacking an academic citation, again we see that it is, at the very least strongly implied, that acquiescence is a morally disreputable form of conduct (hiding the truth about oneself, dissimulating about one's real identity, offering deceptive answers) and, moreover, that conduct of this sort is a dispositional, or inherent, feature of the people in question: 'individuals with developmental disabilities have a tendency . . .'

This is, obviously, a belief with important ramifications, and needs examination. In what follows, recall that the 'traditional school' (as I shall call the secondary literatures, when not referring directly to the particular evidence claimed by Sigelman *et al.*) maintains that people with an intellectual disability as a group, are prone to acquiesce: etymologically speaking, that they are prone to produce answers which 'bow to someone else's will', even though their own preference may be otherwise. I shall resort to the redundant expression 'submissive acquiescence' to make its flavour absolutely clear, and to distinguish it from occasions where something else is going on.

Critique 1. The questions

There are two things to notice about the particular question and answer pairs that are used for evidence in the acquiescence claim. The first is that Sigelman *et al.* thoroughly confound inconsistency with acquiescence: agreeing that you are usually happy and that you are usually sad (to take an example of a pair of their 'acquiescence'–diagnostic questions) is taken to be a simple demonstration of acquiescence on at least one of the questions. But acquiescence is submissive, and inconsistency might not be; it may be the result of the kind of impairment, memory failure, or lack of attention, that serves to make people diagnosable as having an intellectual disability in the first place. And, of course, as Binet (1905) noted, one need not be intellectually impaired to give inconsistent answers (and of course the literature on discourse and rhetoric traces the elegant manoeuvering that inconsistency, or 'variability', might do; see, for example Billig, 1996; Edwards and Potter, 1992). Inconsistency, even outright contradiction, is not, *per se*, a guarantee of motivated, or 'submissive', acquiescence.

The second thing to ask is whether the questions in the original schedule can reasonably bear the weight of the interpretation they were given. Some questions are clearly odd. People of either Caucasian or African-American ethnic origin were asked to respond to questions such as 'Are you Chinese'; residents of long-stay institutions were asked 'Do you know how to fly an airplane'; and so on (Sigelman *et al.* 1981: 56). Similarly 'Nay-saying' is supposedly evidenced by contradictory answers to both 'Are you allowed (is it against the rules) to: (1) hit people? (2) call people ugly names (3) leave here without asking?' The literal-mindedness of the analysis here is breathtaking. It seems not to have occurred to Budd *et al.* that it is entirely possible for it simultaneously to be, formally, institutionally, 'against the rules' to hit people, call them 'ugly names' or abscond, but that, in practice, it is actually 'allowed' in that little sanction follows people being hit, insulted or wandering off (an entirely mundane state of affairs in the long-stay institutions where the Sigelman work was conducted), not to mention that the specific referent of the question is opaque: 'you' can, grammatically, encompass both the singular and the plural. That is, one could say 'no *I* am not allowed to hit people' and 'no it is not against the rules (for staff) to hit people' quite consistently, and validly.[5] Likewise, quite apart from the fact that agreeing that 'yes, I know how to fly an airplane' could be absolutely truthful

---

[5] See Houtkoop-Steenstra (2000: 180ff.) for a discussion of the difficulties engendered by discrepancies between interview designers' intended meanings and those live in actual delivery in survey interviews with 'normals'.

(one only needs to know a little 'theory', one doesn't – in so agreeing – lay claim to being an ace fighter pilot) it also seems to have escaped the grimly serious researchers that neatly symmetrical mickey taking might be an explanation for their results. Again, in a display of research-driven, monolithic meaning management, the very individual relativity of quite what an 'ugly name' might consist in is entirely overlooked. However, leaving aside these possible difficulties, there is also the troubling issue of whether these frankly bizarre questions risk insulting respondents' dignity. One ought also to ask whether the responses they elicit are comparable to responses to sensible questions. As Biklen and Moseley (1988) note, a Q: A pair like 'Are you retarded?', 'No, I'm Catholic' may be entirely sensible. It is answers to sensible questions which are the eventual target of suspicion, but if no good case can be made for extrapolation from the bizarre to the ordinary, then the extension is unwarranted. Indeed, the later papers (e.g. Sigelman *et al.* 1982) that report the asking of 'factual' (1982: 517) questions about everyday activities, suggest that these questions are much more 'successfully' dealt with.[6] These concerns do not seem to trouble the designers of 'acquiescence' scales in contemporary measures – thus bizarre and unoccasioned questions are routinely employed as 'pre-tests' in many measures to eliminate respondents who are likely to respond 'invalidly'. Cummins's (1997) *Comprehensive Quality of Life Questionnaire* for example, requires that people be asked 'Do you make all your own clothes and shoes' and 'Did you choose who lives next door' *before* 'testing' proper commences, with negative responses necessary to 'prove' acquiescence is absent. Similarly, Stancliffe's (1995) *Choice Questionnaire* requires that people respond differently to the following two pre-test questions to prove that they can sensibly answer the questionnaire items that may (or may not) follow. Thus people are disqualified if answers to 'Most mornings do *you* pick what clothes to wear – Yes, Sometimes, No?' and 'Most mornings does *someone else* tell you what clothes to wear – No, Sometimes, Yes?' do not agree. The fact that, in many services, it is entirely feasible for people to choose what they wish to wear, only to be told that it is unsuitable, or that they should get changed and wear something else, again appears to have escaped the diagnostic gaze.

---

[6] Interestingly, in an experimental study conducted around the time of the Sigelman work, Bray and colleagues report that: 'moderately retarded adults were able to consistently communicate which of two objects they wished to obtain . . . severely retarded adolescents initially made some errors but communicated effectively on 100% of the trials by the end of the experiment' (Bray, Biasini and Thrasher, 1983: 13). These authors note that when communication is about real issues, of real interest to participants, then competence may more readily be identified, even in persons described as moderately and severely retarded.

Critique 2. The context

The Sigelman *et al.* work, and the bulk of that which has followed it, barely acknowledges the social context of the interview situation. The nature and demands of the contract between interviewers and interviewees has been the subject of intense study in social psychology. A body of work existed prior to the Sigelman studies which suggested that the social demands of professional–client interactions, and the interpersonal interaction histories of people with intellectual disabilities, might affect the performance of individuals in testing or other interpersonal situations with a clear power differential. Some landmark work then available included Tizard's (1964) pioneering experiments; Gunzburg's (1970) summary of test performance, and Zigler and co-worker's studies of 'outerdirectedness' and 'positive reaction tendency' (e.g. Zigler and Harter, 1969). Subsequent work has been still more emphatic about the impossibility of clearing power-differentials away from the communicative scene, and Marková (1991) reports a compelling case-study showing how even consciously prepared professionals have great trouble effacing their superior communicative power from interaction with people with intellectual disability and, as noted earlier, Hatton's (1998) review of the pragmatics literature suggests that such *communicative environments* are key, if insufficiently attended to, influences on both the quality and variety of interactions observed in many studies of the pragmatic competence of intellectually disabled people.

This is where the real trouble with claims of acquiescence lies. The lack of a comprehensive conceptual or pragmatic analysis (Leudar and Fraser, 1985; Marková, 1991) of acquiescence is troubling, but more serious is the issue of the invisibility of actual interaction in the papers and secondary sources which supposedly cement the phenomenon. There may be something about the actual delivery of question and answer between interviewer and respondent that makes what is happening difficult to cast as submissive acquiescence. For the traditional school, the respondent's tendency to acquiesce comes out in 'inconsistency', in 'nay-saying' and 'yea-saying'; but those two descriptions are analysts' glosses on behaviour that we, as readers, never see. We need to see it.

Observations here on (supposed and actual) acquiescence phenomena must be prefaced by something essential to the interpretation of the data: the participants' orientation to what is going on as a *test*. Thereafter we will examine how it is that an interviewee may, in a testing context continuously refreshed by the interviewer's probes, be shepherded into apparently inconsistent answers by a range of interactional phenomena: the need to formulate and reformulate responses to questions; by the interviewer's pursuit of pre-existing expectations of what the 'correct' answer is; by the interviewer's drive to obtain an answer in the official vocabulary of the interview schedule; and by the interviewer's misconstrual of the interviewee's active engagement with the task of producing careful answers by checking with backchannel responses. In all of these cases the interviewee is shepherded into producing pseudo-acquiescent responses: inconsistencies or agreements that are motivated not by submissiveness or willingness to please, but by the logic of the interviewer's demands. Each is a conversational phenomenon of its own, only united by the superficial (and artefactual) appearance of inconsistency and agreement.

Critique 3. The testing situation

Although barely considered by the traditional school it is clear that the test situation itself fosters interviewees' giving what look like submissive, willing-to-please responses. However, on closer examination it appears that these are either legitimate or indeed rational turns which manage the 'examination', or artifacts thrown up by the interviewer's insistent pursuit of answers within it. That is several authors (e.g. Atkinson, 1988; Leudar and Fraser, 1985) have noted that people with learning disabilities often behave with professional interlocutors as if they were in a formal examination. In many cases that may be what it is: here, it certainly is. The interviewer is in the business of testing the respondent and the result may be highly consequential. First, evidence that the interviewees do indeed orient to the interview as a test. Consider these extracts:

Extract 7: Code: CA/KK/CD, from Rapley and Antaki, 1996

```
18   I    erm (. . .) and I'd ↑like you to ↑answer some questio::ns to tell me
19        how you feel about the   ⌈(unintell)
20   AR                           ⌊they're not 'ard ones are they (.)
21   I    not very  ⌈hard
22   AR             ⌊no:o
23   I    no (.) and ↑if you don't understand ↓them Arthur you can just tell
          me (.)
24   AR   yeus
25   I    and I'll I'll say them differently (.)
26   AR   ym
27   I    ↑ok? (.) erm (. . .) let's °see (wharr) else° ↑erm (. . .) ↑there's no
          right or
28        wrong answers ↑Arthur↓ (.)
29   AR   mm
30   I    it's just to tell me how you ↓feel about ↑things
31   AR   m↑yes
```

```
32   I     allright? and we (.) we can take as ↑long a time as you ↓need↑
33   AR    ↓ye: hm↑=
34   I     =so there's no ↓°hurry    ⌈(. .) °do you have any° ↓ques↑tions? (.)
35                                    ⌊(paper shuffling)
36   I     to ↓ask ↑me?
37   AR    ye: ↑e:r↓:::s
38   I     what would you like to ↓ask me
39   AR    I ↑like being I ↑like being er (. .) in 'ere (.)
40   I     you ↑like  ⌈being=
41   AR               ⌊=(living) in 'ere like I like living in 'ere
```

In this extract, taken from the opening moments of the interview, two points are of note: Arthur immediately orients to being under examination, to being tested, firstly by making a mentionable out of the possibility that the questions are 'not 'ard ones' (l 20) and, secondly, when asked if he has any questions (in lines 34–8) by responding not with a question, but with a (doubly affirmed) statement. The interviewer's confirmatory utterance at line 40 is then met with a further double affirmation by Arthur of his previous utterance, and his offered 'I like being here' may well orient to the interviewer's invitation in line 18 – how Arthur feels about being here. In the context of interviews as perceived threats, Arthur's statement is a telling one: ''Ere' is, of course his own home, not the institution from which he was 'resettled' and from which he knew that the interviewer had travelled to see him. In this, and the following extract, the interviewee clearly establishes a preference for their (new) living environment and, by implication, suggests that they perceive the QOL interview as a 'test' of their suitability for remaining within it.

The second example again reveals the respondent's orientation to the interview as a testing situation. The extract is, again, taken from the opening minutes of a QOL interview. Bob has, some 76 turns earlier, asked the interviewer where he had come from that morning, and been informed that the interviewer had travelled from the institution in which Bob, like Arthur, had previously lived.

Extract 8: Code HB/MR/TT

```
131          (5 secs)
132          (whistles)
133→   BO    hhh (do you know ↑more) than the residents there?
134    I     erm?
135    BO    (at the County ↑Castle)
136    I     I think so   ⌈↑yeah (. .) I know quite a ↑lot of them
137    BO                 ⌊((slurping noise)) eh?
138    I     I know quite a lot of them (.) there's not many ↑peo↓ple
139          left there now ↓though
```

```
140    BO    no: (.) °er°.h >most of< um:: ↓died didn't they?
141    I     hmm ↓died or moved ↑out (. .) °hm?° did ↑you used to (. .) °hhh°
142          be at the Ca↓stle
143    BO    yeh=
144    I     °yeh°
145→   BO    I didn't like it much
146    I     no:?
147→   BO    .hhh I'd sooner be 'ere
148    I     yeah (.) how long have you ↑been ↓here Bob
149    BO    since from nine↑teen eighty nine
150    I     (right) that's a↑bout >(so)< ↓for ↑five ↓years now (. .)
151    BO    ↑yeah
152    I     yeah (1 sec) and you ↓wouldn't wanna go ↑back
153    BO    <no> ((throaty syll)) °ye can: ↑sti-° (. .) you ↑know what you can
             do:
154          ↓with it?
155    I     what's that ↓then
156→   BO    .hh stick it up °where° the monkeys keep their ↑nuts
157    I     °uh huh huh hu° ((sniff)) <↓yeah> it's not ↑ter
158          (1 sec)
159→   BO    er >sh we sh we< make a ↑start ↓then
160    I     ↑yep (.) o↑kay (1 sec) erm=
```

Bob approaches the topic of the institution indirectly. Following a long
(5 second) pause in the conversation he asks a non-committal question
about the interviewer's knowledge of the people at the Castle (line 133).
When it is apparent that the interviewer is prepared to set up a space for
him to pursue this line (136 and 138–9) the scene is set for an exchange
which allows Bob increasingly emphatic avowals of his dislike of his previous institutional experience and preference for his present home. It
seems clear that the issue of the institution has been live for him through
an extended sequence of turns. His first avowal is low key: 'I didn't like
it much.' When this is met with a story continuer a stronger statement,
'.hhh I'd sooner be 'ere' is made (which, note, echoes Arthur's formulation in the previous extract) (line 147). The interviewer's continuation
of the exchange, and the confirmatory reformulation at line 152, releases
the most powerful statement in this escalation: the suggestion that 'you
can stick it where the monkeys keep their nuts'. Note here the delicacy
and sensitivity with which Bob approaches this, his final, appreciation:
in lines 153–4 he checks that he has permission, that it is safe, to state a
strong view. Via the quietly delivered, but truncated, stem of what is to
come (°ye can: ↑sti-°), and then the explicit question 'you ↑know what
you can do ↓with it?' he makes plain his appreciation of his status in the
encounter: that is, he is in the presence of an authority who may not take
kindly to such a characterisation of the service he represents. The extract

shows, then, how Bob elegantly makes the possibility of test-contingent resettlement plain, and, after a series of manoeuvres, gets the interviewer to offer him the chance of articulating his attitude toward it. Then he signals that not only is he ready for the interview to start, but that the interviewer is, accountably, long overdue in his starting of it.

The point is that there is plentiful evidence that interviewees are casting the speech-episode of the interview as a *test*, and furthermore a test whose results they know or suspect to have potentially serious consequences. Against this background, the ordinary expectations of question and answer sequences become heightened. This is the general theme of the interpretations to follow of what otherwise look, at face value, like submissively acquiescent responses, as we shall see in the next sections.

Pseudo-acquiescence 1. Reformulation of responses

We saw above how the participants orient to the interview as a test, and indeed, it is a definitional feature of an interview that the normal, egalitarian distribution of question and answer turns at talk is suspended (Schegloff, 1989). This imbalance will produce pseudo-acquiescence, particularly in those situations where, as here, the interviewer has a schedule to complete which specifies a range of acceptable ('right') responses. Consider this extract:

Extract 9: Code MT/MR/JW

322	I	d'you ↑feel out of ↓place (. .) >out an' about in< ↓<u>soc</u>ial (.) situ↓ations
323	AN	<u>n</u> ⌜<u>o:</u>
324	I	⌞Anne? (.) never?
325	AN	<u>no</u>
326	I	sometimes?
327	AN	↓°no°
328	I	or usually
329	AN	↑<u>some</u>↓times I ↑do:
330	I	yeah? (. .) ok we'll ↑put a two down for that one then (sniff)

The respondent's reply at 323 ('no') is apparently clear, but, by line 329, has changed. Is this submissive acquiescence? On a 'traditional' reading Anne has offered contradictory responses. If it is submissive acquiescence, then the motivation seems to be largely the interviewer's, not the interviewee's; it is the interviewer who does not accept what could be treated as a perfectly acceptably designed answer, which is in fact twice repeated. This is pseudo-acquiescence motivated by the *interviewer* – not the dispositionally predisposed interviewee. Rather than assuming here that Anne is, in some fashion, displaying her incompetence as an inter-viewee, in fact quite the opposite reading is that much more plausi-ble. Anne is, correctly, assessing the combination of the interviewer's schedule-driven need to provide all three of the prescribed response options, his over-ride of her initial well-formed candidate answer, in con-junction with his – situationally unusual – use of her name with a rising intonation and questioning register, as implying that her first answer is in some way, unacceptable or incorrect. Being, in fact, a collaborative con-versationalist – as well as a competent on-the-spot, online analyst – she, quite normatively, reformulates and repairs until the interviewer receipts her hearably rather grudging 'sometimes I do' as acceptable. This is, surely, a demonstration of competence. In passing, one might note that to endorse 'never' or 'usually' in response to such an item is highly likely to draw negative attention to oneself as either accountably disinhibited or as equally accountably agoraphobic: as such Anne's first utterance, 'no', is in effect an endorsement of an unprovided option which is less extreme than the extreme case formulation 'never', and which is, thus, hearable as a carefully crafted response. Would one sensibly ask someone who was not already categorised as 'intellectually disabled' such a question?

Interviewers may pursue interviewees through a number of turns in order to gain an acceptable response for a number of reasons (see Antaki and Rapley, 1996a; Houtkoop-Steenstra, 2000). They may themselves have not comprehended the relevance or meaning of their interviewee's utterance; an interviewee's utterance may constitute a provisionally acceptable answer, but require reworking to conform to the demands of the 'official' one; or, occasionally, because the interviewer knows better than the interviewee what the interviewee thinks. Interviewees, if they are competent conversationalists, will, in the face of the demands set up by the utterances of the interviewer, change their position (and thereby seem to be 'acquiescing' in the motivated sense) until such time as the trouble brought about by these factors has been either averted or resolved. And as we will see below one tactic used by interviewees of whatever 'level' of ability is, simply, to allow difficulties to pass by. This is, however, not always possible: the exigencies of testing are such that there is pressure on interviewers to do it 'by the book', to return what is, in the terms of the schedule itself, what is to count as a countable answer.

Pseudo-acquiescence 2. Shepherding to a 'correct' answer

A researcher's guess at, or stereotype of, what their informant believes can be a powerful factor in any interview, and here we can see it drive responses which might look acquiescent. In the extract below the interviewer is asking about the degree of freedom the respondent has in who can visit her. The interviewer, being aware of the organisational context and the likelihood that staff would need at least to be consulted about the respondent's social schedule, does not accept the respondent's first answer and pushes the interviewee into what, on the surface, appears to be an acquiescent, self-contradictory, response. Upon close examination however, it is not at all clear that Anne's final utterance 'Yeah we have to ask the staff' (line 633) is in fact a contradiction of her earlier 'yes' to the interviewer's question 'Can they come whenever they like?' at lines 622–3.

Extract 10: Code MT/MR/JW

```
616   I     .hh when can your ↓friends (.) visit you (.) here Anne
617   AN    me mum and dad visit me ↓(yis)ter↓day on ↑Wed:: nes↓day
618   I     do you have any ↑friends come to visit?=
619   AN    =me mum and auntie May 'n uncle ↑Chris visit me (yis)te↑r↓day
620   I     do you have any ↑friends come to ↓visit?
621   AN    (yeah syll syll) er auntie May fetched a little ↑ba:↓by
622   I     yeah? can they come when ↑ever they ↓li:ke?
623   AN    yes
624   I     or (. .) d'you have to ask the staff if they can come?
625   AN    yeah they ↓do:
626   I     yeah (. .)   ⌈can they-
627   AN                 ⌊the staff book it down int ↓bo:ok
628   I     right (.) do staff say that's ok (.) or-
629   AN    o↑KA:Y
630   I     yeah?
631   AN    yis they ↓wa:s
632   I     mm (.) d d'you ↑have to ask the staff
633   AN    yeah we ↑have to ask the staff
634         (3.00)
```

There is what looks like a possible contradiction in this extract (visitors can come when they like *versus* the staff must be asked), but inspection suggests a different interpretation. Anne's utterance at line 625 is a continuation of that at line 623 – an apparently acceptable confirmation that visitors may come whenever they like, not a response to the interviewer's further question about asking staff at line 624. The referent in Anne's utterance at this turn is *they*, i.e. Mum, Auntie May and Uncle Chris, and the expanded answer to the question posed in line 622 continues at line 627 with an explanation of the way in which staff enter forthcoming visits in the diary. On this reading it sounds as if the response at line 633 'yeah, we *have* to ask the staff' means that staff have to be asked to 'book it down in't book' as a matter of routine rubber-stamping.

The next example does, however, appear to show, less equivocally, a respondent shifting their ground and offering contradictory responses in the face of the interviewer's demands for reformulation or refinement of an offered candidate answer. It looks, at first sight, like a clear example of submission.

Extract 11: Code: CA/KK/MB

```
342  I   right (. .) °a:o_k:° (. .) ↑what about ↓money Eileen (.) who (.) decides
343      (.) who spends (. .) >↓sorry let me start ↑ag↓ain< (.) ↑how do
344      you (.) ↓deci:de what you spend your ↓money on (.) ↑do ↑you
345      say what (.) you want to b↑u::y (.) or    ⌈does s- staff buy
346  E                                            ⌊°yeh°
347  I   things >for you<
348  E   n↑o:: ↑I do i::t
349  I   you do it (.) >↑do they ↑help you or you< do it all by yours↓elf (.)
350  E   no ↑they help me love th' staff (.)
```

There is an apparent contradiction: Eileen both buys things for herself *and* the staff help her do it. Certainly the interviewer sets these up as contradictions (line 349), but how is that reached? Note that the interviewer's original question is a dysfluent amalgamation of four distinct questions: who decides who spends Eileen's money, how Eileen decides what to spend her money on, whether Eileen says what she wants to buy and finally whether staff buy things for her. The false starts and self-repairs in the utterance make it difficult to know whether Eileen's 'yeh' at line 345 is designed as a reply or a back-channel; and the situation is not much better at 347, since it is not obvious which question is being picked out in Eileen's 'no I do it' response. One might read this as Eileen affirming that she decides what to spend her money on and that she spends it independently. It would appear from the interviewer's response at line 349, a confirmatory 'you do it', that this is indeed her hearing of Eileen's utterance, but one which the interviewer seems not to accept (see the section below on plausible answers). Out of this confusion the interviewer confects the opposition 'do they help you or you do it all by yourself?' (line 349). This gives a context in which Eileen's response 'no they help me love th' staff' will be *heard as* a contradiction even though seeking, or accepting, advice or practical help is an unexceptionable feature of anyone's shopping.

Pseudo-acquiescence 3. Shepherding to a 'competent' official answer

As Sigelman *et al.* (1981) observe: 'gaining valid information from mentally retarded consumers, who almost by definition have difficulty with receptive and expressive communication, is likely to be . . . problematic' (Sigelman *et al.* 1981: 53). It should be noted, however, that difficulty with communication is not limited to people with an intellectual disability (cf. Marková and Foppa, 1991; Hatton, 1998). Interviewers too may express themselves poorly or apparently misunderstand what is being said to them. However, the power differential in the interview situation is such that it is the interviewer who, in cases of failure to comprehend the relevance or meaning of their conversational partner's utterances, has the power to deem such utterances 'irrelevant', 'unintelligible' or 'inadequate'. The following extract demonstrates the ease with which it is possible to rule as irrelevant or extraneous interviewee utterances, and the dangers inherent in assuming, on the basis of these judgements, that people with an intellectual disability are incompetent. Here Anne mishears or misunderstands the term 'guardian' (and thus is probably very puzzled by the conjunction of a question about her garden with a query about 'who looks after' her). Nevertheless she produces two perfectly legitimate candidate answers: she states that she has a back garden (line 682) and after a long pause and an apparently extraneous ('irrelevant') utterance about boots (possibly referring to gardening) answers the second part of the question (someone who looks after you) posed at line 681 by emphasising that (someone) 'PAYS me on Friday' at line 687. In and of itself this utterance might appear to suggest that Anne is off-track, and indeed the interviewer clearly assumes this to be the case by dismissing her utterance explicitly at line 688.

Extract 12: Code MT/MR/JW

```
680  I    oh good (. .) have you got a a ↓guardian or someone who looks ↓after
681       you
682  AN   yes a back garden in:: ⌈dere
683  I                          ⌊↑no:: a guardian
684  AN   no I get boots for me (.) ↑bo::↓y
685       (2.00)
686  I    ↓oh (. .) .hh is there (.) is there someone who (.) is in-
687  AN   (PAYS) me on ↑fri::↓day
688  I    no wha' what I'm ↓asking (.) °Anne° is is there someone who's in
689       ↓charge of you?
690  AN   ye:s
691  I    yeah?
692  AN   they pay me on ↓Fri↑day
693  I    (. . .) .h I don't think we're under↓standing each other (.) is there
694       ⌈↑someone in charge of (.) of you?      ⌈in charge of Anne
695  AN   ⌊oh                                      ⌊yes
696  I    who?
697  AN   the staff
```

```
698  I     yeah? (. . .) are they in charge of you all the ↑time
699  AN    (yis) they (w)are (.) Colette comes here n Helen .hh and Sarah n'
700        Lillian
701  I     mm (. .)⌈and they-
702  AN          ⌊(they're in charge of us)
```

The *interviewer* has clearly failed to comprehend Anne's utterances here. At line 688 the question is repeated (with Anne identified by name and a hearable stress on the key syntactic items in the utterance '↓asking' and '(in) ↓charge') and in the following turn, is answered, with an unambiguous 'yes' at line 690. A further turn on at line 692, an explanation of the previous referent-less 'pay me on Friday' is offered. This is clearly not good enough for the interviewer who, it should be noted does not say 'I don't understand you', but instead suggests a *mutual* failure of comprehension at line 693 and yet again asks the question. Again, the long-suffering interviewee affirms their case at line 695. However, by this point in the exchange it is clear that the interviewer perceives Anne's interview performance to be incompetent as he explicitly asks for collateral confirmation that the question has been understood by asking 'who?' In an elegantly economical response Anne simply states 'the staff' and, when further pressed, fluently reels off a list of the staff members who are in charge. Note also that, in the overlapping final two lines of the extract, Anne completes the interviewer's turn. Such anticipatory turn completion will be discussed at greater length in the next chapter but, for now, it is enough to note that this is an interactional accomplishment which demands a level of pragmatic competence usually withheld in the literatures from people of the 'level' of disability that Anne was officially classified as 'having' (cf. Oelschlager and Damico, 1998; Lerner, 1991).

This extract also offers a clear example of the tendency for interviewers to 'edit' official items described by Antaki (2001). He shows the way in which edited questions frequently result in semantically and grammatically simplified items, which, importantly *project the relevance of agreement*. Thus if 'Do you participate actively in those recreational activities? Usually, most of the time; Frequently, About half of the time; Seldom or never' is replaced with a simple yes/no question 'when you're at your parties, do you have a bit of a drink do you?', (or here 'have you got a a ↓guardian or someone who looks ↓after you' is replaced by 'is is there someone who's in charge of you') the reformulated version is considerably more likely to be answered in the affirmative (if the recipient is a competent interlocutor) than the question it replaces (Antaki, 2001: 446). That is structural alterations to items, when initially met with a response that the interviewer cannot readily match to the official script, can be so fashioned as to actively make sequentially relevant the preferred second pair part, of agreement, to a yes/no question. As Antaki, Young and Finlay note: 'Yes/no questions are easy to agree with, and hard to challenge, whether one has a learning difficulty or not. They tend very strongly to confirmation by the respodent (sic) simply as a matter of the way conversation is organised' (Antaki *et al.* 2002: 448). The net effect of such structural online editings is to project optimism and to create, in so doing, 'happy people' simply by means of attendance to facework (Houtkoop-Steenstra and Antaki, 1998).

However, to suggest on this basis, that replacing yes-no questions on interview schedules with alternative (e.g. either-or, or multiple choice) formats – as seems to have become the norm, and indeed as Heal and Sigelman (1995) recommend – is simply to miss the point that interview questions, even with 'normal' respondents tend to editing and rephrasing in their actual delivery as a consequence of the need for interviewers to 'meet both ends' (Houtkoop-Steenstra, 1995; 2000). Furthermore, to see, as the traditional literature would have us, that such responses are accountably 'acquiescent' is simply to misunderstand the preference structure of interaction.[7]

This extract further shows the danger of assuming that the offering of what appears to the interviewer to be 'irrelevant' or 'unrelated' material renders people who are described as moderately intellectually disabled incompetent to participate in interviews. Here Anne talks of gardens, boots and payments on Friday. Such material could very readily be seen as unrelated to the question asked, which explicitly requested information about caregivers or formal guardianship. Yet it becomes apparent by the end of this extended sequence that Anne is perfectly capable of saying whether she has caregivers (the staff) and of identifying them by name.

This is, again, a problem engendered by the insistence in standardised interviewing with people with intellectual disabilities of importing poorly theorised understandings of actual interaction into research practices, and also of the difficulties caused by an *a priori* failure of imagination. Thus in the meticulously designed and methodologically rigorous standardised interview-based study of acquiescence bias in quality of life assessment reported by Perry and Felce (2002) that was touched on earlier, 'a nonresponse was considered to occur if the respondent said nothing throughout the presentation of pre-test items or if none of their responses was related to the questions asked' (Perry and Felce,

---

[7] In this respect it is remarkable that Heal and Sigelman belatedly note, apparently with some surprise, that: 'question formats make a huge difference in responses given by adults with mental retardation when they are asked about their likes and dislikes' (1995: 338).

2002: 450). As is usual in the mainstream literature, no actual examples of the enactment of these crucially important categories in actual talk-in-interaction is provided. Rather an anecdotal account is offered of a respondent who slipped through the pre-testing net, and who is discussed in order to raise questions about the adequacy of the methodology of pointing to an iconic response card as opposed to reliance on verbal responses, and the necessity of what is described as 'independent corroboration' of people's responses.[8] In the regime of truth that defines psychological testing what is countable as an 'answer' to a 'question' is not to be determined by the normative intersubjective machinery of adjacency pairs, repair and so on. Instead countable answers are, as in intelligence testing, defined *a priori*, by researchers. The walls of this regime of truth, this 'belief in the validity of their tests and procedures' (cf. Goode, 1983), clearly act to constrain the imagination, if not the simple recognition of shared humanness. Perry and Felce (2002) write:

> When one man, who was reasonably articulate and who had passed all the ComQol pretests, was asked how happy or sad he felt about the things he owned (material wellbeing), he began to list his possessions. His response was uninterpretable as a comment on whether or not he was satisfied. In this case, his verbal response to the interviewer demonstrated that he was not answering the question as posed. If the man had responded by pointing to one of the iconic representations of happiness, his lack of understanding would not have been apparent. (Perry and Felce, 2002: 453)

We cannot know, in the absence of a transcript of this interaction sequence, just in what manner such a catastrophic 'lack of understanding' was actually displayed, but surely one might imagine that to set out to list all of the things that one owns may – if allowed to proceed – become a comment which constructs one's 'happiness', 'unhappiness', 'satisfaction' or 'dissatisfaction' with that 'domain' of 'quality of life'? 'Well, I have a yacht, a Maserati, a big house, a lovely wife, three beautiful children, a summer house in the country . . . and I'm still miserable'; or perhaps 'I have the shirt on my back, an old pair of shoes and not a penny to my name . . . but I have friends and am thankful for that.' But of course, we cannot know how the anonymous 'reasonably articulate man' who gave the game away displayed the uninterpretability of his response: we must simply take it on trust. Where in the interaction with Anne reproduced above would the

---

[8] 'Corroboration' is an unusual term to use outside of the context of police interrogation or courtroom cross-examination. Likewise the existence of 'pre-tests' obviously suggests that, at least to the researchers and questionnaire designers, what is going on in the interactions in these studies is 'testing'. As we have seen, people with intellectual disabilities are not unaware of 'testing' and its potential implications. Knowing 'how to keep quiet' (Leudar and Fraser, 1981) may then be an important – and highly functional – strategy.

line be drawn, one wonders? At what point would the interviewer holding to canonical testing procedure have deemed her response 'irrelevant' or as 'failing to answer the question as posed'? It would not be unreasonable to suggest that strict procedure would have such a decision made early on, most probably *instead of* the interviewer's attempted (and successful) repair via his appeal to intersubjective breakdown in line 693. In that case she too would be disqualified, and her entirely competent answer to the 'question as posed' (lines 697–702) would *never have been delivered.* In chapter 6, we will see just how much more imaginatively than the designers of standardised psychometric tests an intellectually disabled man – who is also describable as 'reasonably articulate' – can demonstrate his 'satisfaction' with the 'quality of his life'.

Pseudo-acquiescence 4. Echoing and backchannel responses

In the absence of detailed transcripts of the interactions between interviewers and interviewees reported in the literature as substantiating the acquiescence phenomenon, one can't be sure that previous work has ignored or misunderstood what respondents do with back-channel responses. However, it is possible that misperception of both back-channel responses, and the rehearsal of alternative candidate answers on the part of the interviewee, has had a part to play in sustaining the view that people with intellectual disabilities are, inevitably, incompetent interviewees.

The design of many questionnaire schedules, such as the Schalock and Keith (1993) QOL.Q examined here, is such that interviewers will be forced to employ three-part listings of response alternatives (e.g. 'Do you feel out of place in social situations? Always; Sometimes or Never?'). Houtkoop-Steenstra (2000: 94–5) suggests that this design feature of survey instruments may, in and of itself, result in the receipt of invalid responses when used with 'normal' populations. However, as well as being a standard feature of questionnaire design, such listings also are extremely common rhetorical devices in everyday talk, and, by the use of pauses, set up a series of response slots for the interviewee to indicate their continued attention and understanding. It is not uncommon for these slots to be filled with utterances such as hhmmhh or other non-verbal fillers, but it is also not uncommon for conversationalists to use 'yes' as a filler (Holmes, 1995). As Williamson (2003: np) points out:

Many back channel tokens are thought to exhibit a continuer function. Jefferson (1984: 200) notes that the token mm hm exhibits what she calls passive recipiency, i.e. it 'proposes that the co-participant is still in the midst of some course of talk, and shall go on talking'. Schegloff (1982) proposes that, in addition to this continuer function, tokens such as uh huh, mm, etc., are used to pass an opportunity to initiate a repair. Inasmuch as tokens such as these operate to pass an opportunity to initiate a repair, Schegloff suggests that they betoken the absence of problems and, therefore, they are seen as signalling understanding of the prior talk.

In the example below it is apparent, from the rapidity of his utterance, that Arthur is indeed using 'yes' as backchannel, merely to indicate that he has understood the response alternative, no repair is required, and that his interlocutor should proceed to the next item. The unwary, the inexperienced, or the overly persuaded of acquiescence ('yea-saying') as a deterministic phenomenon, may well be forgiven for reading these 'yes's' as 'acquiescent' responses and thus as 'invalid'. On such a reading he has answered 'yes' to two, contradictory, response alternatives, whereas in fact he indicates clearly at line 225, by virtue of his rising intonation and repetition of the affirmative 'yeah the ↑best yeah yeah' overlapping with the interviewer, that he has understood the alternatives and made a decision to reject two of them.

Extract 13: Code CA/KK/CD

```
213  I    o↑kay >can ↓I< >shall ↑we< do some of these questions then?
214  AR   yeah
215  I    okay (.) overall would you say ↑that (.) ↓life brings ↑out (.) the ↓best
216       in you
217  AR   ↑yes
218  I    treats you like everybody ↓else=
219  AR   ↑=yes:
220  I    or doesn't give you a chance
221  AR   eh:?
222       (1 sec)
223  I    what >do you think ↓that< (.) life (.) brings out the best in ↑you (. .)
224       ⌈or (syll syll)
225  AR   ⌊yeah the ↑best yeah yeah
226  I    right (. .) so that's ↑your (.) your answer ↑yeah   ⌈life >br< life
227  AR                                                       ⌊↓yes yes
```

Problems with 'yes' are, again, not restricted to interviews with people described as intellectually disabled, nor is the manner in which they may be taken awry by interviewers and, importantly, allowed to pass uncontested by the 'respondent'. Hanneke Houtkoop-Steenstra's data contain the following example:

Extract 14: (20) Culture PandP Survey 23, question 6, from Houtkoop-Steenstra, 2000: 124

1	I	a:nd I mention a list of museums in Amsterdam,
2		please indicate which ones you have ever
3		been to.
		(. . .)
4		d- Tropical Muse↑um
5		(1.0)
6	R	yah, that was in primary school uh
7		(1.2)
8		ya:h yah sixth grade or something ( )
9	I	abou:t ten years, say
10	R	⌈yah
11	I	⌊.hh and u:h that was with your primary school?

In line 9, the interviewer formulates the age of the interviewee when in sixth grade 'as about ten years say', to which what might appear to be an unproblematic 'yes' response token is forthcoming at line 10. Houtkoop-Steenstra notes that: 'in the old Dutch school system, a pupil was approximately twelve years old in the sixth grade'. The interviewer does not await the respondent's evaluation of this reformulation and proceeds to the next question. Simultaneously, the respondent says 'yah'. Although this may be a confirmation of the reformulation, the rising intonation suggests that the 'yah' is the beginning of a longer turn (Houtkoop-Steenstra, 2000: 124–5). And let's see what happens: the respondent, faced with an interviewer who has taken the floor, does not produce a correction to the interviewer's formulation, but rather stops his turn and allows the interview to proceed. A further extract illuminates the use of 'yes' as a checking filler quite clearly.

Extract 15: Code CA/KK/CD

357	I	no? (.) ((sniff)) (.) o↓kay (. .) ↑(just) ↑one more ↓question yeah?
358		(. .) would you say: (.) life was really ↓good
359	AR	⌈yes ↓yeah
360	I	⌊o- o↑kay or ↓useless
361	AR	↓yes
362	I	yeah?
363	AR	>er<↑really ↓good
364	I	↓okay (.) that's ↑great (.) that's ↑me finished

Another way in which submissive acquiescence may be inferred is by the interviewee's repetition of response alternatives. The following example shows how, if care is not taken to pursue legitimate candidate answers, this repetition may be taken as indicating either incomprehension or implicit acceptance of the interviewer's offered candidate answers. Here Arthur may, on a superficial reading, be accused of 'parrotting' the interviewer's talk (at lines 361 and 363), thus opening the way to a negative judgement about the competence of his answer. However such a dismissal would be rash.

Extract 16: Code CA/KK/CD

```
359  I    ↑oh right (.) ok ↑then (.hh) right ↓then (.hh) so Arthur would
360       ↑°you ↓sa:y that ↑your ↓li:::fe (. .) >↓brings out the best< in ↓you↑ (. .)
361  AR   ↑brings ↑out the ↓best in (you)=
362  I    or ↑treats you like ev'ryone ↑else↓ (. .)
363  AR   (↑ 2 sylls) anybody e::lse
364  I    or ↓doesn't give you a ↓cha:nce (. .)
365  AR   >°uh er°< ↑treats yer (.) uh u::h al- all↑right
366  I    the same as everyone ↑else?     ⌈(syll) you (syll) the middle one?
367  AR                                   ⌊ye:ers
```

At line 365 it becomes apparent that Arthur, far from merely echoing the alternatives offered to him by the interviewer, is engaged in a more sophisticated strategy. The pause at the end of the interviewer's utterance at line 364 sets up a response slot for Arthur: his hesitation would appear to be buying time for him to search among the previously offered alternatives for his preferred answer. This he offers, not as a 'parrotted' response but as a competent paraphrase of the response alternative offered at line 362. This reformulation suggests that he has indeed comprehended the items offered and his repetition of alternatives along the way may, rather, be construed as rehearsal.

Interviewees' resistance

It is important not simply to correct a misapprehension about the apparently acquiescent responses of people with intellectual disabilities, but also to report positively on their competencies in persisting in their version of events even in the face of some pressure. Several extracts follow which illustrate that, for these individuals at least, they have at their disposal the wherewithal to countenance the breach of two major conventions of conversation management, the production of preferred second parts of adjacency pairs, particularly with regard to agreement with formulations and acceptance of requests, and the provision of an explanation or justification for the implied failure or inadequacy of a previous response (cf. Antaki, 1994). Again, in this context it is important to remember also that, as we saw in the first part of this chapter, these encounters are understood by the interviewees as tests – with possibly unpleasant upshots: that is as encounters with a pre-given power asymmetry, and moreover, one that is not balanced in their favour. It is also important to recognise that in all of the literature of the traditional school, submissive acquiescence is a 'strong disposition' presumed to be residing within the interviewee, which will have ruinous effects, if not detected by careful testing (Heal and Sigelman, 1995: 335). The implication of this state of affairs, then, is that the normative sequential expectancies of interaction (the preference for agreement for example) are magnified (Marková, 1991). It would then be expected that, if people with an intellectual disability were indeed strongly disposed to be interactionally incompetent, that under *these* circumstances we should see not levels of 'response bias' at the 41.7 per cent–50.9 per cent suggested by Heal and Sigelman (1995: 335); the two thirds of their sample identified by Perry and Felce (2002: 445) as 'unable to respond or exhibit[ing] response bias' or the average 25 per cent reported by Matikka and Vesala (1997) but rather something much more pervasive. What we should not expect to see is resistance or disagreement.

The following two extracts illustrate the interviewer deploying the conversational device described by Schenkein (1978) as a 'pass' in order to solicit an explanation of the previous speaker's last utterance. Here, by implication, the previous speaker's utterance is cast as being, in some sense 'wrong' or in some other fashion, inadequate. It is of note that this device, although apparently an innocuous echo, very specifically locates some part of what the client has said as requiring accounting, but sidesteps the responsibility of naming it. In these circumstances, then, there is a clear onus on the speaker so made accountable to exonerate themselves, or in some other way to justify their position. They are, in terms of our present concerns, under pressure to meet the interviewer's demand for an *alternative* answer to the one they have offered.

Extract 17: Code HB/MR/TT

```
125   I     ri:ght    ⌈(. .) oh that's ↓good (1 sec) ↑do ↑em: (1 sec) do >↓you<
126   BO              ⌊((hhhhh))
127   I     ever feel ↑lone↓ly (.) Bob
128   BO    ↑eh?
129   I     ↓do you ever feel ↓lonely
130   BO    ↑no:
131   I     ↑no (. .) not ever
132   BO    ↓no:
133   I     ↑no:
```

In a rather dysfluent delivery the interviewer makes a dispreferred query (Antaki and Houtkoop-Steenstra, 1997), followed by a 'pass' at line 131.[9] The interviewer's utterance here is signalling, by use of the apparently innocent repetition, that the unambiguous candidate answer offered by Bob at line 130 is perceived as inadequate and requires justification. The interviewer is, however, not content with this and, after a short pause to allow Bob an 'explanation slot' (Antaki, 1994), offers a reformulation. Despite this pressure, Bob's non-take-up of the offered slot at line 131, and his utterance at line 132, firmly restates his earlier position and explicitly rejects the interviewer's proposed reformulation (no (. .) not ever?)

The extract below again illustrates the operation of this process, but also illustrates an alternative way of resolving the trouble it occasions. Here the interviewer overrides the candidate answer to his question offered at line 142, only coming in with the 'pass' when he has finished the questionnaire item, by which time he has had a second (consistent) overlapping candidate answer.

Extract 18: Code HB/MR/TT

```
138  I        yeah?
139  (3 sec)
140  I        .hh ↑are there people living with ↓you who (.) who ↓bother you (.)
141           sometimes (. .) or hurt you or: (.)      ⌈m-
142  BO                                                ⌊↑no
143  I        make you ↑angry or     ⌈(pes↓ter you) (.) no? (1 sec) ↑so ↓y-
144  BO                               ⌊↓n:o
145  I        y' ↑like the people you live ↓with
146  BO       yes:
147  I        yeah?
148  (2 sec)
```

Here, however, the interviewer reformulates positively, by effectively reversing the polarity of the question (y' ↑like the people you live ↓with), to check – for the third time – that the answer to his question which Bob intends to give is, in fact 'no'. In the face of this pressure Bob again remains resolute.

As a final example of a respondent attempting to get his concerns onto the agenda and resisting the interviewer's formulation, consider the following.

---

[9] Houtkoop-Steenstra (2000: 154) notes that of the two alternate forms of an enquiry (e.g. A. Did you have a nice holiday?; B. Did you have a bad holiday?) that the marked, B form, is not only less likely to be asked, but is also likely to elicit a response such as 'what makes you think so?', whereas the A form is the default, unmarked, format which projects the relevance of agreement.

Extract 19: Code CA/MR/WM

554	I	how much control do you have (.) over what you ↓do
555	MA	what (.) ↑'e::↓re?
556	I	↑well (.) (li-) (.) ↑yeh (. .) wha- (.) things that- like going out (.) an'
557		(.) when you get up an'
558	MA	well I (go out) (.) on a ↑Wednesday::=
559	I	=yeh
560	MA	up ↑Merchant↓man
561	I	right ↑so (.) are you in charge of doin' that?
562	MA	↓yes
563	I	yeah? (. .) ↓you don't have to ask anyone if you can
564	MA	↑no no
565	I	right right
566	MA	(see) on a Thursday (. .) I go to 't (. . .) club
567	I	mhm
568	MA	(they- they) complained said I- >not s'posed to (go in) in< club (.) they
569		said (you're- you not the boss) (. .)
570	I	⌈HHhhh (. .) right so ↑you're in charge
571		⌊(rustle)
572		(rustle)
573	MA	(cough) if I (syll) club (syll) on a ↓Thursday I ↑would
574	I	°right°
575	MA	nothing to do with ↑them
576	I	°ok°=
577	MA	=↑is ↓it?
578	I	↑no::↓ I think you're ↑right
579		(2 secs, including some rustling)
580		↑ok (. . .) ↑when- when can friends come over and ↓see you

Note in this final extract the degree to which Malcolm's statement about the problem he faces at the club ('they complained said I- not s'posed to (go in) club. .') is resisted by the interviewer as germane to what is, after all, supposed to be an interview about Malcolm's Quality of Life. The interviewer reformulates the complaint in the terms of the official question (lines 554 / 561), but note that he has entirely missed its spirit: Malcolm is complaining about something like the lack of acceptance or access, yet the interviewer casts it as Malcolm being 'in charge'. However, rather than accept this formulation, Malcolm signals non-acceptance by leaving a hearable pause, giving a cough, then taking up the issue again, though in a way which, as competent conversationalists do, avoids other initiated repair of the interviewer's turn ('if I (syll) club (syll) on a Thursday I would'). This is given minimal encouragement by the interviewer, occasioning a blunter restatement of Malcolm's grievance (nothing to do with them). Still there is no positive up-take, and the interviewer effectively ends the narrative at 578, moving onto the next question at 580.

This exchange demonstrates a number of issues not least of which is the degree to which the interviewer can decide what is and is not pertinent to the interviewee's quality of life and direct the interaction accordingly; but the other key point here is that it also demonstrates the interviewee's persistence with their business in the face of such direction. Again, of course, we have it open to us as analysts to decide how to characterise this resistance: it would not be difficult, were one so minded, to read this as further, damning, evidence of Malcolm's interactional incompetence.

The aim of this chapter was to look again at the influential notion of 'acquiescence bias' in the language of people with learning disabilities. This notion, current since the mid 1980s, has encouraged a climate of opinion in which what people with intellectual disabilities have to say is (at least) open to the suspicion that they are merely offering what the questioner wants to hear. The evidence given for this notion in the literature has been, and continues to be, based on an inadequate picture of language and language use. It is certainly possible to identify points in the interactions reproduced here where responses might look submissively acquiescent on a superficial reading, but are, on closer inspection, more persuasively interpretable as a complex interplay of respondents' strategy and interviewer demand. There is no single thread that ties all the strategies together; they are all taken from the normal repertoire of conversational management. It is only their surface appearance of inconsistency and agreement that would tempt someone into calling them all acquiescent. And, of course, if we heed Schegloff's (1999) warning about the interactional dynamics peculiar to formal assessments, and take cognisance of Simmons-Mackie and Damico's speech therapy data, we may see that the formal interview (test) *qua* formal interview (test) may itself be centrally implicated in, if not constitutive of, the production of what one might choose to call dispositional acquiescence.

Although it is a strongly implied part of the traditional school's thesis that the person with an intellectual disability is acquiescing as a matter of spontaneous preference, or a strong dispositional tendency, independently of the position she or he is put in by the interview situation, we can, alternatively, see that the social context of the interview situation is crucially important in that it was perceived by people as a test situation, and oriented to as such. Thus interviewees often found themselves in a position where their initial candidate answers were subject to a series of reformulations by the interviewer. There were two ways this could happen: one was that the first answer given looked incompetent against the official vocabulary of the interview schedule, so was queried, setting up a chain of candidate answers. The other way was generated by the interviewer's pre-existing expectations of what the 'correct' answer 'actually' was, encouraging them to pursue a line of questioning until an 'appropriate' response was given. In both these circumstances, the respondent's utterances may have looked contradictory and the final utterance 'acquiescent', but this is an artifact of the complex manoeuvres into which both interviewer and interviewee get enmeshed.

Similarly, an important part of the management of any interaction is the provision by the listener to the speaker of 'back-channel' responses to indicate that attention is being appropriately given. In the case of these interviews, a number of points can be identified at which such ordinary conversation-management signals might be misconstrued as submissive acquiescence by researchers rigidly importing the criteria of the ideal interview, in which all interviewers' utterances are questions and all interviewees' utterances are answers. This is patently not the case in the data, and it is important not to take all 'yes' tokens (for example) at face value.

Indeed, even in studies conducted within the uncritical 'mainstream' paradigm, such possibilities are canvassed – while retaining the notion that the issue is, at base, one of a dispositional characteristic of intellectual disability. Chong *et al.* (2000), whose work was considered earlier, suggest that:

Response switching following a repeated question might have been inadvertently learned through everyday interactions with adults and teachers. It is quite common for an adult to repeat a question when a child or student gives an incorrect or undesirable response. If the child or student provides an alternative or different response to the repeated question, he or she is more likely to be 'correct'. This may be further strengthened by receiving an adult's approval and/or by escaping the adult's persistent questioning.

And as we have seen not only is 'escaping persistent questioning' precisely one of the major problematics of interviews identified in the general (e.g. Krosnick, 1991) and conversation analytic literatures (Houtkoop-Steenstra, 2000) with 'normal' respondents, but it is, in and of itself only a problem if one is inclined, *a priori*, to treat it as a moral accountable, rather than as an entirely understandable human response to aversive circumstances. That is to say, saying 'yes' to one's interrogators may be a smart interactional strategy.

Finally, an important aspect of the data is its demonstration of respondents' resistance to interviewer-led questions and response alternatives, even in this situation of power asymmetry and 'test' conditions. For an interviewee to 'hold out' against an authority figure is in any circumstances hard, and here must be seen to be doubly so. It may even be that displays of resistance or anti-acquiescence of this kind are strategic self-presentations of a rather macro kind, designed to orient to the very general motivation of the interview as a whole by showing the respondent to be 'independent' – and in chapter 4 this issue is explored in greater detail.

The long-unexamined assumption in the literature is that people with intellectual disabilities cannot be expected to answer validly in interviews, because they tend to acquiesce submissively to questioners. This assertion, repeated mantra-like in the literature, is conceptually cloudy, based in an entirely discredited model of interaction and, where clear, empirically false. In the data examined here, where there is inconsistency and agreement, it is understandable as the result of joint manoeuvering by the questioner and an assiduous, if often frustrated, respondent. In sum, then, the general case is that the behaviour of people with intellectual disabilities in interviews ought not to be characterised as 'acquiescent' in the traditional school's sense of submission to others or automatic yea-saying. If there is inconsistency and agreement, it is not of necessity a matter of a general, unoccasioned submissiveness, but rather a demonstration of attention to the manner and sequence of the way that test questions are put, and the large amount of surrounding material in which they are embedded. In spite of any cognitive limitations they might be said to have, people with an intellectual disability demonstrably try to make sense of what they hear the interviewer do and say, respond accordingly, and try to get their own concerns onto the agenda of the interaction. This having been said, it is important that the type of interaction studied here be recognised: these interviews may not be – and indeed it is an important part of the argument of this book that such methods are not – adequately representative of the mundane doing of social life that is psychology's self-appointed task to explain. Accordingly, it is important to look at interaction that *is* adequately representative of the mundane business of everyday life, and chapter 5 does just that. Prior to that analysis however, in chapter 4, we examine interaction which more closely approximates to everyday talk – unstructured interviews – and, remarkably, it appears that here people with an intellectual disability seem to show much less evidence of a putative dispositional willingness to please.

4   Matters of identity

'Retard' . . . is a common expression of derision among today's youth.
It is no surprise, then, that those who bear this diagnostic label, and
understand its stigmatizing quality, wish to avoid it.

(Baroff, 1999 cited in Schroeder *et al.* 2002: 90)

The truthful rendering into speech of who one is . . . is installed at
the heart of contemporary procedures of individualization. In the act of
speaking, through the obligation to produce words that are true to an
inner reality . . . one becomes a subject for oneself.

(Rose, 1999b: 244)

This chapter turns to look at the manner in which people with intellectual
disabilities themselves describe and account for their identities as such
persons, drawing on both ethnographic and interview data. Of course,
such an approach takes the very real risk of failing what Jonathan Potter
has called the 'dead psychologist' test, or, as David Silverman (2001)
would have it, of lapsing into soppy – or at least questionably rigorous –
romanticism.[1] Attentive to the dangers of romanticising sound bites, and
perhaps of being accused of treating talk as a window onto the soul, we will
start with a preview of the issues at hand. In a widely quoted summation
of his decades-long ethnography of persons discharged from Californian
institutions, Edgerton states in the revised and updated edition of *The
Cloak of Competence* that:

The label of mental retardation not only serves as a humiliating, frustrating, and
discrediting stigma in the conduct of one's life in the community, but it also
serves to lower one's self-esteem to such a nadir of worthlessness that the life of
the person is scarcely worth living. (Edgerton, 1993: 132)

Accounts such as this have set the tenor for an entire literature. The taken-
for-grantedness of the stigma attached to 'being intellectually disabled'

---

[1] The 'dead psychologist test' is a criterion against which the naturally-occurring-ness of
data can be gauged. Ideally data should exist even if the psychologist / researcher who
wishes to study it died prior to its occurrence. In other words the data are not set up by
the analyst.

can be seen in Todd's characterisation of stigma as 'a pervasive, limiting and daunting influence' (Todd, 2000: 604). Thus we also see that Davies and Jenkins (1997) suggest, in their account of 'how people with learning disabilities see themselves' that:

People with learning difficulties carry a label and an associated social identity which is a major determinant of their material prospects and the character of their social relationships. This label is a 'master status' (Hughes, 1945) which affects most of their other social identities, such as gender and social adulthood. (Davies and Jenkins, 1997: 95)

Such structuralist theorising is again a recapitulation of the billiard ball theory of action-in-the-world criticised by both discursive psychology and second wave disability studies writers. Under this account, a social identity is a fixed thing, like a handbag perhaps, which people 'carry', and which 'determines' not only life's practical material outcomes, but also the sorts of relationships that people may have. Intriguingly, while relying conceptually on Edgerton's (1967) early work for this account, Davies and Jenkins and other workers in this genre tend to overlook the fact that the reports from the latter stages of the decades long ethnography that Edgerton has conducted (e.g. Edgerton and Gaston, 1990) suggest that, if anything, the lives of people with intellectual disabilities may be characterised not by stasis, and an impoverished life 'determined' by their 'social identity', but (like 'normal people', perhaps?) by change, fluidity and a remarkably mundane, yet heterogeneous, set of material outcomes and social relationships. The totalising, homogenising, and hence utterly misleading, effects of this way of conceiving of 'social identity' and its 'effects' may be illustrated by a simple thought experiment: if we could even think it, what sense could we make of describing 'being normal' as 'a label and an associated social identity which is a major determinant of . . . material prospects and the character of . . . social relationships . . . a "master status" . . . which affects most . . . other social identities, such as gender and social adulthood'? Clearly this says everything – and, hence – tells us nothing.

But is not only in sociology that such deterministic accounts of identity are to be found. Craig et al. (2002: 63) offer perhaps an apogee of this work when they describe their study thus:

The aim of this study is to explore the relationship that the people with an intellectual disability have with their intellectually disabled identity and to examine the influence services for people with intellectual disabilities have on this relationship.

Here we see again the matter-of-fact reification of the notion of an 'intellectually disabled identity': such a putative 'thing' is spoken of as if it were a piece of clothing, a pet or a neighbour. It is, further, taken for granted *a priori* that such an identity is something that all people described as 'intellectually disabled' *really* have, whether they know it or not. What is also absolutely evident is the manner in which studies such as these are predicated on what Nikolas Rose describes as our 'contemporary procedures of individualization'. That is, these studies both demand of their participants 'the truthful rendering into speech of who one is' and lay upon interviewees 'the obligation to produce words that are true to an inner reality'. Again, in a context of asymmetric rights to determine what is and is not sayable as truth, what we see is an endeavour which calibrates a person's status as a co-equal member in terms of the faithfulness of their words to an inner reality defined, *a priori*, by the researcher.

Thus, perhaps unsurprisingly, Craig *et al.*'s (2000) account of talk in a service users' focus group – while couched in terms of 'tendencies', 'appearances' and 'allusions' – is presented as 'confirming' that people used phrases they had picked up from staff, compared themselves favourably to other service users ('stating one's own difference to more severely people intellectual disabilities [sic]', p. 70), accounted for their inclusion in services via reasons that played down intellectual disability, and displayed 'obvious discomfort . . . discussions . . . became stilted and awkward when the phrase "learning disability" was used' (p. 65). If this were not enough, a follow-up survey of staff in a learning disability service revealed that twenty-one of the forty-eight surveyed: 'agreed with the assertion that many people with intellectual disabilities do not see themselves as intellectually disabled' with twelve agreeing that 'clients often struggle with accepting that they are intellectually disabled' (p. 69). Quite aside from the fact that, as we have already seen, talking of 'identity' as some fixed thing is in violation of the logical grammar of the term's proper use, and that the delicate management of a potentially disreputable membership is everyone's ordinary mundane business (cf. Silverman, 1998; Sacks, 1992), here it is only by professional fiat that utterly unremarkable focus group talk (itself notoriously problematic, see Puchta and Potter, in press; 2002) becomes a diagnostic indicator of an accountable breach in moral conduct.

That is, people here are held accountable for their 'denial' of the 'truth' about their 'intellectually disabled identity'. This is to proceed as if a focus group discussion of a new soap powder which contained no explicit reference by participants to their gender could sensibly be said to demonstrate the difficulty that women, say, have in coming to terms with their 'female identity'. And this before the sound bites which pass for 'data' are examined. Here is the evidence that Craig *et al.* (2000: 66–7) reproduce to illustrate '[T]heme 3: There was a tendency to concentrate on the differences between other service users and oneself, comparing oneself favourably and rarely acknowledging one's own difficulties.'

Extract 20: Box 5. From Craig *et al.*, 2000: 66. line numbers added, transcription as in original

1 **a** Were they noisier? A – <u>Yes</u>. B – <u>Yes, a lot of people were noisy when I was</u>
2 <u>there</u>. A – <u>But there's not as many there now that's noisy</u>.
3 **b** The people who are noisy, why are they noisier? B – <u>Some of them used to</u>
4 <u>scream, yes</u>.
5 **c** So what kind of people were they? B – <u>I'm not quite sure what it is . . . .</u>
6 **d** What do you think [participant's name]? A – <u>The one's that can't talk to</u>
7 <u>you</u>.

In line 1 participants A and B provide straightforwardly descriptive accounts of the 'noisiness' of users of a day service setting. Notably, neither A nor B takes up the projected relevance of the moderator's initial utterance which makes relevant an upgraded assessment. While 'were they noisier' invites a response such as 'Oh, yes, *much* noisier' (Pomerantz, 1984b) which, imaginatively, might be taken as a 'favourable comparison with the self' despite the fact that the moderator specifies no referent ('were they noisier' – than what or who?). Instead we see a simple proposition that there were indeed a lot of noisy people (A) and that the proportion of noisy people has now reduced (B). Similarly, in lines 3–4, the moderator's fishing expedition 'the people who are noisy, why are they noisier?' (which clearly projects the relevance of an 'honest' response such as 'oh, they're intellectually disabled'), is instead met by B with what, on the face of it, is an entirely acceptable amplification of the content of A's prior turn, that '*some* of them used to scream, yes'. Line 5 sees the sharpening of the moderator's focus on eliciting a confession of the category 'intellectually disabled' and again is met with a perfectly unremarkable, but incompletely formed, claim by B of unawareness, unawareness of precisely what we do not know. As Beach and Metzger show, claiming insufficient knowledge is a complex and ambiguous interactional device, and one which 'may have little or anything to do with not knowing, because claiming and demonstrating knowledge (or lack thereof) can be revealed as distinct sorts of activities' (Beach and Metzger, 1997: 562). Indeed, in chapter 6 we will see an extended *demonstration* of knowledge of a range of culturally normative, and interactionally subtle, forms of conduct by an officially diagnosed 'intellectually disabled' man, in the complete absence of any formal claims to such knowledge. However, in the case of the data Craig *et al.* (2000) provide (and again this is a perennial problem of 'sound bite' data 'analysis'; cf. Antaki *et al.* 2003) we cannot know with any certainty from the material provided just what 'I'm not quite sure what it is . . .' is doing in the interaction in hand: any interpretation of this utterance can only be speculative. The final exchange in the extract again arguably shows a straightforward and unambiguous candidate response: the 'kind of people' that the noisy people are, are simply, 'the ones that can't talk to you'. Given that, as Sacks (1992) points out, all persons can, correctly, be identified by an almost infinite number of characterisations, this description by A surely attends to B's *previous* characterisation – 'some of them used to scream' – and simply, collaboratively, extends it. The suggestion that this reveals a favourable comparison of self to others, and a denial of (failure to acknowledge) 'one's own difficulties', is simply fanciful. Quite how this exchange can be said to 'demonstrate this distancing phenomenon' (Craig *et al.* 2000: 66) is opaque: such a 'demonstration' is, in truth, only available to analysts (particularly those of a psychodynamic persuasion) who already 'know' that their interlocutors 'have' an 'intellectually disabled identity' as a 'master status', and that they are wont, accountably, to 'deny' this 'fact' about themselves.

Such accounts tend to locate this accountable failure within the individual with an intellectual disability: like the supposed tendency to 'acquiescence' bias being a 'strong disposition', so too denial or lack of awareness is held to reside in the person. Another stream in this literature holds direct care staff (Todd, 2000) and parents to account for either engaging in 'fictional identity building' (Todd and Shearn, 1997) for their children, of otherwise failing to inform their children or charges about who, or what, they really are (despite in Cunningham, Glenn and Fitzpatrick's (2000) study of parental telling about Down's Syndrome, only five of seventy-seven respondents actively avoiding such a disclosure); of playing the role of 'maintaining a "protective cocoon" (Goffman, 1968) in a style similar to that of parents' (Todd, 2000: 617); of engaging in a 'benevolent conspiracy' (Edgerton, 1967: 172) to conceal the 'truth' of people's identities or acting as 'tour guides' to 'insulate' young people with an intellectual disability from the 'real world' (Todd, 2000: 616) and collaborating with fictitious and incredible claims to typical identities to shield people from the 'emotional injuries disclosure would inevitably lead to' (Todd, 2000: 615).

Let us look at how these matters are handled by staff and a parent in a group home in Western Australia. In extract 21, Kylie's mother – who we will meet again in chapter 5   is talking to Anne, a member of care staff, about her about recent dealings with the social security agency, Centrelink. Kylie had previously taken a call from Centrelink and had experienced difficulty understanding what was wanted. Anne is relaying her follow-up call with Centrelink worker Rachel to Kylie's mother, with Kylie herself present throughout the exchange.

Extract 21: KA/Mum/AB/1998

```
 1  ANNE  I want Rachel in: Bun↓bury so I ↑got to her and I ↑said (.) so I ↓told
 2        her ↑don't ring Kylie and (1.5) and give her messages like ↓that
 3        because she is: ↓totally stressed out about ↑it and she said oh well I
 4        I ↓realised when I ↓spoke to her that I shouldn't have done ↑it but it
 5        was the ↑only contact number I ↓had (.) so (0.5)
 6  MUM   But I mean they ↑must know that these kids are ↑Activ kids. They
 7        must ↓know (.) they are ret↑arded.
 8  ANNE  ↓Yeah well
 9  MUM   And any message you give ↓them is goin to be ↑totally
10        miscon↑strued you ↑know (.) sort ↓of (.)
11  ANNE  Oh ↓no (.) Kylie did ↑all the right things
12  MUM   ↑Yeah
13  ANNE  ↓She rang Mar↑ie because she didn't want to give out Marie's
14        ↓number
15  MUM   Yeah.
```

In lines 6 and 7 Mum identifies Kylie as one of these 'Activ kids', Activ Foundation being the name of the agency providing the supported housing in which the 'moderately intellectually disabled' Kylie lives. In line 7 her characterisation of 'Activ kids' as '*retarded*' is clear, making quite visible her assessment that among the accountable social consequences of 'being retarded' are the inability to receive, competently, important telephone calls and to make rational decisions. Mum outlines her views on the concomitants of intellectual disability with 'any message you give them is going to be totally misconstrued you know' and actively ('you know') solicits a collaborative agreement from Anne. Such a damning assessment of Kylie's competence (no parental 'fictional identity' building here) is *resisted* by the staff member not only with the bald statement that 'Kylie did all the right things', but also via the provision of behavioural evidence (in line 13) that Kylie is also sufficiently competent to be aware of agency practices and to consider other people's privacy. If this is indeed maintaining a protective cocoon, then it would appear to be based, in this interaction at least, not so much in a sentimental desire to shield Kylie from the emotional damage that frank assessments of her incompetence may inflict, but rather in a behaviourally grounded assessment of her actual capacities.

In Extract 22 the conversation continues, with Mum continuing her reference to people receiving services from Activ as 'kids' (line 4). If it wasn't clear to Anne, the staff member, that Kylie is not only to be included in the group, but also the incapacities which this group are invested, in line 5 her mother points to Kylie while asking whether 'Centrelink think that the kids are actually going to get grow brains over night?'

Extract 22: KA/Mum/AB/1998

1	ANNE	But they ↑do̲ s: trange ↓things Centre↓link.
2	MUM	Yeah ↑it does (.) does
3	ANNE	⌈I mean they ↑send out ↑these forms ↓to̲ the ↑clients-
4	MUM	⌊The ↓Centrelink think that (.) the kids are actually going to get (.)
5		grow↑brains over ↑night and be pe̲r↑fect ↓again I ((points at Kylie))
6		mean ↑I wish that was the ⌈case
7	ANNE	⌊Well (1.5) because they a̲l̲↓ways tell
8		↑us=
9	MUM	=Yeah
10	ANNE	That we̲ (.) are not allowed to know any of these ↓things (.) they
11		↑can̲'̲t̲ give us the information (.) we can't pass on any infor↓mation
12		they ↑send̲ the forms straight to the clients them↓selves (.) so

Anne once more ignores, and in so doing withholds her agreement with, Kylie's mother's direct reference to her suspect intellect and ability and in line 10 returns to the sequence she started in line 1, a complaint about the process used by Centrelink. Again, as noted above, this cannot be seen as cocooning, quite the opposite. It may well be, and indeed arguably is, the case that Kylie's mother is seeking to enrol Anne into a 'conspiracy', but this is hardly one deserving to be described as 'benevolent'. Here, the mother of an adult woman not only refers to her in her presence as a 'kid' and as 'imperfect', but also as having 'no brains'. We see a similar analysis of the capacities of people with intellectual disabilities in data reported Davies and Jenkins (1997: 98–9). Here their informant has been asked to say 'what mental handicap' is. They write that: 'Ellen James, a 20-year-old woman with Downs Syndrome, raised the topic herself and provided one of the definitions closest to conventional understanding' and provide the following data.

Extract 23: From Davies and Jenkins, 1997

ELLEN JAMES	I'll be in the Fun Run tomorrow.
CD	You will?
EJ	Fun Run.
CD	Oh, Fun Run. What's that?
EJ	Sports.
CD	Yes?
EJ	Let me think now.
CD	And you have to run?
EJ	Yes. To raise money.
CD	Oh that's good. To raise money for what?
EJ	Let me think. People with a mental handicap.
CD	I see. What does that mean?
EJ	Help to raise money for charity.

CD Yes. But . . . for charity, for people with a mental handicap. Yes. What does it mean to have a mental handicap do you think?

EJ They haven't many . . . My father told me Saturday. They haven't got . . . brains.

CD I see . . . What do you think about people with a mental handicap?

EJ I feel sorry for them.

Davies and Jenkins (1997: 99) note that this interaction apparently reveals Ellen offering 'a "folk" understanding of mental handicap' but of doing so in such a way as to exclude herself from the category. While it certainly appears that Ellen is at pains to stress that she needs to 'think about it' on two occasions, if we look at this exchange closely what is called *her* 'folk understanding' is actually *her father's* reported speech (Holt, 1996): it is her father who, like Kylie's Mum, holds that 'they haven't got . . . brains', an utterance about which the most we can safely say is that Ellen simply reports it. 'I feel sorry for them' is insufficient a basis to suggest, as Davies and Jenkins do, that this is a definition shaped by Ellen to exclude herself. Again, if we ask an 'Englishman' 'what do you think about English people' and we are told 'I feel sorry for them', we would under no circumstances hear this as a *necessary* denial of co-membership in that category. To see the point let us examine another exchange where the interviewee is asked about the 'meaning of mental handicap'. Davies and Jenkins (1997: 101) report this exchange with June Price, the mother of an intellectually disabled woman.

Extract 24: From Davies and Jenkins, 1997

1 CD   What do you think it means to have a mental handicap?
2 JUNE PRICE   Hard work. Hard work, frustration and tears.

Strangely, June Price is not described as providing a 'folk' theory of mental handicap, of not knowing what the term means – despite the fact that, just like the majority of the interviewees identified as intellectually disabled in the rest of the study – she offers a 'meaning' which bears absolutely no resemblance to their criterion 'more generally accepted interpretations' of the condition (Davies and Jenkins, 1997: 100). Why might this be? It would seem that parents may permissibly use metaphor, but their children must, rather than offer accounts unacceptable to the researchers, produce – on demand – words that are true to an inner reality defined by the researcher. That is, in keeping with the picture theory of reality which underpins this sort of 'identities are things in people's heads' research, the researchers seek to have people confess their status as impaired, and a refusal so to do is taken as a moral failure – as a denial of an unarguable truth. And yet, at least for Davies and Jenkins, there is a paradoxical awareness that whatever may or may not be avowed in an interview may or may not (and from a discursive psychological perspective most certainly cannot) faithfully render into speech hidden psychological truths. Thus they observe:

Comparison[s] with siblings was often cited by parents as evidence that young people knew they had learning difficulties, irrespective of whether or not the young person gave any indication of such an identity being framed in relations of communication. (Davies and Jenkins, 1997: 105)

Taking the phrase 'identity being framed in relations of communication' to mean that the identity was (not) talked about, what we see here is one of discursive psychology's core points: that 'things' like 'identities' can only exist as such, in and for talk. That people may, or may not, talk about a candidate identity in interaction with a researcher thus can tell us very little other than that an interviewee has, or has not, made a candidate identity relevant. It can tell us nothing, whatsoever, about what people do, or do not, "really know".' That is we can see interviews such as those reported by Todd (2000); Todd and Shearn (1995; 1997); and Davies and Jenkins (1997) as sites not where we can use talk as a window onto the soul, but rather as interactions where matters of (morally troublesome) identity are negotiated.

In the data that follows I focus on both the renegotiation – rather than the explicit repudiation – of bald ascriptions of a disabled identity when the status is offered by the interviewer, and also the locally contingent management of 'intellectually disabled' category membership avowals where these may be hearably to the interactional 'benefit' of the interviewee. For in these interactions it is not only the interviewers' talk that makes the possible status of membership in the category 'intellectually disabled person' live, at stake and morally accountable. Interviewees too may, where interactionally occasioned, deploy such identity claims.

Overarching this, however, is some other business. As noted, Edgerton and Goffman have elaborated the notion of 'passing' to describe the identity management practices they have observed among people with intellectual disabilities, and much of the literature would seem to have taken 'passing' to be a set of practices peculiar to people so described. However, examination of the conversation analytic literature would suggest that what has come to be known as 'passing' (with its clear implications of deception and the intent to mislead – these people are not, after all, 'really' normals) may be nothing other than common members' practices. Sacks (1992) has suggested that 'doing being ordinary' is a pervasive feature of the accomplishment of everyday social life – the presentation of self as merely an ordinary actor, with the implication of normalcy, of being just like other folks, and as such, not particularly accountable. As he puts it:

It is almost everybody's business to be occupationally ordinary . . . people take on the job of keeping everything utterly mundane . . . no matter what happens pretty much everybody is engaged in finding only how it is that what is going on is usual, with every effort possible. (Sacks, 1984: 419)

Let us now look at the way in which some people with intellectual disabilities take on that job. Under analysis is data from interviews with people living in supported accommodation in Australia (all described as moderately or mildly intellectually disabled), and also data provided by Todd (2000) and Todd and Shearn (1995). The observations here are organised around the basic question: to what extent can it persuasively be argued that the interviewees here have a 'limited knowledge of their disability and its consequences'? Inspection of the data suggests that it cannot; rather, as I shall try to show, the respondents gave clear evidence of their understanding of (and their dissatisfaction with) their social standing and its consequences for their lives. Chapter 5 will show in more detail this dissatisfaction and its management outside of artificial, interview-based, encounters. Here two main features of this understanding in their talk will be examined: (a) their mobilisation of other people's perceptions and (b) their management of different identities for themselves.

Mobilising relations with others

One strong theme to emerge is the way in which both the interviewer and the respondent call upon other people – not in the interaction – as witnesses and warrants for the respondent being describable as 'having' a disabled identity. In extract 25, consider how Simon manages his grievance about being denied parenthood. According to the 'invisibility' hypothesis, this could be simply because he does not know he is disabled, and the parental prohibition must seem like an arbitrary cruelty. But if we see what he actually says, we see that he manages the dilemma of both acknowledging his own 'abnormality' and complaining about others' prejudices about it. In line 6, the interviewer asks him directly whether being disallowed from having a baby is 'because you have a handicap'. This requires what Brown and Levinson (1978) call a bald, on-record, statement – that is, one that confronts a threat to face directly and publicly. Simon, however, does not shirk from it, answering 'yes'. Note, however, how he immediately turns attention back on the faults of the other parties in the dispute: 'they not talk to us they make up the mind for themselves'. The combination of acknowledgement and return accusation displays Simon's appreciation of his own status and his rejection of other's prejudice against it; a complex combination difficult to square with a notion that the 'toxicity' of his 'handicapped' identity is 'invisible' to himself.

Extract 25: PK/SM/MR1997

1	SIMON	Tina's not allowed to have a baby
2	INT	She's not allowed to have a baby
3	SIMON	Tina's mum and dad said
4	INT	They have said (.) OK (.) Tina's mum said
5	SIMON	They say it's not fair for the baby
6	INT	Not fair for the baby (. .) is that because you have a handicap
7	SIMON	Yes (.) they not talk to us (.) they make up the mind for themselves
8	INT	They didn't talk to you about it
9	SIMON	They told us after
10	INT	Do you want to have children (.) is it something you would like
11	SIMON	I can't have children (.) I've been fixed
12	INT	You've had a vasectomy
13	SIMON	Yes
14	INT	Whose idea was that
15	SIMON	Tina's Mum (.) Tina's Mum (.) She said you can't have children
16		because you're handicapped

Indeed, at lines 15–16, Simon is quite clear about others' perceptions of him and his wife: he puts into direct reported speech (a vivid, but complex, rhetorical device; see Holt, 1996) the injunction 'you can't have children because you're handicapped'. Again, note how other people are being used as sources of evidence for the speaker's own understanding of his situation.

The same theme is visible in the next extract, where Steve – the only other married participant – comes to acknowledge the difficulties that Mary might have with looking after children. Once again, it is other people's reactions and judgement that force the issue: 'The mother, Mary's mother. No, it wouldn't be allowed' (lines 7–9). There follows an exchange in which Steve attributes the judgement of Mary's incompetence to 'the mother', at one point acquiescing with it: 'and I agree with the mother', line 11, but later, in response to a direct question about *his* estimation of Mary's competence, saying 'I don't really know mate (.) Don't really know' (line 21).

Extract 26: PK/ST/MR97

1	INT	Steve (.) you were saying before that you were married to Mary
2		(.) this year (. .) and how are you enjoying married life
3	STEVE	Good (.) good I enjoy it (.) I really do (.) it's good
4	INT	That's a nice part of your life

5	STEVE	Yes (.) it's good (.) it's good
6	INT	Are you planning to have any children
7	STEVE	No (.) no I don't think that (.) the mother (.) would be allowed
8	INT	Who won't allow it
9	STEVE	The mother (.) Mary's mother (. .) no (.) it wouldn't be allowed
10	INT	She wouldn't want you to have any children
11	STEVE	Well (.) Mary wouldn't be able to cope (.) and I agree with the
12		mother (.) too (.) cause Mary's mother wouldn't agree with it
13		know what I mean
14	INT	Does Mary's mother think that it would be too difficult for
15		Mary to look after the child
16	STEVE	Yeah (.) yeah
17	INT	And what do you think about that
18	STEVE	Well (.) I don't know
19	INT	Do you think Mary could look after the child (.) or children if
20		you had children
21	STEVE	I don't really know (.) mate (.) don't really know.

The interviewer sharpens the issue to its most direct point again, as in Extract 27, asking for a bald, on record, statement (lines 22–3)

Extract 27: PK/ST/MR97

22	INT	Do you think that Mary's mum would be saying that because
23		Mary has a disability
24	STEVE	Yeah (.) could be (.) yeah it is (.) she can read and that (.) it's
25		just that she has that (syll syll syll) (.) you know that business
26		so she's got that problem
27	INT	Would you like though (1.0) would you like to be a father
28		perhaps sometime in the future
29	STEVE	Yeah (.) one day I'd like to (.) but (1.0) its just that (1.0) it's the
30		Mother

Steve deals with the interviewer's face threat (though here the imputation of a courtesy stigma as partner of a discredited adult may be a more appropriate analytic gloss) just as Steve did in extract 27; in line 24 he acknowledges the disability identity ('yeah, could be (.) yeah it is') and then introduces his own evaluation of it ('She can read and that it's just that she has that (sylls) you know that business'). Steve is acknowledging disability and, once again, setting it squarely in the interactional world: clear evidence that there is no failure of appreciation of the label or its social consequences.

A description of the less severe social consequences of the application of a 'toxic identity' to self was offered by Sally in her discussion of her experiences in community settings. In acknowledging that being identified as a disabled person might account for the (negative) reactions of people out shopping who, by implication do not treat her as a 'human being' like the people at church (line 23), she is also careful to position herself as 'knowing her own mind' and 'not giving a heck what they think'. In extract 28 she is, as she discursively constructs a version of self, an independent agent who knows her own worth – that is, like Simon and Steve, she mobilises the views of others to set against and contrast with her own.

Extract 28: PK/SF/MR/97

1	INT	How do you find when (. . .) say you are out shopping (.) how
2		do you find people are towards you (.) accepting of you (.) like
3		you (.) or do you find people aren't very accepting perhaps (.)
4		and I'm talking (.)
5	SALLY	Some of them are not very accepting
6	INT	Some are (.) some are not?
7	SALLY	Most people are
8	INT	Most people are accepting
9	SALLY	Yeah
10	INT	Some people aren't (.) is that because you have a disability
11		that sort of thing (.) do you think that
12		(0.3)
13	SALLY	That might be the reason why (.) but I don't give a heck what
14		they think (. .) I just go on (.) blow them (.) if they don't like me
15		(.) fine ((sounding angry))
16	INT	So most people you find accept you (.) but those who don't
17		then=
18	SALLY	=that's fine (.) if I have a bit of a disagreement (.) fine
19	INT	Yeah
20	SALLY	Fine (.) I don't care what you think
21	INT	And you find people here (.) and at work (.) and at church are
22		accepting of you as a person
23	SALLY	Yep (.) they treat me like a human being

As before, we see the respondent faced with a direct question about their disability (in line 10) deal with it by a combination of acknowledgement ('That might be the reason why') and moral assessment ('but I don't give a heck about what they think'). In other words, Sally's interview repeats the pattern of direct question met by acknowledgement and moral evaluation, showing, once again, that the informant is aware of their own status by virtue of their awareness of their social treatment; this is the very opposite of people being 'invisible to themselves'. Note again Sally's demonstration of her ability at instantaneous online analysis in the joint completion of Patrick's assessment of her estimation of others in lines 17–18.

While, in extract 28, for Sally her status as a 'person with a disability' might be acknowledged as visible and accountable when made relevant by the interviewer, Simon himself makes his identity as a 'handicapped person' interactionally relevant (and highly visible) in his talk about his accomplishments and his experience as the butt of others' humour.

Extract 29: PK/SM/MR97

1	SIMON	The supervisor made fun of me
2	INT	He made fun of you
3	SIMON	He said never get a car license (.) not me (.) I not pass.
4	INT	But you did!
5	SIMON	Yes I did
6	INT	Why do you think that is (.) why do you think the supervisors
7		are like that?
8	SIMON	They say us handicapped are a different sort
9	INT	So if you're handicapped (.) you're not good enough to do
10		things
11	SIMON	Yes
12	INT	What do you think of that
13	SIMON	It's not true

Simon's awareness that others' low expectations of 'normal' achievements (lines 3, 11), being seen as 'different' (line 8), and being 'made fun of' (line 1) follow his being identified as one of 'us handicapped' is absolutely explicit. What we see in these extracts is that the respondents' use of other people's views shows not only that they are perfectly aware of their own standing in society, but that they dislike and resist it; this can hardly be 'invisibility to themselves'. Let us at this point look at some of Todd and Shearn's 1995 data. In the interview with Kathleen, the issues of social embarrassment and 'being made fun of' are also directly specified by the interviewee. That is, the social–moral consequences of intellectual disability as a category membership are made relevant as a part of locally contingent interview business. In Simon's case the making relevant of his status as 'handicapped' can be read as doing some nice contrast work with the magnitude of his achievements (gaining his driving licence) and the unpleasantness of supervisors. Let us remind ourselves of Kathleen and Julia's interaction in Todd and Shearn's data:

Extract 30: From Todd and Shearn, 1995: 21

21	JULIA	Does your boyfriend have a mental handicap?
22	KATHLEEN	I don't know. I don't know him that well. I know him from
23		school but not that well.
24	JULIA	So you're not sure if he has a mental handicap?
25	KATHLEEN	No I wouldn't like to ask him
26	JULIA	Why not?
27	KATHLEEN	It might embarrass him poor boy
28	JULIA	What do you think it means to have a mental handicap?
29	KATHLEEN	If people make fun of you that's what it means. Like blind

30		people. It's not nice to make fun of them. I don't make fun
31		of anyone who's blind. I help them. And I help deaf people.
32	JULIA	So what does it mean if you have a mental handicap
33	KATHLEEN	It means you get made fun of, like blind people.

Again we see (in lines 32 and 33) a version of the question–answer sequence we saw above. Here the questions are more abstract ('What do you think it means to have a mental handicap?'; 'So what does it mean if you have a mental handicap?') but the response, again, squarely faces up to the societal risks the avowal of such an identity runs. For Kathleen, the issue appears to be clear cut: while again 'making fun of' is a morally sanctionable action ('unfair' for Simon, 'not nice' for Kathleen) the implications of category membership are not disputed: 'mental handicap' is embarrassing, 'it means you get made fun of'. This is, in practice, not far from the estimation of the meaning of mental handicap offered by June Price to Davies and Jenkins (1997) that we saw earlier: 'mental handicap' means: 'hard work, hard work, frustration and tears'. Jim, in extract 31, while again accounting for prejudice against people with disabilities, as a given, on the basis of an absence of knowledge (about the 'truth' about handicapped people for Simon, about self for Jim), manages the issue of his 'toxic' identity by a partial disavowal.

Extract 31: MR/PK/JG1997

1	INT	What about people in general (.) do you find people in the
2		general community accept you OK (. .) do they like you
3	JIM	Sometimes (.) I find it strange (.) sometimes ohhh (.) people
4		look at me
5	INT	Do they (.) and in not a very nice way
6	JIM	Some don't know (.) sometimes they look at me strange
7	INT	Do they (.) yeah (.) do you think that it's because you have a
8		disability
9	JIM	Because they don't know me
10	INT	They don't know you (.) OK (. . .) and if they got to know you
11		(.) would they (. . .) perhaps like you a bit more
12	JIM	Yeah
13	INT	And how do you feel about that (1 sec) not very (. . .)
14	JIM	Oh (. . .) it doesn't bother me
15		(0.5)
16	INT	Sometimes it does
17	JIM	Yeah
18	INT	I guess that it's pretty unfair isn't it (.) that people do that?
19	JIM	Yeah

Jim's statement that people stared because 'they don't know' him (line 9) may perhaps be taken, if we so wish, as suggestive of the 'invisibility' to him of his intellectual impairment. It is, potentially, hearable as a denial

that he has a disability. It may equally be argued that Jim's partial disavowal of the proffered identity (he does not after all say – as he could have
done – 'but I don't have a disability') in such a way as to attribute staring
to others' lack of knowledge of him is a precise example of the availability
of the 'visibility' of social identities as a discursive resource. Jim confects, with the significant qualifier 'some' (in line 6), others' behaviour as
reflecting a lack of knowledge of him as an individual (his 'real', invisible,
identity as a likeable person) rather than accepting the interviewers' proffered account of staring (by 'people in general', 'the general community')
being consequential upon a 'visible' aspect of self ('because you have a
disability'). Jim's talk thus reconstructs the interviewer's global assessment of him as being 'unliked' by the 'general community' 'because you
have a disability' as a hard-to-explain ('strange') discourtesy by 'some'
people who do not 'know' him. In passing, Jim's subtle discounting of
membership in the category of 'disabled persons' here, we would suggest,
may tell us as much about his possession of knowledge about the moral
status accorded to such memberships as it implies ignorance of them. It
would certainly seem that he does not, like Kathleen and Simon earlier,
experience his support staff as tour guides, shielding him from everyday
prejudice and the potentially 'devasting truth' about himself.

Let us see another extract from Todd and Shearn (1995) before we
leave this section on the respondent's use of *other people*'s perceptions as
warrants, or evidence, of their own standing.

Extract 32: From Todd and Shearn, 1995: 20–1

1	JULIA	Are there any people at college who have disabilities?
2	KATHLEEN	Yeah! Sometimes I see people in wheelchairs there. And
3		there's a girl on oxygen. She's got heart trouble.
4	JULIA	Have any people got learning difficulties there?
5	KATHLEEN	The deaf people. They don't understand what we say to
6		them. They need to communicate with a tutor.
7	JULIA	Has anyone got a mental handicap at college?
8	KATHLEEN	I don't think so.
9	JULIA	Has anyone said you have a mental handicap?
10	KATHLEEN	I don't think so. They haven't said.
11	JULIA	Do you think you're disabled at all?
12	KATHLEEN	I can't do my shoelaces up, that's the problem. I've got to
13		have some help with that.

This is one of the most powerful pieces of evidence that Todd and Shearn
offer. It does, it must be said, look as if Kathleen is either denying she
has a handicap (line 10), or failing to understand what a handicap is
(lines 2, 5–6, 12–13). But firstly let us observe in the interviewer's utterances the lexical indeterminacy of the target concept under examination

and secondly its fluidity of reference: In line 1 a general enquiry is made about whether any people at college have 'disabilities'. In line 4 the interviewers' (still unvoiced) target is respecified as again a general query about whether any people have got 'learning difficulties'. The target construct is yet once more reformulated in line 7 as (a still general) enquiry about whether there are any people with a 'mental handicap' at the college. This is doing indirection (Bergmann, 1992; Schegloff, 1988) or discretion (Maynard, 1991; 1992) at its most laboured: when, despite this fishing for an utterance like 'well, I have' continues to be unsuccessful, the question is posed somewhat more directly, with Kathleen herself as a referent, but with a hearable indeterminacy, in line 9: 'has anyone said you have a mental handicap'. This personalised, potentially face threatening, but still somewhat underspecified, query (anyone at college, anyone at home, anyone on the street?) is met with a perfectly well-formed candidate answer indicating – as a gloss – that no-one has said 'you, Kathleen, have a mental handicap'. This is, more than likely, absolutely true. Others may not have directly told her that she is 'mentally handicapped'.

However, with the interviewer failing again to achieve a personal avowal of any of the three candidate identities on offer (people with 'disabilities', 'learning difficulties', 'mental handicap'), in line 11 Kathleen is at last asked, directly, whether she thinks she's 'disabled at all'. To which a perfectly well-formed response is forthcoming, specifying with precision a particular task which she finds problematic. It is, perhaps, of note that the category of persons analytically at issue – those who are 'learning disabled' – is at no point specified in the exchange above. Todd (2000) also offers similar data to suggest that the special school pupils he interviewed 'had not yet learned to appreciate the stigma potential of special schools or of intellectual disability' (Todd, 2000: 610). Specifically, pupils were identified as unaware of their 'real' identity on the basis of either a flat denial of 'handicap' or of the identification of a physical impairment.[2] Let us examine these fragments.

In the first fragment we are told Alan demonstrates, 'paradoxically', that he is aware of the nature of the school he attends, but that he does not, thereby, view himself as 'handicapped'. It is suggested that 'Alan felt that a "handicap" referred to a physical or sensory impairment . . . since Duncan (sic) had no such impairment, the term "handicapped" was not applicable to him' (Todd, 2000: 610).

---

[2] In so doing these interviewees may alternatively have been described as having both a good grasp of the WHO's distinction between 'impairments' and 'handicaps' and also of the social model of disability.

Extract 33: From Todd, 2000: 610

1	STUART	What kind of school is this Alan?
2	ALAN	For the handicapped
3	STUART	Handicapped? What does that mean?
4	ALAN	Dunno.
5	STUART	Does that mean you have a handicap?
6	ALAN	No.
7	STUART	Do your brothers come to this school?
8	ALAN	No.
9	STUART	Why not?
10	ALAN	Dunno. I've got to come on a bus. They don't.
11	STUART	On a bus? Are there any handicapped children on the bus?
12	ALAN	Yeah, in wheelchairs. And my mate Frankie, he can't talk
13		properly.
14	STUART	What about you? Do you have a handicap?
15	ALAN	No, I can walk.
16	STUART	Have you ever heard of people who have a mental handicap?
17	ALAN	Yeah, people who are thick and the like.
18	STUART	Is there anyone at Afton Lodge who has a mental handicap?
19	ALAN	Yeah, William. But my mum tells me to stay away from him
20		because he hurts me.
21	STUART	What about your brothers? Would they like it here?
22	ALAN	(rubbing his hands): Yeah.
23	STUART	Why?
24	ALAN	'Cos it's a good school.

Let us note first the promptness with which Alan identifies the school as being 'for the handicapped' in line 2, his specification of 'handicapped students' as including those with mobility and speech impairments (in lines 12 and 13) and his description of 'people with a mental handicap' (which surely would have pleased Davies and Jenkins, 1997) as people who are not only 'thick and the like', but who also display 'maladaptive behaviour' ('he hurts me'). It seems here that Alan *actually* demonstrates quite clearly that he understands 'handicap' to refer to both physical and sensory impairments, communication difficulties, and being 'thick' (cognitive impairments). The ignorance and denial of the brute reality that he is, really, 'handicapped' imputed to him appears to turn on the interpretation of 'dunno' in line 4, the 'no' in line 6, and the statement that 'I can walk' in line 15. What are we to make of these utterances?

It seems obvious that Alan's 'dunno' in line 4 is not, actually, reporting a state of ignorance of the meaning of 'handicapped' because, as we have just seen, he goes on to demonstrate with remarkable clarity that, in fact, he *does* know the commonly accepted referents of the term. As we have seen previously, 'I don't know' is a complicated rhetorical object

(Beach and Metzger, 1997; Edwards, 1997) and – as here – may, in use, make absolutely no direct claim to knowledge (or its absence) as such. 'Dunno' here may rather be heard as a non-continuer: an indication that Alan would rather not pursue the topic. Rather than accept this Stuart issues the now familiar direct, face-threatening, enquiry: 'does that mean you have a handicap?' And, if we so wish, we can hear Alan's 'No' in line 6 as a straight denial of the imputed stigma's applicability of the term to him. But *sequentially*, it is also perfectly possible for 'does that mean you have a handicap?' to be heard as 'does not knowing what "handicapped" means, mean you have a handicap?' To which, of course, 'no' is an entirely sensible answer.

But let us note what is done with the apparent 'denial' of his handicap that Alan has offered. In line 7 an indirect fishing expedition commences, is refreshed at lines 9 and 11, and meeting with no success, is bluntly restated again at line 14: 'what about you, do you have a handicap?' Given that Stuart *has not attempted to repair* Alan's candidate definition of 'handicapped children' in line 12 (people in wheelchairs and those who can't talk), it is only reasonable for Alan to assume that it is *this* definition which is consensually agreed to be in play. For Alan then to disavow a handicap by virtue of his ability to walk is, thus, simply for him to tell it like it is in terms of a definition uncontested by Stuart, and hence (at least for Alan) currently operative. However, Stuart's fishing for an identity confession restarts in line 16, with an apparently innocuous general query about Alan's general knowledge: 'have you ever heard of people who have a mental handicap?', which again secures a promptly delivered and perfectly well-formed response indicating that far from 'not knowing', Alan knows very well that intellectual impairment is the generally accepted referent of the term. But an entirely appropriate response, and in precisely the general terms requested, is taking the assiduous interviewer no closer to a confession from Alan that he, really, is best described by the term 'handicapped'. Hence the disingenuous enquiry of Stuart's in line 18, which while on the surface appears to be a simple, unmotivated, asking sequentially clearly projects the requirement for Alan 'spontaneously' to include himself in the category 'thick and the like'. Instead, having identified William as mentally handicapped, Alan gently distances himself from William, on account of his mum's instructions. In the face of this subtle refusal to be pigeon-holed alongside William, Stuart makes his final attempt to secure Alan's compliance in applying the term 'handicapped' to himself in this fragment. Having established earlier that Alan's brothers do not attend the school, asking 'would they like it here' clearly specifies that only a response like, 'no, they wouldn't want to be associated with all of these handicapped people' will be taken as evidence that Alan understands his true nature. Instead, and with a display of sophisticated tables-turning, Alan looks back to Stuart's initial query about the type of school that Afton Lodge is and identifies the high quality of the school as the reason his brothers would like it.

The second fragment Todd provides is similar to the interaction between Julia and Kathleen which we saw earlier. Here Robbie is described as 'another student who associated the term handicap with a sensory or physical impairment . . . something which might have been applicable when he was younger, but had no current relevance in terms of self-labelling' (Todd, 2000: 610).

Extract 34: From Todd, 2000: 610

```
1   STUART   Has anyone ever said to you that you were handicapped or
2            anything like that?
3   ROBBIE   I think my mum told me something once upon a time. She said I
4            had a bad toe or something. Do you want to see it? It's better
5            now anyway. I'm a young man now.
```

Robbie agrees that his mum told him he was handicapped (or something like that) once upon a time. Given that Stuart's 'handicapped or anything like that' does not, explicitly, rule out reference to physical impairment (indeed it is an utterance of potentially all-encompassing reference) it is simply curmudgeonly to hold Robbie to account for choosing to take Stuart's question as indexing a physical injury. That is, to confidently suggest on the basis of this exchange that, 'for Robbie, "being handicapped" was something he had grown out of' (Todd, 2000: 610) is simply unwarranted analytic extension.

Constructing alternative, 'competent', identities

In the section above we saw respondents mobilise accounts of other people's perceptions to display their understanding of their position in society (and their frustration with it) and the ways in which they negotiated that knowledge with interviewers intent on identity confessions. Now let us see the other main theme in their talk, the issue of competence and competent identities.

The interviewees whose talk is reproduced here took pains to construct versions of self as doing typical, ordinary, activities and as being the sorts of persons who were hearably and unremarkably 'at home' in these ordinary identities. Simultaneously attention to the moral accountability of identity was evident in the careful interactional management of questionable identities. In extract 35 Mel, who works part-time for a cleaning company, orients to a set of normative expectancies about the competencies of ordinary members. Her description of relations with colleagues and supervisors at work displays that she is aware of the fact that competent members are expected to make attributions about the psychological make up and motivations of others (Edwards, 1997) (for example being able to tell when a manager's behaviour is a 'joke', and in passing thus positioning herself not only as a discriminating individual but also as one who can 'take a joke') and also to respond to them appropriately and in kind ('you just turn around and tell him to piss off').

Extract 35: MR/PK/TW/1997

12	MEL	The people are really nice (. .) and he (the supervisor) is really
13		nice (.) I mean he likes a person who can take a joke (.) like he'll
14		come up to you and squirt you with a bottle and tell you to
15		hurry up (.) and you just turn around and tell him to piss off
16	INT	You'd want to be a morning person then wouldn't you to put
17		up with those sort of jokes
18	MEL	He jokes around with you all the time (.) and that's really good
19		to joke around in your work

Mel's positioning of self, of her identity, as a 'typical worker' who is also a 'good sort' who can 'take a joke', is further underlined by her final move in lines 18–19 from describing the specifics of her present position ('he jokes around with you all the time') to her summary statement about what makes for a good job in general (that it is 'really good to joke around in your work'). In so doing not only is Mel able to display herself as possessing a sensitivity to the possible interactional ambiguities in her current position, but she also positions herself as being sufficiently experienced a worker to be capable of drawing broader inferences about what makes for a good working environment more generally (cf. Alan's estimation of why pupils would like a given school).

The presentation of self as competent, and claiming membership in conventionally high status social categories is also visible in Shane's talk about his unpaid work with a voluntary organisation. Shane's talk in particular does some important defensive rhetorical (Potter, 1996) work in fending off versions of himself as dependent upon others for help, as inarticulate and incompetent. Such attributions would be clearly inconsistent with the identity he constructs in the following extract.

Extract 36: MR/PK/LC/1997

1	SHANE	Yes (.) sometimes during the week we come up and talk about
2		the Lions Club
3	INT	The Lions Club (.) yeah
4	SHANE	We talk about thing (.) things we can do

```
5    INT      Yeah (.) what sort of things do you do at the Lions Club
6    SHANE    The dog show at the Showgrounds (.) and Bungaree Show (.)
7             we do all the cooking (.) all the cooking out there
8    INT      The cooking (.) OK (.) do you have a stall there
9    SHANE    Under the grandstand
10   INT      And do you cook the food and sell it to people
11   SHANE    Yeah (.) and we do barbecues to help people out
```

Shane's talk makes both formal membership claims (as a member of the Lions Club) but also, in passing, a number of other implicit claims of membership in the categories of persons glossable as 'charity worker', 'public speaker' (lines 1–2, 4) and 'stallholder/business operator' lines 6–7, 9, 11). A number of lexical selections help to emphasise both the issue and scope of his competence – such as the repeated '*all*' describing the extensive catering operation at the Dog Show or the Bungaree Show (we do all the cooking (.) all the cooking out there) – and also the fact that this charitable activity is conducted by virtue of his membership of the Lions (the repeated use of the possessive 'we' indexing the Lions Club in lines 1, 4, 6 and 11). His social status as a competent social actor – as someone who helps *others* – is cemented in place with the seemingly casually tossed off 'yeah (.) and we do barbecues to help people out'. Recall that the positioning of self as a helper of others, as opposed to being a recipient of such assistance, was also to be seen in Kathleen's talk in extract 30: 'I don't make fun of anyone who's blind. I help them. And I help deaf people' (lines 30–1).

The interactional utility of 'voluntary/charity-worker' status in constructing a competent identity was also illustrated by Albert, who spoke about his attendance at Alcoholics Anonymous (AA). Though it remains unclear whether he 'really' acted as a volunteer, or was simply an AA member, when volunteer worker status was offered by the interviewer in extract 37 below, it was *implicitly* claimed, by virtue of non-denial, correction or repair. This is, in line 9, clearly a straightforward manipulation of an accountable moral status (as an 'alcoholic'), which is revealed as strategic in line 20 by the doing of his 'expert status' on alcohol's categorisation as a 'drug' and its deleterious effects on marital relationships ('husbands leave them').

Extract 37: MR/PK/AA 1997

```
1    INT      Umm (.) do you have meetings each week (.) each month (.)
2             Albert at AA
3    ALBERT   Well (.) meetings we have on Tuesday nights (.) one at
4             Cleveland (.) one in town
5    INT      Twice a week
```

6	ALBERT	Yeah
7		(1 sec)
8	INT	And that's all voluntary work
9	ALBERT	Yeah
10	INT	What sort of things do you do at the meetings? Do you
11		sort of (. . .) talk to people?
12	ALBERT	Yeah (.) talk to people(.) about what we're like when
13		we drink (.) what we're like when we're sober (.) and
14		then after that we have a cup of coffee and then (. . .) we
15		get into groups and talk to each other (. .) especially the
16		girls (. .) married ladies (.) we've got about eighteen
17		married ladies that come to our meetings.
18	INT	Eighteen married ladies who have problems with
19		alcohol?
20	ALBERT	Yeah (.) husbands leave them (.) it's a drug (.) alcohol's
21		a drug.

Albert's talk thus not only implies his understanding of the effects of alcohol, and other people's alcohol-related problems, but also makes direct knowledge claims. These claims serve to position him as someone who is – literally – knowledgeable. The selection of 'eighteen' as the highly specific number of 'married ladies' who attend 'our' (rather than 'the') meetings (in line 16) also serves to add to the sense of Albert's knowledge – and hence Albert – as precise, factual and detailed (see Pomerantz, 1984a, on the use of 'precise' numbers as evidence of expert talk). His apparently overt, and problematic, moral status – or social identity – (an 'alcoholic') is finessed into that of experienced and knowledgeable 'volunteer worker' and maintained as such both by his final display of 'technical' knowledge or 'expertise' and also, intersubjectively, by the interviewer's *non-pursuit* of the contradictory material offered in lines 12 to 15 (talk[ing] to people about what we're like when we drink) which would seem to establish Albert as an AA member rather than as a group leader, volunteer worker or therapist.

While the AA talk may have presented a particularly acute need for delicate social identity management, much more mundane topics were also the site for the presentation of self as an 'expert' or as a 'connoisseur'. Suzie's detailed discussion of her favourite TV shows – and her reasons for liking them – allowed the presentation of self as a discriminating and thoughtful viewer.

Extract 38: MR/PK/TV1997

1	INT	Do you watch much television besides the videos
2	SUZIE	Umm (.) Blue Heelers (. .) umm (.) Australia's Most Wanted (.)
3		Water Rats (.) umm (. .) Profilers (. . .) seen that one

4	INT	I've heard of it but I haven't watched it
5	SUZIE	Umm (. .) One Way Ticket (.) the Sunday movie I like because
6		it was made in Brisbane (0.2) umm (.)
7	INT	What about Neighbours or Home and Away?
8	SUZIE	Oh (.) no. I don't like them any more

In the next extract, Michelle's discussion of her attendance at TAFE[3] also closely attended to issues of the management of self, and particularly to the presentation of self as both someone with an acknowledged impairment and also as an effective social actor. Michelle's lexical choices carefully position her and Judy as collaborators: 'we work on my typing' (lines 4–5); as a recognisable and competent individual who has preferences and who can get their needs met: 'there's only me. I prefer to work in a room by myself' (lines 12–13). Her talk thus attends to constructing herself as a person not only with tastes and wants, but also as someone who knows (and can negotiate about) her own learning style, her tuition preferences *and* her weaknesses in this area. Her implicit assent (line 7) to the upgraded career choice offered by the interviewer – Michelle's 'typing practice' becomes the interviewer's 'looking for some work as a typist' – as a both a socially 'typical' (and thus, for a person with an intellectual disability, non-normative one) is however qualified, by Michelle herself, with an estimation of her capacity to get such a job in line 22.

Extract 39: MR/PK/TAFE/1997

1	INT	You were saying before that your job at ((sheltered workshop))
2		was OK, but you would like a change to something different
3	MICHELLE	Yeah, I've been doing typing practice down at ((employment
4		agency)) with Judy (.) I go there every second Monday and
5		we work on my typing
6	INT	So you're looking for some work as a typist
7	MICHELLE	I go to TAFE as well
8	INT	And what do you do there
9	MICHELLE	On the computers (.) I have lessons on the computers
10	INT	So you go to a TAFE class and learn how to use the
11		computers
12	MICHELLE	Not a class (.) there's only me (1 sec) I prefer to work in a
13		room by myself
14	INT	Just you and the teacher
15	MICHELLE	Just me and the teacher
16	INT	Are you doing this training to get a better job
17	MICHELLE	Yes (.) of course (.) Why do you think I'd be doing it
18	INT	Is it important to try and improve yourself
19	MICHELLE	Yes (.) it is

[3] College of Technical and Further Education.

20	INT	And if you are able to get a typing job sometime in the
21		future (.) that will be improving yourself
22	MICHELLE	Yeah (.) but I have to learn better than I am now (.) then I
23		might get one.

It is then Michelle, in lines 22–3, who volunteers the information that 'I [will] have to learn better than I am now, then I might get one.' Such an utterance might, should we so wish, perhaps offer evidence for the self-avowal of an intellectual disability. Yet these surface features of the text are overshadowed by the most delicate piece of identity management in the extract. Michelle makes a further, but extremely subtle, implicit claim to her place in the membership category of 'ordinary persons' with her barbed invocation of 'common knowledge' in line 17. This is the interactional claim of a jointly shared epistemological warrant of the first water. 'Why do you think I'd be doing it' not only neatly turns the tables on the interviewer (by positioning him as stupid) but also sharply positions her as someone who shares membership in the same category of persons as all other members (everyday folk, who naturally – 'of course' – know why people would do TAFE courses).

A similar attention to the subtleties of social identity work was evident in Shane's talk of his former employment. His account of his duties as a member of a motel's waiting staff was constructed in a manner which emphasised his mastery of the skills involved in silver service waiting, but with an exquisite attention to the socially normative understatement of his achievements and popularity.

Extract 40: MR/PK/LC/1997

1	SHANE	Yes (. .) and I didn't have any trouble with the trays (1 sec) I
2		walk up (.) get the tray like that can ((gestures tray balanced on one hand))
3		they showed me how to do that (.) ⌈knock on the door
4	INT	⌊and serve the people in
5		the motel rooms (.) yes
6	SHANE	knock on the door (.) good morning (.) it's breakfast time
7	INT	excellent (.) that's good (. .) and you found people you served=
8	SHANE	=yeah=
9	INT	=quite liked you (.) and accepted you (.) and that sort of thing
10	SHANE	people was fair (.) and staying there came and said hello to me

In line 9 note that the interviewer's utterance projects the relevance of an upgraded response (Pomerantz, 1984b). Shane, however, offers not an upgraded response, but a dispreferred moderation (disagreement) of this formulation, suggesting not that people were 'wonderful' or 'totally accepting', as might normatively be expected – or indeed as might a person seeking to stress their success in 'passing' as normal – but merely that they were 'fair'.

Indeed bald claims to 'normality' are, in themselves, non-normative. Why, one wonders, would one expect people (who, as we have seen) demonstrably have a clear understanding of the precarious nature of their moral status, to threaten that by a noticeably unusual identity claim? However, such claims may occur, and, if we are not careful to examine what utterances like 'dunno' or 'I'm normal' are *doing*, sequentially, we may be misled. In their discussion of the presentations of self by people with learning difficulties, Finlay and Lyons (2000) reproduce a fragment of a conversation between a researcher and 'P'.

Extract 41: From Finlay and Lyons, 2000: 143

1	I	You also told me that you'd like to marry a redcoat, from holiday.
2	P	Yeah but I'm not a redcoat I'm a normal person.
3	I	You're a normal person.
4	P	Yeah.
5	I	You're not a redcoat.
6	P	Human being.

Once again it would be easy to read P's claim to be a 'normal person' (lines 2 and 4) as somehow denying that she is describable as 'intellectually disabled'. But as Finlay and Lyons argue, to do so would be to take far too simplistic an approach to the deployment of categories in interaction, not least by making the familiar mistake of assuming that meaning can be read, straightforwardly, off semantics. Rather than 'normal person' being set up here as a contrast to 'disabled person', here the category is doing the work of providing a contrast case to 'redcoats', who, as members of *that* category, are readily distinguishable from ordinary, 'normal', holidaymakers. Of course this does not exhaust the sorts of interactional work that the explicit invocation of the category 'normal' can do, nor the range of parties who might deploy it. In his analysis of HIV counselling sessions, Silverman reproduces the following exchange between a counsellor and an HIV-positive 'client'.

Extract 42: From Silverman, 1994: 435 (7) [53B WH6]

C	And what's your behaviour been like (.) since you've been
P	Nor ⌈mal
C	⌊In X [[city]]?
P	Normal
C	Meaning?
P	Working, (0.2) and going out with one person.
C	And have you been engaging in
P	Uh huh

C   unsafe ( ). =
P   =N(h)o. .hhh=
C   =No.
     (0.4)
P   No (I've had) a <u>bor</u>ing lifest ⌜yle.
C   ⌞heh heh heh

As Silverman (1994: 435) points out, here the characterisations of a life as 'normal' and 'boring' work alongside the emphasis placed on by the speaker on 'normality' and 'can be heard as running contrary to the category-bound activity of being tested for HIV', that is 'being normal', being embedded in normality, attends to the possibly negative moral evaluation that may be forthcoming upon an individual identified, in this context, as leading a 'colourful' or 'risky' lifestyle. That is to say, it would appear that persons with an intellectual disability may be just as alert to the possibilities of negative evaluations of their (moral) character as 'normal' people who have HIV, and that the deployment of claims to being 'normal' by both (artificial, but morally disreputable) groups are attentive to precisely this problematic. One would not, however, be tempted to suggest that Silverman's P, in claiming 'normality' twice was 'denying' his HIV status nor that his seropositivity was 'invisible' to him.

In the final extract here, we see again the way in which people with an intellectual disability (unlike many sociologists, it seems) may demonstrate their acute appreciation of the way in which membership in the category 'normal' is not to be had by simply, verbally, claiming it, but rather may be ascribed or achieved on the basis of its category-bound predicates and activities. Davies and Jenkins report on interviews with Christine Lewis, described as 'a woman in her early twenties who attended an Adult Training Centre' who 'made it clear that the terms "handicapped", "mental handicap" and even "learning difficulties" were to be applied to people attending special clubs and centres, but had nothing to do with any other characteristics of these people' (Davies and Jenkins, 1997: 101). They reproduce the following data from a discussion of a social evening at the ATC.

Extract 43: From Davies and Jenkins, 1997: 102

1 CD   No. This is new . . . What kind of people from outside will
2   come? Do you know any of them?
3 CL   No. They're all strangers.
4 CD   Are they? Yeah . . . Are they different from people who come to the
5   ATC?
6 CL   Yeah.
7 CD   Yes? How are they different?
8 CL   They're normal people.

9   CD   I see. What does that mean? They're normal?
10 CL   Yeah. They, they've got normal jobs, haven't they?
11 CD   I see. Yeah.
12 CL   Here, it isn't a job really.
13 CD   It isn't a job?
14 CL   No.
15 CD   Why not?
16 CL   They, they've got, the only people come here to train . . . // . . .
17 CD   So what makes them normal, the other people?
18 CL   They can go to different . . .
19 CD   To different places? . . . Could the people here in the ATC be normal?
20 CL   Yeah. . . . // . . .
19 CD   What about Jonathan [her boyfriend], can he be normal like the
         others?
20 CL   Yes.
19 CD   If he could get a job?
20 CL   And I could.

Here Christine makes plain the fact that statuses like 'normal' – and indeed its converse – 'handicapped' – are then to be had not by confession, but by virtue of having normal jobs, normal freedoms and all of the other predicates of the category, which she also, all too clearly, makes plain do not accrue to herself or Jonathan.

In summary

The careful management of a possible identity as 'disabled' or 'handicapped' in their lives strongly suggests that the people whose talk we have examined here were only too well aware of the 'toxicity' of the category, where the 'reality' of one's disability is to be disavowed. Participants displayed an awareness of the differentness of their social experiences, and the negative effect that their identification as 'intellectually disabled' has had in their lives. Some of this orientation was overt – as in Simon's talk of 'us handicapped' and discussion of his sterilisation – and on other occasions lexically implicit, yet intersubjectively salient. This interactional salience is visible in, for example, Shane's subtle attention to downplaying the interviewer's over-enthusiastic version of the public's acceptance of him and Sally's careful acknowledgement, and discounting, of the fact that her disability might be the reason for people being intolerant.

Importantly, however, an orientation to differentness and its social consequentiality is also visible in Todd and Shearn's (1995) data: Anne (in talk not reproduced here) tells us that 'being handicapped' means 'I can't do things like other people . . . I can't go out' and specifies clearly that a consequence of this inability is what might be glossed as parental management of potential experiential disconfirmation ('If I want to go to the pub I have to ask my Dad'). Similarly, 'I don't think so', Kathleen's first response to the question 'Do you think you'll ever get married?' is sufficiently unambiguous to attribute a clear understanding of the normative trajectory of a 'disabled career' if we so wish. It is only further probing by the interviewer – and the equally unambiguous projection of the relevance of assent ('perhaps one day to someone else?') – which shepherds Kathleen into a (hedged and not terribly emphatic) incompetence-revealing utterance that 'maybe yes' she might 'perhaps one day' marry 'someone else'.

As in the Todd and the Todd and Shearn data, the people here can then be seen to 'do knowledge of disability' and, at the same time, clearly orientate to 'doing being ordinary', to offering a version of self which is 'occupationally ordinary'. The presentation of Albert's participation in AA as 'voluntary work' and Mel's extrapolation from the particular to the general offer examples of this. While they may not have offered their interviewers a textbook diagnostic definition of the term 'intellectual disability', close examination of what is said actually reveals clear understandings not only of what 'handicapped' actually means, but also of the interactional and social realities of their lives: and such attention is also clearly to be seen in the Todd; Todd and Shearn; Davies and Jenkins and Finlay and Lyons transcripts.

Indeed, recognising that people with intellectual disabilities may actively seek to manage the ascription of a 'toxic' identity by 'passing' as 'normal', implicitly acknowledges that such identities are not necessarily fixed things that people 'carry' with them, but rather are both contestable and situationally constructed. What the literature has failed to do is to follow through this reasoning to recognise that identity ascription of any kind, and by academics as much as by anyone else, is always occasioned by some interactional or institutional circumstance. That is to say that identity categories – and disability categories no less – are essentially fluid. The import of this is that a person's 'toxic' identity is no less worked-up than another person's 'normal' identity; that 'passing as ordinary' is no less an interactionally occasioned judgement than is 'being intellectually disabled' (though, ostensibly at least, the sources of evidence might be different). However, as ever, in such situations of power asymmetry as research interviews inherently are (Marková, 1991; Oliver, 1992; Stone and Priestley, 1996), it is, at the last, the interviewer who disposes the power to deem 'doing being ordinary' as either unexceptional 'ordinariness' (with consequent membership in the category of ordinary persons) or – alternatively – as the morally disreputable and hence accountable form of such social action, 'passing'.

In their discussion of disability more broadly, Shakespeare and Watson (2002) argue that:

> Many disabled people do not want to see themselves as disabled . . . they downplay the significance of their impairments, and seek access to a mainstream identity . . . This refusal to define oneself by impairment or disability has sometimes been seen as internalised oppression or false consciousness by radicals in the disability movement. Yet this attitude can itself be patronising and oppressive . . . What is wrong with seeing yourself as a person with a disability, rather than a disabled person, or even identifying simply as a human being, or a citizen, rather than as a member of a minority community?

In other words, we should acknowledge that the ascription of 'real' identities – such as 'intellectually disabled person' – is both to engage in the (contestable) construction of a version of 'identity' (as an enduring, dispositional, characteristic of persons) and also to oversimplify the complexity of the manner in which the deployment of versions of personal identity is a central component of *all* members' interaction-management. 'Doing being ordinary', as Harvey Sacks (1984) observed, is a pervasive part of the business of everyday social life because there is, pervasively, always the possibility that you will be seen to be not ordinary. For people already identified *a priori* as definitionally 'non-ordinary' such normative social demands must be seen as heightened: of course the difficulty for persons so identified – and here the fundamentally moral nature of such judgements becomes evident – is that the psy professions construct their attention to the everyday business of being mundane as accountable moral action.[4] As Bogdan and Taylor have it: 'to be called retarded is to have one's moral worth and human value called into question. It is to be certified as "not one of us"' (Bogdan and Taylor, 1994: 14). And, as we have seen, to fail to confess this status on demand, is to be doubly disqualified.

That people orient to the need to do being ordinary may be taken to imply that they are 'invisible to themselves'. Alternatively, we can suggest that people are, rather, very much aware (by virtue of both acknowledging and contesting their ascribed membership category 'disabled' or 'handicapped') of the societal consensus on the toxicity of the imputed identity, not necessarily that they are in some sense unaware that they can be classed as intellectually disabled. Equally, the very attention seen here

---

[4] The apparent difficulty that many academics have with these ideas is exemplified by the complete misreading of this point by Craig *et al.* (2002) who suggest that Rapley *et al.* (1998) (an earlier version of this analysis) argued that 'participants in their study tended to orientate themselves to being ordinary, to try to become invisible or to pass for "normal"' (p. 62).

to doing 'being ordinary' in and of itself, positions people not as incompetent social actors – or 'the sociological form of "strangers"' (Todd and Shearn, 1997: 343) – but, to the contrary, very much as members of a shared social order. Indeed it seems somewhat contrary to employ as evidence of incompetence (that people are 'invisible to themselves' or 'in denial') the fact that people with intellectual disabilities demonstrably attend to, and effectively manage, issues of identity construction in talk. Such attention might rather be taken to emphasise the commonality of membership with ordinary folk which these interviewees interactionally accomplish – rather than the essential 'otherness' – of people with intellectual disabilities.

As Shakespeare and Watson ask: 'what is *wrong* with seeing yourself as a person with a disability, rather than a disabled person, or even identifying simply as a human being, or a citizen, rather than as a member of a minority community?'

5   Talk to dogs, infants and . . .

> Authority, that is to say, becomes ethical to the extent that it is exercised
> in the light of a knowledge of those who are its subjects . . . The exercise
> of authority, here, becomes a therapeutic matter: the most powerful way
> of acting upon the actions of others is to change the ways in which they
> will govern themselves.
>
> (Rose, 1999a: np)

> But co-membership can be at stake, rather than presumed.
>
> (Edwards, 1997: 295)

This chapter examines data collected in community-based group homes
for adults described as having moderate and mild intellectual disabilities. Review of sixty hours of videotaped interaction between staff and
residents of the homes suggests, in line with the literature on staff–client
interaction, three broad classes of staff behaviour which may – in order of
their relative frequency – be glossed as: (1) babying/parenting; (2) instruction giving, and (3) collaboration/pedagogy. While such descriptions may
be taken to imply that these are readily discriminable and categorically
distinct genres of action this is not what is intended here. Rather these
interactional styles shade into each other, and particular episodes of interaction may show evidence of aspects of more than one 'style'. However, in
broad terms, these interactional registers not only form an inverse hier-
archy in terms of commonly advocated human service 'best practice',
but also raise further questions about the reliance to be placed on the
collection of standardised data quantifying 'competence', the validity of
notions such as dispositional acquiescence, and the prevailing accounts in
the psychological literature of the 'impaired' interactional and pragmatic
abilities of persons with intellectual disabilities.

This chapter then turns away from testing, from interrogative or otherwise artificial encounters between psychologists, researchers and people
with intellectual disabilities, to examine the fine grain of everyday mundane interaction in supported housing. What is immediately apparent in
these data is that issues of asymmetry in dialogue are not absent from

these encounters, but rather the issues are still live. Their management, however – in a different communicative environment (Leudar, 1989) – is distinctly different. What is immediately visible in the interactions examined here, then, is the sophisticated management, in interaction, by people defined by their 'incompetence', of issues of power, member- ship and its entitlements, and their status as competent human beings. The negotiation of this co-membership with staff – who can frequently be seen to work to withhold it – is managed in a range of ways and, unlike the simple-minded notion that category membership is accomplished (or not) by avowal or disavowal that we have seen in the work discussed in chapter 4, these ways are often subtle, sophisticated and, ironically, invisible to 'normal' interlocutors. This chapter, then, analyses the dis- play of everyday competence and the tenacious resistance of people with intellectual disabilities to what they clearly make relevant not just as staff 'well-intentioned condescension' (Sabsay and Platt, 1985) but rather the exercise of straightforward *force majeure*.

Staff–client interaction – 'babying' and 'parenting'

A number of features of talk have been identified as characteristic of asymmetric, institutional, talk (e.g. Caporael, 1981; Marková and Foppa, 1991), and by Mitchell (2001) as characteristic of the talk of adults to dogs and infants (see also Blount, 1977; Caporael and Culbertson, 1981; Caporael *et al.* 1983; DePaulo and Coleman, 1986; Fernald and Mazzie, 1991). Such talk, suggests Mitchell, tends to serve four functions: con- trolling the addressee by maintaining a persistent focus on an object or activity; facilitating communication with an inattentive addressee, or one with limited understanding; 'pretending' that the other is a conversant; and tutoring (Mitchell, 2001: 197–8). Of particular relevance throughout this chapter are the control and tutoring functions of support staff talk, and, particularly features identified in 'institutional' talk: (1) asymmet- rically distributed control over topic and topic shift, (2) asymmetries in turn length, (3) asymmetric rights to ask questions, (4) the adoption of simplified semantics and lexical choices by the 'competent' interlocutor and (5) a 'sing-song' intonation contour. Specifically, throughout the data discussed in this chapter, we see an overwhelming reliance by staff upon a set of devices which have a very limited class of preferred seconds – most commonly agreements – which, in and of themselves, cannot but produce the 'intellectually disabled' interlocutor as closer to a puppy or a babe-in-arms, than a competent adult conversant. Despite this, and the unremittingly negative expectations that might be engendered by the bulk of the psychological and sociological literatures we have seen earlier, this chapter (and the next) demonstrates clearly that people with intellectual disabilities are not only demonstrably aware of upshot of the forms of interaction prosecuted by staff, but are also perfectly prepared to resist, in subtle and artful ways, their social construction as incompetent.

As an introduction to staff–client interaction data, an example of a 'real' parent 'being a parent' is provided to offer a template against which the interaction styles used by staff may be measured. As is apparent from the data, this style of interaction offers little in the way of opportunity for the demonstration or development of autonomy by the intellectually disabled person; maintains asymmetric positions of power and control in favour of the non-disabled interlocutor; and produces, promotes and sustains the incompetence of the person with an intellectual disability.

In the following extract, Kylie's mother (whom we met earlier in chapter 4) has come to visit her daughter in the group home where she lives, and is making arrangements for an outing the following weekend. This interaction follows the Centrelink data seen earlier.

Extract 44: KA/Mum/1998

1	KYLIE	An (.) an (.) ↑what time (.) ↑next Saturday mum
2	MUM	Right (.) next Satur↓day
3	KYLIE	⌈Yep
4	MUM	⌊Now (.) what I want you to ↓do
5	KYLIE	Yep
6	MUM	O↑kay (.) is get ↑all packed what you need to do
7		for ↑two days and ⌈I'll -
8	KYLIE	⌊Yep
9	MUM	Pick ↑that up Wednes↑day
10	KYLIE	Yep
11	MUM	Now (.) on Satur↓day
12	KYLIE	Yep
13	Mum	I need you to ↑walk to the PCY↓C
14	KYLIE	Yep
15	MUM	O↑kay
16	KYLIE	Yep
17	Mum	↑Only with your hand↓bag
18	KYLIE	⌈Yep
19	MUM	⌊Cause ↑I'll have all your gear
20	KYLIE	Yep
21	MUM	The walk'll do you ↑good
22	KYLIE	Yep
23	ANNE	( )
24	MUM	And you better ↑be there by ten to ↓eight
25	KYLIE	Mm ↑mm

In this extract we see that after her initial enquiry, Kylie accepts her mother's instructions without question, not being required to contribute to the interaction other than by showing her understanding of the instructions she is given with a minimal assent token (most often 'yep'). Further, the provision of such an indication was sufficient for her mother to move on to the next instruction, with occasional evaluations of the benefits to Kylie of the arrangements she is requiring, with complete maternal control over topic shift. It is, further, notable that – even if we were to remove the PARENT + CHILD identities from this encounter, that what remains is, if not explicitly 'parental', then very clearly an interaction between a figure of authority who takes both their right to issue orders for granted and also their unquestioning acceptance by a compliant other: SERGEANT + PRIVATE, perhaps.[1]

The following extracts show the way in which staff may also assume a 'parental', authoritative, register in their interaction with residents. This style of interaction has also been observed in staff behaviour with other populations who may be seen to be dependent and helpless – such as residents of elderly people's homes (Caporael, 1981). This communication style is again characterised by use of a simplified lexicon, and a prosodic register characterised by a high pitch and exaggerated 'sing song' intonation contour. In addition to the phonemic and syntactic aspects of staff talk in this register, such an interactional style often conveys an assumption of incompetence, with the staff being produced as the interlocutor with both the competence and the authority both to make decisions on behalf of the 'less able' party to the interaction, and to issue instruction on 'correct' modes of behaviour. This interactional style also works to convey an expectancy that the 'dependent' party will acquiesce to the wishes of the 'parent'. Caporael (1981) further notes that while the use of 'secondary baby talk' (cf. Ferguson, 1977) may perhaps be understood as a strategy to teach language and to convey 'difficult' concepts, it also promotes a strong expectation of dependent behaviour (cf. Mitchell 2001; Mitchell and Edmonson, 1999).

While the interaction in extract 45 is taking place, Jenny is seated at the dining table with paperwork in front of her. Mary is seated on the floor patting her dog on the opposite side of the room. Jenny continues writing throughout the encounter and her tone takes on an 'absent' quality as evidenced by some unusually long pauses (tenHave, 1999). As tenHave points out, such a quality may be taken to indicate that the 'absent' interlocutor is offering less than their complete attention to their conversational partner.

---

[1] My thanks to Charles Antaki for this point.

Extract 45: MM/JS/1998

```
1    JENNY    Um (2.0) well Mary I'm go↑ing to allow ↓you (.) an extra
2             fifteen dol↓lars that's for your ↑two tax↓is plus your
3             shopping taxi and you pay for the shopping taxi this
4             ↑week and Trev↓or parts with his fifty cents for the
5             phone ↓call
6             (4.0)
7             O↑kay
8             (1.5)
9    MARY     ⌈Yep
10   JENNY    ⌊Take ↓turns (.) be↑cause that's that's fair ↓then
11   MARY     But we some↓times do
12   JENNY    Yep o↑kay (.) so an extra fifteen dol↓lars for (.) taxi↑s
13            and I must check into that (1.5) taxi subsidy for ↑you
```

In line 1 Jenny takes responsibility for directing the conversation about Mary's budget and payment for taxis. In line 6 she offers a long 4.0-second slot which hearably projects the relevance of agreement with her proposition that she *allows* Mary to pay for the taxi, in addition to suggesting that Trevor should 'part with' his fifty cents for the phone call, a somewhat infantilising semantic choice. The use of the term 'your shopping taxi' also produces the interaction as involving a less and a more competent interactant: Mitchell (2001) notes that while rather infrequent in talk to infants, such constructions are not uncommon in talk to dogs. When this agreement is not immediately forthcoming, her next utterance ('okay') reinforces the demand for agreement. Mary's response is non-committal ('yep') in line 9, again given after a significant pause. Jenny's response to this in line 10 is a statement packaged in such a way that doesn't require a response or continuation from Mary. Rather it is a hearably 'parental' formulation of the 'fairness' that turn taking offers. Mary's response ('but we sometimes do') can be understood as her offering resistance to Jenny's instruction on the value of turn taking (in line 10) which offers an opportunity to collaboratively formulate turn-taking arrangements which Jenny does not take up, but rather closes the topic abruptly with a rather absent 'Yep okay' (line 12) and restates her earlier 'offer' of extra money.

The same pattern is evident in extract 47 when Jenny and Mary are completing Mary's weekly budgeting. In line 1 Jenny asks Mary if there is there is anything else she requires money for. Again, her main preoccupation here is writing. Mary's account of her actions is met with high grade assessments (HGA's) (Antaki, Houtkoop-Steenstra and Rapley, 2000) from the staff member in line 8 ('Excellent'); in lines 10 and 12 where stress is placed on '*good girl*'; and again in line 15 where stress is placed on 'That's *right*', all of which seem somewhat excessive for the circumstances reported. Antaki *et al.* (2000) suggest that the

Use [of] a high-grade assessment (like 'brilliant' or 'jolly good'), possibly delivered in some contracted form, without a newsmark, and in tandem with an immediate move to next-business-in-a-series . . . is not a comment on the content of the preceding talk, but rather a signal that there is something noteworthy about its production . . . [W]hat is it about these data that might make sense of one speaker's orientation to the well-foundness or otherwise of another speaker's talk? There seems, we would say, something irredeemably 'institutional' in such an orientation . . . that this sort of receipt manifests that what is going on – the relation between the two speakers, their rights and obligations – is indeed currently official and institutional, with a strong asymmetry between question asker and answer-giver. (Antaki *et al.* 2000)

Antaki *et al.* (2000) offer an extensive corpus of instances of such high-grade assessments drawn from formal psychological assessments (though these assessments are somewhat paradoxically ordered such that their very informality is stressed). While the talk examined here does not come from formal assessment encounters, and hence the employment of the device as move-to-next-topic-in-a-series is not pertinent, the interactional effect of the high-grade receipt device seems to be similar. One of the fragments reproduced by Antaki *et al.* (see extract 46, below) shows the device (in line 7) particularly clearly.

Extract 46: CA/KK/MB 254

```
1   SS    °they don't ↑stop so long° (. .) _____↑°no° (.) d'they
2         ↑d'they make you feel imp↓ortant (. .) at all (.)
3         do they d'you think that they ↓care a lot about ↑you
4   E     yeh ['querulous']
5   SS    ↑they d↓o
6         (5 secs)
7         °right° (.) o↑k ↑then (.) brilliant (.) d'you go to ↑work
8         at all Eileen (.)
```

In extract 47 then we see that Mary's position as subordinate vis-à-vis Jenny is cemented by the use of the HGA device. Mary's status as non-adult is also firmly established in Jenny's estimation, twice repeated, that she is a 'good girl' for what, in any ordinary circumstances, would appear to be rational and entirely mundane decisions not to order from the Avon catalogue.

Extract 47: MM/JS/1998

```
1   JENNY    And (.) anything ↑else
2            (2.0)
3   MARY     Not that ↑I know ↑of
4   JENNY    Not that you know ↑of (1.5) ah (.) it's not rent ↑week
5            (0.5)   [that was last week yeah
```

```
6    MARY         ⌊No that was last week
7                 (0.5) a:nd (0.5) there's ↑no ↓Avon
8    JENNY        Excellent (.) and you've not order‗ed ↑any
9    MARY         N↑o::
10   JENNY        Good girl
11   MARY         I told them I didn't want the book ↑eith↓er
12   JENNY        Good girl Y↑e:p  ⌈It costs too much
13   MARY                         ⌊Because (.) looking at the book is
14                too ↑tempting
15   JENNY        That's right (0.5) good think↓ing
```

Mary responds to Jenny's rather underspecified request for information in line 1 after a lengthy pause of two seconds by stating 'not that I know of'. In mundane conversation between equal interlocutors one might have thought that this utterance would be sufficient to close the topic. However, Jenny repeats what Mary has said in line 4, deploying a variant of the conversational device described by Schenkein (1978) as a 'pass' and by Williamson (2003) as a 'restatement'. Such an innocent sounding repetition, preserving the intonation contour of the prior turn, can serve to mark the previous utterance as accountable – as insufficient in some way. In other work on interviews with people with intellectual disability, discussed in chapter 3, Rapley and Antaki (1996) have shown how the 'pass' may be deployed by interviewers to apply pressure for the reformulation of candidate answers.

Indeed, in his study of talk between instructors and trainees in an Adult Training Centre while it is noted that a restatement or a 'pass' may, in what he terms 'instalment contribution sequences' function as a continuer,[2] Williamson (2003: np) similarly noted that 'in certain sequential contexts trainees appear to orient to the restatement as highlighting a trouble source and as having full turn status. In such contexts the restatement does not assume a continuer function . . . trainees may orient to restatements as having full turn status and as signalling other-initiated repair'. Rapley and Antaki (1996) illustrate the employment of the device with a data fragment drawn from a formal quality of life interview. In the fragment the pass occurs in line 131, with the repetition of Bob's 'no' in line 130. That the interviewer's utterance is hearably applying pressure for reformulation is confirmed by his offer of a candidate parameter for a revised response from Bob ('not ever') when the offered explanation slot is not immediately taken up.

---

[2] See Schegloff (1982) Discourse as an interactional achievement: some uses of 'uh huh' and other things that come between sentences. In D. Tannen, *Analysing Discourse: Text and Talk*, Georgetown University Round Table on Language and Linguistics (Georgetown: Georgetown University Press).

Extract 48: From Rapley and Antaki, 1996: 221

```
125   I      ri:ght ⌈(. .) oh that's ↓good (1 sec) ↑do ↑em: (1 sec) do> ↓you<
126   Bob           ⌊((hhhhh))
127   I      ever feel ↑lone↓ly (.) Bob
128   Bob    ↑eh
129   I      ↓do you ever feel ↓lonely
130   Bob    ↑no:
131   I      ↑no (. .) not ever
132   Bob    ↓no:
133   I      ↑no:
```

The long (1.5 second) slot offered by Jenny in line 4 of extract 47 is then hearable as the offering of a slot in which Mary *should* expand her previous candidate answer. When Mary does not take up the slot, Jenny proceeds to offer a pair of candidate matters that Mary 'should' have volunteered.[3] Again we can hear resistance from Mary to this project in her utterance in line 6 ('no that was last week') in overlap with Jenny's confirmation of her *prior* knowledge that rent was not an item in line 5. In line 7 after a short pause Mary co-operatively goes on to offer the additional information that Jenny has demanded ('and there's no Avon').

The parental tone of Jenny's utterances reaches its peak in the following sequence. Ascribing to Mary the identity 'good girl' in lines 10 and 12 automatically differentiates her from someone of equal status to Jenny, with the loudness and emphasis of Jenny's delivery working to further emphasise Mary's status (Caporael, 1981). The HGA receipt of the news that there's no Avon in line 7 ('excellent') is, again, out of keeping with the triviality of the matter reported.

Extract 47: (detail)

```
6    MARY     ⌊No that was ↑last week
7             (0.5) a:nd (0.5) there's ↑no ↓Avon
8    JENNY    Excellent (.) and you've not order↑ed ↑any
9    MARY     N↑o::
10   JENNY    Good girl
11   MARY     I told them I didn't want the book ↑eith↓er
12   JENNY    Good girl Y↑e:p ⌈It costs too much
13   MARY                     ⌊Because (.) looking at the book is
14            too ↑tempting
```

---

[3] Williamson (2003: np, my emphasis) notes that: 'restatements may be partial or full (verbatim) repeats of the prior utterance and they may occasionally include structural reformulations of the prior utterance including, for example, proforms and other determiners. In contrast with tokens such as uh huh, mm and mm hm, the non-continuative interactional outcome of the use of a restatement in certain contexts has been noted. Robson (1989) highlights the stultifying effect on the flow of conversation between teachers and pupils in that the *teachers may deploy restatements in order to end conversations*, thereby demonstrating their awareness of the generally non-continuative function of this token.'

As in the previous extract, Mary's utterances are mundane reportings of the facts of the situation, as in lines 11 ('I told them I didn't want the book either') and lines 13 and 14, ('because looking at the book is too tempting'), offering further evidence of her ability to make rational decisions. In doing so she again demonstrates her recognition of, and resistance to, staff attempts to parent her.

In extract 49, which occurs shortly after Mary has been identified as a 'good girl' for making sensible, if minor, decisions for herself, she is being asked by Jenny to try a new drug to control her seizures. The strength of Mary's opposition to this move is evident in line 3 by her clear 'Nuh' delivered with neither delay nor other dispreference markers (Pomerantz, 1984b). During this interaction Jenny gives Mary her full attention by turning around in her chair to face her, crossing her legs and leaning forward. Note that Jenny self-repairs her utterance in line 1 ('So they need to put you on the teg– the other ones to control your seizures.') This self-repair, which terminates the brand name of the proposed medication (Tegretol) and substitutes the pro-term 'the other ones' for it, simultaneously produces Mary as both too incompetent to comprehend a proprietary medication name and also as not needing to know even the name of the drugs she is being told she 'needs' to take. What we see in this utterance then is that while Jenny's *simplification* is describable as being recipient-designed to aid Mary's understanding (Caporael, 1981), it also serves to establish and maintain Mary's status as incompetent.

Extract 49: MM/JS/1998

1	JENNY	So they <u>need</u> to put you ↑on (.) the teg– the other
2		↑ones >to control your seiz↓ures<
3	MARY	Nuh
4		(0.5)
5	JENNY	So you'd rather (.) have (.) seiz↓ures
6		(2.0)
7	MARY	I'd rather stay on ↑these ↓ones
8	JENNY	<u>Why</u>
9	MARY	Because I ↑<u>want</u> ↓to
10		(1.5)
11	JENNY	For (.) what what reas↓on
12	MARY	Because I <u>don't</u> like the ↑other ones
13	JENNY	What <u>don't</u> you ↑like about ↓them
14		(0.5)
15	MARY	I just ↑<u>don't</u>
16	JENNY	No I need to ↓<u>know</u> what you don't like ab<u>out</u> ↓them
17	MARY	Cause they always make me seel ↑<u>feel</u> sick
18	JENNY	No (.) you only took you only took one ↑night

```
19                of medi↓cation (.) we need to try a↓gain
20                (1.5)
21   MARY         But I don't ↑like ↓it
22   JENNY        Yeah well I ↑know you don't like ↓it (.) but we really
23                need to try a↓gain to con ⌈trol your seiz↓ures
24   MARY                               ⌊No Daniel told me to try for
25                one ↑day(.) ⌈and I ↑did
26   JENNY                   ⌊M↑m m↑m (0.2) and the doctor wants you
27                to try  ⌈again
28   MARY                 ⌊Nuh (.) I'm not ↑goin' ↓to
```

Line 1 is packaged as a bald announcement, where initially, responsibility for decisions about medication is attributed to an unspecified 'they' – with Jenny merely acting as a messenger. After Mary immediately rejects this instruction (in line 3) Jenny's next line is remarkable: the extremity of the formulation and the 'measured' delivery: 'So you'd rather (.) have (.) seizures' – positions Mary as a wilful and perhaps slightly stupid child, the micro pauses within the turn adding emphasis to the seriousness of Jenny's proposition. Again, there is a considerable pause after Jenny has presented Mary with an opportunity to respond before she actually does so with what, in other circumstances, may be heard as a reasonable account of her preferences.

However, in lines 8, 11, 13 and 16 Jenny reinforces her demands that Mary provides *reasons* for reluctance to try Tegretol again: of course, such repetition positions Mary as accountable and her wants as secondary to what 'we' (line 19) are described as 'needing' to do. That 'we' here clearly only indexes the addressee, *Mary*, is reminiscent, again, of Mitchell's (2001) work on talk to dogs and infants, where such lexical features are frequent. Mary's responses (lines 9, 12 and 15) appear to be received by Jenny as evidence that Mary is 'childlike' (for example, in a turn that would be highly unusual in everyday interaction between co-equal inter-locutors, her utterance at line 16 very carefully spells out the reason *why* she requires the information she is seeking). When her persistent pur-suit of an account and the specification of the reasons for her pursuit do not solicit a more 'acceptable' response than Mary's claim that the medication 'always' makes her 'feel sick', Jenny changes tack. Following a blunt rejection of Mary's account ('No' in line 18) Jenny's attribution of responsibility for the need to try Tegretol again shifts – from the vague 'they' in line 1 to 'we' in line 19 – in what is potentially hearable as a concession: 'we' in Jenny's turn (lines 18–19) appears to be an attempt to secure collaboration. That 'we' is not, in practice, an invitation to Mary to participate on equal terms with staff and the now specified 'doc-tor' (line 26) in decision-making about the management of her epilepsy becomes apparent in lines 22–3: '*we* really need to try again to control *your* seizures'. That 'we' is now not inclusive of Mary is perhaps most clearly evident here in lines 24–7: Mary's utterance in lines 24–5, with the clear specification of the instructions that the explicitly named *Daniel* (who is, in fact 'the Doctor') gave her, is over-ridden by Jenny *prior* to turn completion with Daniel's institutional role (the Doctor) deployed to trump Mary.

The 'irredeemably "institutional"' (Antaki *et al.* 2000) nature of the interaction here is then manifested in the assiduous manner in which Jenny strives to sustain a cover identity (Sacks, 1992) as 'collaborator' while at the same time establishing and maintaining a strong asymmetry between question-asker and answer-giver. It is Jenny who determines the adequacy or otherwise of Mary's accounts, who specifies the parameters of membership in the category 'we' who need to control the seizures, and who stipulates – by virtue of her discounting of Mary's claim to equal status participation by the use of the name 'Daniel' and its replacement by the term 'the doctor' – the parties to *real* decision making about medication.

In extract 50 – a continuation of extract 49 – we see both Mary's explicit recognition of, and resistance to, the asymmetry evident in this interaction. In line 31 Mary offers a further challenge to her infantilisation under the cover of putative collaboration implied by Jenny's re-deployment of 'we' in her opening utterance. Resistance is evident in both the extremely long (10.5 second) silence that Mary allows prior to her first turn, and also in her assumption of responsibility for telling 'him'.

Extract 50: MM/JS/1998

```
29    JENNY    So::: ↑what do we ↓do
30             (10.5)
31    MARY     I don't ↑know (0.5) but ↑I'll tell ↑him
32             (1.0)
33    JENNY    You'll tell ↓who
34             (0.2)
35    MARY     I'll tell the ↑doc↓tor
36    JENNY    You could have told ↑him when (.) when we were at
37             the ↑surgery but you refused to go ↑in
38             (2.8)
39    MARY     But you didn't ↑tell me that (0.5) ↑we were going in for that
40             reas↓on
```

That Jenny's 'we' in line 29 is another *rhetorical* usage and is not in fact the collaborative question that the wh- form may seem to imply, is made apparent in her failure to appreciate the referent of the deictic 'him' in Mary's turn at line 31. In the sequential position that 'him' occupies the only possible person who could be indexed by the usage is 'Daniel' or 'the doctor'. As is apparent, Mary's attempt to take responsibility for her decision by reporting that *she* will convey it to the doctor is initially met with incomprehension by Jenny as to the intended recipient of the news, followed by an immediate disqualification by her of such autonomy on Mary's part by reference to what is constructed (lines 36–7) as Mary's prior irrational intransigence – 'you could have told him . . . but you refused to go in'. Again, in a nice twist on Jenny's earlier insistence on the provision of rational *reasons* for actions, we see Mary offer (lines 39–40) what in any other circumstances may be hearable as an entirely reasonable account for her unwillingness to co-operate on that occasion: she had not been told *why* she had been taken to the surgery.

Again, the institutional asymmetry of this encounter is evident a little further into Mary and Jenny's exchange. We have seen thus far that it is not just Jenny's direction of question:answer (Q:A) sequences which produces the interaction as recognisably institutional, despite its occurrence in a supposedly domestic residential setting, but also her lexical choices, her high-grade receipts of trivial news reports and her assiduous refusal to allow Mary to present herself as an autonomous adult with her own wants, preferences and rights to mundane matters such as confidential decision-making with her general practitioner. All of these markers may be taken as indirect evidence that, despite Jenny's routine (but increasingly thin) rhetorical appeals to collaborative cover identities, what Sacks (1992) describes as an 'omni-relevant device' is operative in the encounter: to this point a device such as STAFF + CLIENT may be offered as a charitable reading: in extract 50 it becomes apparent that, through Jenny's direct invocation of Mary's identity as a person whose competence at self-care is compromised, and the resort to what may only be glossed as threats of sanctions in the face of continued non-compliance, a device more akin to MOTHER + CHILD is present (cf. McHoul and Rapley, 2002).

In extract 51 Jenny initiates a new Q : A sequence in line 1 by bringing into the argument Mary's ability to care for her dog if she experiences a fit (lines 1–9). In a remarkable shift from her earlier line that Mary's capacity to communicate sensibly with her doctor was compromised, Jenny now appeals to Mary's *responsibility* for her pet's welfare. While earlier in the conversation Jenny explicitly called attention to Mary's irrationality and unreasonableness *directly*, here the capacity to provide pet care is equated with Mary's level of responsibility only by implication (lines 1–9). By indirection Mary's global responsibility and competence – as indexed by her care for her dog – is called into question because of her decision not to change her medication. Yet again, while it may appear on a superficial glance that Jenny is here employing rational argument (thus positioning Mary as her co-equal) on closer inspection it is of note that, particularly in lines 5 and 6, not only is her delivery characterised by a very clear sing-song stress and intonation contour, but also the content of this utterance is semantically simplistic and resolutely pedagogic.

Extract 51: MM/JS/1998

1	JENNY	Well what a↓bout what a↓bout your ↑dog (1.5) what
2		happens to your ↑dog when when you (.) when you're
3		having ↑fits (0.5) when you're (.) ↑out (.) all day in ↑to↓wn
4		(.) taking her for a ↑walk or (.) or (.) tak↑ing her to the
5		vet (0.2) or (.) taking her to visit ↑friends (0.3) and <u>you</u>
6		have a ↑fit (.) What happens with your ↑dog (4.2)
7		because <u>you</u> are res<u>pons</u>ible for the ↑<u>care</u> of your dog
8		(.) and to do <u>that</u> (.) you↑<u>need</u> to be res↑<u>pons</u>ible for the
9		<u>care</u> of your ↓<u>self</u>
10		(3.0)
11	MARY	Nuh
12	JENNY	((Clears throat)) (4.0) Cause I'll I'll I'll I'm I'll ↑have to <u>tell</u>
13		you this Mar↓y (0.2) but if if (.) it's shown that you can't
14		<u>care</u> for your ↓dog (0.2) that ↑you can't be res↑<u>pons</u>ible
15		for your ↓dog (3.0) d'↑you know what'll hap↑pen (.) if
16		people can't ↑care for their ↑pets (4.5) she will ↑need to
17		go <u>back</u> where you got her ↓from
18		(1.5)
19	MARY	No
20		(0.5)
21	JENNY	Well so (0.2) what are you go↑ing to ↑do (8.5) cause
22		you ↑need to be res↓<u>pons</u>ible to look after a ↓dog (1.0)
23		and for ↑you to be responsible you to be res↓<u>pons</u>ible
24		for your ↓<u>self</u> in looking ↑after (.) yourself to (.) to be
25		↑heal↓thy to be able to look after your ↑dog (2.0) and
26		↑<u>that's</u> all we're try↑ing to ↑<u>do</u> (.) is ↑change your
27		medi↑<u>cation</u> so you ↑<u>don't</u> (.)have ↑seiz↓ures
28		(20.5)
29	MARY	N↓o
30		(1.5)
31	JENNY	So you would ↑<u>rather</u> have ↓fits and have your dog
32		taken a↓way
33	MARY	↑Nuh
34		(4.0)
35	JENNY	Well ↑that's what it sounds like (.) to ↑me (.) because
36		you're <u>not</u> wil↓ling to try this medi↑<u>cation</u> to see if we
37		can get these fits under con↑tr↓ol
38		(0.2)
39	MARY	Cause I don't ↑<u>want</u> ↓to
40	JENNY	So you ⌈don't -

41   MARY   ⌊That's all there is ↑to ↓it ((Gets up))
42   JENNY   So you ↓don't so you don't want your ↓dog
43   MARY   Yeah I ↑<u>do</u> want ↓her (0.1) but I <u>don't</u> ↑want to try the
44   new medi↑<u>cation</u> ((Mary walks out))

Mary's refusal to collaborate with the equation of her competence in
pet and self-care with acquiescence to a medication change proposed by
Jenny is clear in her declining to take the floor when it is unambiguously
offered in lines 1, 3, 5 and 6. When she is unable to sway Mary on her
decision not to try the new medication, after a lengthy pause, and in a
strikingly dysfluent delivery – in which she again sidesteps any personal
accountability for the consequences she is describing – Jenny issues a
threat which she presents herself as being forced into delivering. In much
the same way as a parent might resort to explanations for sanctions based
in what Sacks describes as Type 1 ('natural') causality (if you touch the
stove you will burn your hand) when in practice Type 2 ('moral') causality
(if you are insincere no one will love you) is operative (for example a claim
to a naughty child that a forthcoming beating is occasioned, caused, by
the child's *disobedience* rather than by parental fiat – such statements as 'I
don't want to have to do this, but' frequently indexing such transpositions;
McHoul and Rapley, 2000), Jenny presents the putative removal of the
dog as *required* by Mary's unwillingness to care appropriately (in her eyes
at least) for herself. The script formulation (Edwards, 1994) 'she will
need to go back where you got her from' (lines 16–17) thus works to
position Jenny as not only *able* to make this decision but also as *reluctantly
forced into it* by *Mary's* accountable refusal to behave in accordance with
her wishes: a classic Type 1/Type 2 causality manipulation device.

Mary's monosyllabic utterances (in lines 11, 19, 29 and 33) may be
heard as implying her reluctance to be engaged in what becomes a relent-
less pursuit of acquiescence (though by line 21 capitulation or uncondi-
tional surrender may more adequately capture the flavour of what Jenny is
demanding). It is again of note throughout this exchange (which explicitly
denigrates Mary's willingness and ability to care for her dog, offers a lesson in how to be responsible, and culminates in the bald threat of having
her dog taken away) that Jenny consistently attributes not only a wilful
pursuit of ill-health (e.g. line 31) but also an accountable *irrationality* to
Mary's wishes. This reduction in Mary's status in the interaction to that
of a petulant infant turns on the local production of a contrast pairing of
the magnitude and incomprehensibility of Mary's intransigence with the
utter reasonableness and triviality of the change proposed. Thus we see
qualifiers which serve to minimise the course of action she proposes, such
as '*all* we're trying to do' (line 26), paired with manifestly unreasonable

corollaries 'so you would rather have fits and have your dog taken away' (lines 31–2) as their proposed upshot. Yet Jenny routinely also endeavours to shroud such strategic manipulation of Mary's identity as incompetent adult in a veil of apparent collaboration. In lines 21 to 27 Jenny returns to the sequence she began in line 1 on responsibility. However, this is prefaced by a turn in question-form (line 21: 'well so what are you going to do') which on the face of it appears to propose that Mary does, in fact, have the agency and autonomy to make an informed choice based on the information she has received. That Mary recognises not only the transparently illusory nature of the 'choices' she is rhetorically being offered, but also the sleight of hand in play in Jenny's causality transposition is eloquently demonstrated in her final turn before leaving the room: 'Yeh, I do want her . . . but I don't want to try the new medication.' Again, as was noted in chapter 3, such interactions cast an entirely different light on the notion that people with intellectual disabilities are in some fashion dispositionally prone to acquiescence bias. Here, where *real* issues, for *real* people, are the matter in hand, rather than inane questions such as 'Do you make all your own clothes and shoes?' (Cummins, 1997; Perry and Felce, 2002) in interrogative testing contexts, we see that far from simply 'saying yes', people can – and demonstrably do – state a case and sustain their position in the face of extreme pressure from staff who clearly *demand* acquiescence.

In a continuing effort to get Mary to agree to a medication change, the assistance of a senior staff member (Sally) is sought to change Mary's mind, by having them 'drop by' Mary's house after she returns from work. In contrast to the frankly coercive approach seen in the extracts above, the exchange in extract 52 below opens in line 1 with a news-marked pre-announcement ('So apparently'). Sally works then from the outset to construct the encounter with Mary as an informal 'chat' about a matter of which she has only hearsay, but which noticeably does not eschew 'technical' matters: it is a 'slower release' medication that the doctor is suggesting – 'so apparently the doctor wants to change your medication into the slower release one?' This turn then acts as a preface to instruct Mary on what's to come, but the projected relevance of an affirmative, acquiescent, answer – maybe something like 'oh, OK then' – is disappointed.

Extract 52: MM/SB/1998

1	SALLY	So ↑apparent↓ly the doc↓tor wants to change your medi↓cation
2		into the slower rel↑ease ↓one
3	MARY	Nuh
4	SALLY	Wh↓y

5	MARY	Because I I've ↑tried (.) two times be↑fo↓re
6	SALLY	And what ⌈hap-
7	MARY	⌊and <u>both</u> times haven't ↑wo↓rked
8	SALLY	So ↑what are you telling me you want to ↓do (1.0) you want to
9		stay with your ↑old medi↓cation
10	MARY	Mm::

Initially Mary continues with her monosyllabic rejection of the proposed change. However when asked 'why' as Sally's second turn (contrast this with Jenny's fourth turn in extract 51: 'so you'd rather have fits') she co-operatively expands her answer to indicate she has tried two times before. Sally's continuer in line 6 is overlapped by Mary prior to completion (with an absolutely sequentially relevant) reinforcement of the fact that – with stress on the *both* – each time the changes have been unsuccessful. In line 8 Sally works to *show* that she is taking a collaborative approach to the medication issue by formulating Mary's position in such a way as to demonstrate that she is not presuming to have understood, but rather that she, Sally, is looking to Mary to confirm that she has understood her views in this situation ('so what are you telling me you want to do (1 sec) you want to stay with your old medication?'). Mary accepts this version as accurate and offers an agreement token 'mm'. However, this is not the end of the matter: it rapidly becomes apparent that Sally's emollient approach is merely superficially collaborative as Mary's assent to her formulation does not close the conversation, but rather is taken by Sally as the opportunity for further questioning.

Extract 53: MM/SB/1998

1	SALLY	Has he given you a rea↑son why he ↑needs ↑to
2	MARY	↑Nuh ((Shakes head, looking around))
3		((Gets up and walks towards door))
4		(1.5)
5	SALLY	↑Don't get up↓set (.) I'm just trying to help ↑out here ↑eh
6		(3.5)
7		What are you up↑set a↓bout (0.5) the medi↑cations
8	MARY	((Shakes head and walks out))

Sally's utterance in line 1 of extract 53 again shows the characteristic exaggerated intonation contours (Caporael, 1981; Mitchell, 2001) of interaction between unequal interlocutors. Mary adds stress to her negative response by shaking her head and looking around as if to find an escape route, gets up from the table and moves towards another room. In response to Mary's obvious distress Sally's utterances in lines 5–7 construct her as occupying a neutral, 'helping', role rather than one of authority, again utterances which strategically redirect the focus of the interaction and its possible upshot away from one of potentially coercive decision-making by staff towards a solicitous and caring puzzlement. Her apparent efforts to calm Mary in line 7 by asking what is upsetting her do not offer a distressed Mary much time to respond before providing a closed option response ('The medications?'). Mary's prompt disagreement token and departure would seem to suggest that a more accurate identification of the source of Mary's 'upset' may be something more to do with staff *management* of her decision regarding her medication than the medication itself.

These encounters share a remarkable similarity to the detailed analysis of a conflictual speech therapy session reported by Simmons-Mackie and Damico (1999). In their analysis of the escalation into open hostility of a difficult therapeutic encounter between 'C', a fifty-year-old woman with severe aphasia consequent upon a stroke and 'L', her speech and language therapist, we see many of the features identified above. Over the course of a 203 line transcript Simmons-Mackie and Damico (1999) show how L fails to hear and to recognise the efforts that C makes to register her dissatisfaction with the progress of both the specific therapeutic session, and with the therapy process as a whole. In extract 54 we see an early failure by L (in line 64) to entertain the possibility that C can, and is, exercising her right as 'client' to request an amendment to the therapy session, a failure which is then compounded (as we have seen above) with a what is only describable as a patronising display of L 'doing being therapeutic' in lines 126–9.

Extract 54: From Simmons-Mackie and Damico, 1999

```
59    L   Can you read that sentence for me now?
60        Read that whole sentence.
61    C   (pause) ((downward gaze, leans forward))
62        ((clears throat, eyes closed))
63        Is NE::::W ((lifts 'sleeping' card))
          ((looks at L then down then up and down rapidly))
64    L   New? ⌈What ya mean.
65    C        ⌊Yeah, plea::se ((tense voice))
66        I don know ((nods no rapidly))
67        is is alu ((gestures stop))
68        ((writes 'enough')) ((loudly drops pencil))
69        PLEA:::SE
70    L   Enough?=
71    C   Yeah
72    L   =What ya mean?
73    C   Isy ((pointing to 'sleeping' card))
74        is is is good ((speaks rapidly, points to tablet then to card))
75        is NE:::W ((points to L))
```

```
76   L   What's new?
77       What ya  ⌈mean it's new?
78   C            ⌊Is is too
         ((leans forward and sweeps hand across cards on L's side of the table))
79   L   You want anoth ⌈er one?
80   C                  ⌊Yeah, plea::se.
. . .
83   C   ⌊I know (pause) I don kno::w ((gaze down))
84       O::h o:h no:::: ((grabs head))
85   L   Too frustrating today?
86   C   Yea- ((clipped, terse))
87   L   Okay. The couple is sleeping in bed.
88       That was good. Perfect sentence.
89       Nothin wrong with it ((sing-song intonation))
90       Awright lets look at this one
. . .
124  L   Is that what you were going to tell me?
125  C   I don know is is
         ((crying, looking down at lap, body turned to side))
126  L   Is it frustrating today?
127      (pause) C, it's okay (pause) All right? ((said in soft voice))
128      ((pause)) Just take each day as it comes
129      ((places a box of tissues directly in front of C))
         and we just do as much as you can do, okay?
. . .
144  C   Is PLEA::SE NE:W (pause) ah CARD
         (pleading intonation))
145  L   Oh you want different ⌈pictures?
146                           ⌊PLEA:SE! YES ((nods))
147  L   O:::::H. Oh Okay
. . .
169  C   Isy, I don know isy. Is bye bye
              ((waves with rapid expansive gesture))
170      Is MONEY ISY ((gestures grasping money to self))
171      BYE BYE ((waves))
172  L   About money?
173  C   YEA::: IS ME. PLEA::SE
174      IS NEW (leans forward stares at L))
```

In this interaction Simmons-Mackie and Damico pick out a series of features that are also evident in the conflictual encounters between Mary and her care staff Jenny and Sally. Like Mary, C engages in attempts to assert her independence (the physical rejection of the 'help' proffered in the form of the box of tissues); equally C's utterances and actions are receipted by the therapist not as those of a 'dissatisfied customer' unhappy with the repetition of therapy, but rather as expressions of 'aphasic incompetence' in the same manner as Mary's refusals to countenance a change of medication are receipted as accountable insolence rather than the choice of a 'patient'. As Simmons-Mackie and Damico put it, we see the: 'creation of incompetence by expectation. That is, the therapist expected C to be incompetent, and interpreted the talk in the light of this expectation. The expert failed to recognize the interactive competence of her client.' Further, Mary, like C, demonstrates her competence via her deployment of normative resources for the doing of argument which is, after all, itself a preference-organised form of talk-in-interaction (Schiffrin, 1990). Both make assiduous efforts to indicate their position, offer reasons for the position they are advancing and, only after such argumentative resources have been exhausted, do both adopt the only course of action available to them in the face of 'therapeutic' dominance – and remove themselves from the room. Both situations then show us 'a competent human being struggling to extricate herself form a dependent social role' (Simmons-Mackie and Damico, ms 31).

Extract 55 takes place in the home of Marie and Rae. Marie is lying on the couch in the living area and Rae is watching television in the lounge room. Marie started telling Janet, a visiting research worker, about a holiday she had been on recently on a cruise liner. Throughout the extract Janet uses exaggerated intonation and a high pitch in her responses to Marie's descriptions of her sickness, common features of 'baby' talk with people who are seen to be dependent or less competent in their communicative ability.

Extract 55: RK/MW/JU/1998

```
1    MARIE    On ↑my ship I got sea↓sick
2    JANET    You got ↑sea↓sick (1.0) ↑did ↓you o::h yuc↓ky
3             (2.0)
4    MARIE    Every↓where
5    JANET    E↓oo
6             (1.5)
7    RAE      She (.) she does↓n't want to know ↑that
8             (7.5)
9    MARIE    I's sick every↓where
10   JANET    O:h were ↑you
11   MARIE    In a ↑buck↓et
12   JANET    Eoo: de↓ar
13   MARIE    In the ↑toi↓let
14   JANET    ↑Oh de↓ar
15   RAE      Oh (      ) I ↓didn't want to know ↑that
16   MARIE    (hhh) and diar↑rhoea
17   JANET    ↑O↓h ↑gre:↓at
18   RAE      (hhhh)
19   JANET    So did you en↑joy your holi↑day
20   MARIE    (hhh) Diarr-  ⌈Throwing up
```

21	RAE	Mar ⌊ie we don't want to ↑kno:↓:w
22	MARIE	And diarr↓hoea at the same ↓time
23	JANET	Oh ↓dear (1.5) you were a ↑mess
24	MARIE	I was a ↓<u>mess</u>
25	JANET	Big ↓<u>mess</u>
26		(7.5)
27	MARIE	↑And a black ↓out
28		(0.5)
29	JANET	And ↑what
30	MARIE	↑And a black ↓out
31	JANET	↑<u>And</u> a black ↓out
32	MARIE	Mm
33	JANET	Did ↑<u>you</u> black ↓out
34	MARIE	Mm
35	JANET	Oh ↑de↓ar (.) you're ↓not a born ↑sail↓or ↑are ↓you
36	MARIE	↑Nuh

Both characteristic semantic features (e.g. the repetitions of 'you got sea-sick', line 2 and 'and a black out' in line 31) and a greatly simplified lexicon (i.e. 'oh yucky' in line 2 and 'eoo:' in lines 5 and 12) of 'baby-talk' are obvious – as indeed is the rather patronising closing formulation, delivered in the familiar sing-song intonation, of this tale of woe in line 35 (Oh ↑de↓ar (.) you're ↓not a born ↑sail↓or ↑are ↓you).

In extract 56 Jim is preparing dinner with his social trainer, Jenny. In this extract we see an intriguing instance of Jim ironising Jenny, who continues the conversation apparently unaware that Jim's utterances make explicit his receipt of her 'solicitude' as patronising. In line 1 Jenny claims responsibility for chopping the vegetables: note the sing-song intonation contour; the unusual use of the nominal as attention getting device to index Jim (Antaki and Rapley, 1996; Mitchell, 2001), the twice repeated stress on *I*, and the deployment of the mental state term 'I think' (in what is clearly a strategic interactional usage rather than a reference to the state of her mentation, cf. Coulter, 1979; Edwards, 1997; McHoul and Rapley, 2003).

Extract 56: JM/JS/ 1998

1	JENNY	Jim ↑<u>I</u> think ↓<u>I</u> might cut ↑these=
2	JIM	=Ye::s ↓mum
3	JENNY	=Because (.) ↑this knife (.) is dread↓ful (0.5) and it is↑n't (.) isn't
4		very sh↑arp
5	JIM	We'll have to ↑<u>buy</u> more
6	JENNY	And I'm just con↑cerned that you ↓might-
7		(2.0)
8	JIM	Buy a ↑sharp knife (2.5) at the ↑shop
9	JENNY	If ↑you'd like to peel <u>that</u> ↓for me
10	JIM	Yes ↓<u>mum</u>

This apparently unremarkable seven word utterance (Jim ↑*I* think ↓*I* might cut ↑these=) thus achieves a number of social actions: it positions Jenny as acting on the basis of rational (fore)thought and concern for the welfare of her charge; it locates in Jim a potentially self-injurious incapacity; and it asserts possession, for her, of the authority to permit – or not – certain mundane actions. In short line 1 proposes and produces Jim as incompetent. That this is not an analyst's fancy is demonstrated in line 2 where Jim's 'ye::s ↓mum' is surely hearable as ironising Jenny (who is not, after all, Jim's mum): in short 'yes mum' – in both receiving Jenny's utterance as patronising and commenting on it as such – produces Jenny's utterance as an insult. Let us turn now to an instance of an extraordinarily similar data fragment. In his *Lectures on Conversation* (1992) Sacks reproduces the following exchange from a group therapy session for 'delinquent youths'. What we see here is a near identical deployment of the second part seen above: 'ye::s mum' – 'yes mommy' in both instances addressed directly to an interlocutor who is quite evidently not a biological relative.

Extract 57: From Sacks, 1992: 420

1	ROGER	Ken, face it you're a poor little rich kid ( )
2		((cough))
3	KEN	Yes Mommy. // Thank you
4	ROGER	Face the music

In their analysis of this extract McHoul and Rapley (2002) note that:

The key to finding how it is that 'Mommy' is referring to Roger turns on questions of *conversational sequencing* as a form of cultural order (as opposed to formal correspondence). That is, 'face it you're a poor little rich kid' is produced by Roger as an *insult* and, in cases of an insult being issued in a first conversational slot, only a small number of possible utterances can be expected in the second, following, slot. And in fact, the most likely second (or 'return') is a counter-insult [. . .] So what we have to do (as analysts *or* as co-participants), in order to find Roger as designated by 'Mommy', is attend to the *cultural rules* for the practice of insulting: that is, to such things as 'insults come in pairs' and 'return insults can use kinship misidentifications'.

Thus we find ourselves in the paradoxical position in extract 56 where it is the participant formally identified as 'intellectually disabled' who displays both his orientation to, and his mastery of, the rules of both conversational sequence *and* 'the cultural rules for the practice of insulting' and it is the formally identified 'normal' staff member who demonstrates her incapacity to attend to the same. Indeed so insensitive is Jenny to the receipt of her utterance as insulting that Jim is moved to reiterate his turn – and this time with stress on *mum* – in line 10 when his demonstration of competence (via his clear appreciation of the fact he is being told he's

incompetent and his explicit demonstration of his cultural knowledge of
at least one remedial strategy for ownership of blunt knives) is met by
being asked to peel rather than chop.

In community houses one of the assumptions made is that residents
are somewhat independent in basic living skills. Yet, massively routinely,
throughout the data under consideration here mundane tasks such as
dinner preparation, meal planning and decision-making are undertaken
by staff. The next extract is a good example of this. The support worker,
Brenda, is in the kitchen serving up a takeaway dinner. Dan and Gwen
are watching television while Terri is in her room. After being called to
dinner in lines 1 and 2, all members of the household make their way to
the dinner table, seat themselves and wait to be served.

Extract 58: DY/TG/GP/BC/1998

1	BRENDA	O↓kay dinner's ready darl would you like to take ↑yours (3.0)
2		↑Ter↑ri (.) ↑Dan din↓ner's ready ↓loves
3	DAN	⌈'Kay we're ↑co↓ming ↓merry ↑Christ↓mas
4	TERRI	⌊'Kay
5	BRENDA	((Putting plate down)) ↓Ga↑il
6	GWEN	Not be long 'till Christmas ↑now ↓Bren↑da
7	BRENDA	What ↓love↑y
8	GWEN	Next month it's ↑Christ↓mas
9	BRENDA	Oops ((Nodding, keeps dishing up and putting plates on table,
10		residents sit))
11	DAN	↑This came in the (.) in the ↓mail
12	BRENDA	There you go darling (.) sorry ↑love
13	DAN	( )
14	BRENDA	Do you ↑want to open it up at the (.) ↑table or (.) open it
15		la↓ter
16	DAN	A:h do it la↑ter
17	BRENDA	Do it la↑ter (.) ↑Just put it on the desk ↓Dan and I'll ↑look at it
18		la↓ter

Perhaps the first observation to be made about this extract is the strikingly *mundane* nature of this interaction. Lines 1–4 capture a moment of
entirely unremarkable domesticity: an exchange that might be heard in
any family kitchen when the evening meal is ready. Equally, when Gwen
tries to engage a busy Brenda in conversation in line 6 with a seasonally relevant pre announcement ('not long till Christmas now Brenda')
we are struck by the overwhelming *ordinariness* and *orderliness* (tenHave,
1999) of the initial turn, Brenda's 'absent' response ('what lovey?' in
line 7) and her successful sidestepping of an exchange following Gwen's
topical expansion in line 8 ('next month it's Christmas) by explicitly *showing* that she is re-directing her attention to the task in hand (the nodding

and the 'oops' in line 9, to which candidate termination point Gwen accedes with a pertinently *absent* third turn). Similarly when in line 11 Dan tries to get Brenda's attention, this time showing her correspondence that came in the mail (line 11 – 'this came in the mail') both he and Brenda *collaboratively* manage both Brenda's serving of dinner and the conversation about the mail simultaneously.

Yet what is clearly hearable as – and arguably essentially indistinguishable from – a scene of domestic tranquillity as a mother calls her children to the dinner table is *not* such a scene. Whilst both the distribution of tasks and the lexicon that Brenda employs suggest a warm familial intimacy ('dinner's ready darl'; 'what lovey?'; 'there you go darlin''), an intimacy which is dependent upon being *collaboratively co-produced* by Dan and Gwen, these are not Brenda's children but rather adults for whom she is paid to 'care'. That Gwen and Dan can and do display the fine-tuned sensitivity that they do – in naturally occurring talk – to the moment-by-moment, turn-by-turn, requirements of conversational management in such a way as to produce such evident (if mundane) order, rather than conversational chaos, suggests once more that prevailing notions of an essentialised (in)competence require respecification.

Instruction-giving

Given that people with intellectual disabilities are most frequently conceptualised (if not specifically so defined (cf. AAMR, 2002)) as deficient in some areas of functioning, and as requiring assistance to carry out domestic tasks, one of the very real functions of staff working in community homes is to teach 'adaptive' skills. Giving 'instructions' may then be understood as a necessary part of skills teaching. However the frequency with which staff members implement this interactional style has been well documented in the literature as excessive, if not exclusive (McConkey *et al.* 1999; Kuder and Bryen, 1993): data reported here suggest that this is substantially correct, and that while the term 'instruction' appears to be used as a synonym for 'teaching' in much of the literature, frequently the pedagogic value of what may also be (and perhaps more accurately) glossed as 'directive giving' appears limited. As such, opportunities for house residents to collaborate with staff members in reaching a shared understanding of task requirements and to actively participate in the development of task skills, are often missed, with staff positioning themselves as not only more knowledgeable, but also as having the unquestioned authority to make decisions on the behalf of the 'less able' party. As with 'parenting', this interactional style also conveys the presumption of incompetence. As we have seen above, the 'intellectually disabled persons' with whom such an interactional strategy is pursued may make evident both their appreciation, and dislike, of it.

The second most commonly observed interactional style evident in the data considered here was either direct or indirect instruction-giving. As noted by Schegloff (1999) in his detailed study of the pragmatic competence of Alvin, a commisurotomised man, data collected in this study suggest that preconceptions about the pragmatic (in)competence of people with an intellectual disability become more difficult to sustain if the fine detail of mundane interaction is analysed. In particular, data collected here suggest that, like Alvin, intellectually disabled people demonstrate a considerably greater orientation to the pragmatics of social action, for example, in responding to indirection, than is assumed in the literature.

However, as was noted earlier, the apparently straightforward distinction between interactional registers that may be assumed to be implied by the glossing of a range of phenomena with a title such as 'instruction giving' should be approached with caution. As we have seen in the extracts considered above (particularly extract 58, for example) neither the doing of 'parenting', nor the issuing of 'instruction' by staff, is unambiguously describable in *a priori* terms. It is not just that apparently 'instructional' single utterances may be met by intellectually disabled participants with second pair parts that indicate that the 'instructions' are received as 'parental', but also that single speech episodes may contain exchanges which are co-produced by both participants as 'parental', 'instructional' and as we shall see in the final section, as 'collaborative'.

The following extracts show a variety of different situations where staff have assumed a more knowledgeable position, and project the relevance of acquiescence on the part of house residents. Of note in the data was the manner in which, rather than adapting their interactional style to individual contexts, staff members working across a number of different houses were observed to use similar techniques in all homes in which they worked.

In extract 59 Anne is seated at the table with Kylie doing some paperwork when Susan walks through the house with a basket of washing. Anne stops what she is doing to ask Susan where she wants to fold her washing. However, although the first part of the two-part turn is delivered in the semantic wh form of a question, and the second part preserves both the question form and a 'questioning' intonation contour, the second part of Anne's utterance in lines 1 and 2 ('where did you want to fold them (.) do you want to fold them over there on the sofa') is *not* a check on Susan's plans for her washing, but rather acts to *direct* her to an appropriate place to fold. That Susan doesn't verbally respond to this indirect request, but rather dutifully turns around and folds her washing in the suggested place is in itself a demonstration that Anne's utterance has been received by Susan as such.

Extract 59: SK/AB/1998

1	ANNE	Where did you want to ↑fold ↓them (.) do you
2		want to ↑fold them over ↑there on the so↑fa (.) ↓that'd be
3		al↓right are they all ↑dry
4		(2.0) ((Susan walks towards sofa))
5	ANNE	Susan (.) Susan (.) are they all ↑dry (1.5) are they all ↑dry (.)
6	SUSAN	↑yeah

In extract 60 Anne uses a similar interaction style to that seen in the previous extract when it is time to make breakfast and lunches for the next day. Here, she is in the kitchen with Susan discussing lunch options. The first of her three questions in line 1 ('shall we make breakfast and lunch?') is not so much *giving Susan a choice* of whether or not to make breakfast and lunch, but rather Anne is *proposing the course of action that should be taken*. Again, while Anne does not use the excessive intonation contours we have seen in previous extracts, both her prosody and her actions in the exchange are – as with Kylie and her mother – primarily concerned with *directing* both action and interaction, with Susan's participation limited to single word or non-verbal receipt tokens.

Extract 60: SK/AB/1998

1	ANNE	Shall we make ↑breakfast and ↑lunch do you ↑want some
2		of that la↑mb ((Susan nods)) (5.0) bread ↑roll or ↓bread
3	SUSAN	Roll
4	ANNE	↓Roll (.) which ↓one (.) you (.) you pick which one you
5		↓want and I'll (.) de↓frost it for ↓you
6	SUSAN	((indicates a roll))
7	ANNE	One of ↑those (1.0) now we've got roast ↑lamb (. .) want
8		some roast ↑lamb
9		((Susan nods))
10		Was that ↑nice (.) ↑yeah
11		((Susan nods)) (1.0)
12		((Cough)) Are ↑you having a roll (.) Ky↑lie ((Anne places rolls in microwave and switches it on))

While in line 2 Anne provides Susan with a binary choice of 'bread roll or bread', following Susan's indication that she would prefer a roll, the interaction becomes less a conversation than a running commentary by Anne on her activities and, like Kylie's mother in extract 44, a checking on Susan's receipt of her commentary rather than an active solicitation of her participation. This is perhaps best demonstrated by Anne's actions in line 12 where, as she has prefigured in lines 4–5, rather than recruit

Susan as a participant in defrosting the bread she takes responsibility for microwaving the rolls, perhaps as a way of taking on the aspects of lunch making which are too 'difficult' for Susan and Kylie but, simultaneously, continuing to render these activities beyond their competence.

The indirect request as directive is also demonstrated in extract 61. Jenny issues an indirect instruction to Ida in lines 1 and 2 by combining a wh- utterance with the implicit proposition that the directive is reasonable on the grounds of equity.

Extract 61: IL/JM/JS/1998

```
1    JENNY    I↑da (.) would you like to set the ↑table now that (.) since
2             Jim ⌈has prep↑ared din↑ner
3    JIM          ⌊↑This ((showing staff salad dressing))
4    JENNY    ↓Oh ↑yeah
5    IDA      Mm::
6    JIM      Sa↑lad
7    JENNY    Yeah (.) we'll take the cheese out ↓first 'cause otherwise it will
8             go all sog↓gy
9    JIM      Sog↓gy
10   JENNY    Yeah
```

A receipt from Ida such as 'well, actually I'm very grateful to Jim for preparing dinner, but no I wouldn't like to set the table' would clearly be incongruous and, as we see, no such receipt is forthcoming. Rather, having displayed her orientation to the overlapping exchange between Jenny and Jim about which salad dressing to use, and waited for the completion of their side-sequence, Ida promptly offers a positive receipt at the first available turn (a simple 'Mm' in line 5) and complies.

It is also of note in this interaction sequence that *forms of instruction* are co-occurring with the issuing of the *directive* to Ida. Jenny's utterances in line 4 ('oh yeah') and in line 7 ('yeah we'll take the cheese out first 'cause otherwise it will go all soggy') do not necessarily display a semantic form that may be immediately recognised as the doing of instruction: they are, however, both receipted by Jim in such a manner (albeit differently on each occasion) as to warrant the suggestion that he has heard Jenny's utterances as offering him 'instruction' (in the sense of issuing feedback that comments upon action and offers guidance for future performance). Let us examine these micro-sequences a little more closely:

Extract 61: IL/JM/JS/1998) (detail 1)

```
3    JIM         ⌊↑This ((Showing staff salad dressing))
4    JENNY    ↓Oh ↑yeah
5    [. . .]
6    JIM      Sa↑lad
7    JENNY    Yeah (.)
```

In the first sequence Jim's utterance (line 3: 'this') is delivered with a rising intonation contour, and accompanied by showing Jenny a bottle of salad dressing which is receipted by Jenny with 'oh yeah' (line 4). That the utterance 'oh yeah' here functions to perform instruction is demonstrated by the sequential use to which Jim puts it: that is 'oh yeah' is taken as offering confirmation that Jim's prior action (the selection of the appropriate salad dressing) was correct and it is *also* taken as a marker that, one subtask having been successfully completed, it is time for a move to the next item of business, a move that Jim promptly proposes with the utterance in line 6: 'salad' – again delivered in a rising ('questioning') intonation contour. We can thus reconstruct this exchange along the following lines:

Extract 61: IL/JM/JS/1998 (detail 2)

```
3   JIM     Have I selected the right dressing to go with the salad we're making
4   JENNY   Yes Jim, that's the correct salad dressing
5   [. . .]
6   JIM     So now we get on with putting the salad together do we
7   JENNY   Yeah (.)
```

Similarly, with the second detail, we can see that Jim receipts Jenny's more apparently 'pedagogic' explanatory utterance 'we'll take the cheese out first 'cause otherwise it will go all soggy' with a token designed to *demonstrate* his *comprehension* of the information imparted to him.

Extract 61: IL/JM/JS/1998 (detail 3)

```
6    JIM     Sa↑lad
7    JENNY   Yeah (.) we'll take the cheese out ↓first 'cause otherwise it will
8            go all sog↓gy
9    JIM     Sog↓gy
10   JENNY   Yeah
```

As is evident in line 9, Jim's receipt recycles *the key word* in Jenny's utterance, 'soggy', and retains precisely Jenny's intonation contour in so doing. Again, reconstructing this exchange allows us to see that what Jim is 'saying' with the recycle of 'soggy' is something like: 'I want you to know that I appreciate that I have been told that there is a good reason for taking the cheese out first and starting with that, because if we don't do it that way it will become soggy and unpleasant.' Jenny's prompt utterance at line 10, 'yeah' is, similarly, sufficient to indicate that she has heard 'soggy' as doing precisely such an adequate demonstration of understanding. The instructional episode is complete.

Such demonstrations or declarations of understanding are not always an uncomplicated matter for staff members, nor is the question of instruction necessarily always a matter of imparting skills. In the following extract the question of what a resident knows is revealed to be designed not as a prelude to instruction, but rather to the issuing of a directive; further, when the resident in question shows her appreciation of this and manages a 'question' about her knowledge as the strategic enquiry that it is, the 'instruction' that follows may perhaps be better understood as an issue of the maintenance of *staff authority* rather than as an opportunity for necessary or opportunistic skills teaching.

At the start of extract 62 Jenny and Jim have dinner in its final stages. Jenny has been preparing to leave the house and arranging for the meal to be completed without her direct oversight. Here we see Jenny issue a typical pre-request (Antaki, 1994) as a prelude to what becomes a directive + instruction sequence. In line 1 she (doubly) nominates next speaker (naming Ida and placing stress on *you*) and asks: 'Ida do *you* know how to cook rice?'

Extract 62: IL/JM/JS/1998

```
1   JENNY    I↑da (.) do you know how to cook ↑rice
2   IDA      Ye:::↑ah
3            (1.0)
4   JENNY    O↓kay (0.2) well (.) ↑since Jim and I have made ↑this (.)
5            we're going to let ↑you cook the ↑rice
6   JIM      Yeah I cook ↓that
7   JENNY    O↑kay (0.2) and ↑I'll show you how much rice to put ↓in
```

Antaki (1994) notes that pre-request + request sequences usually take the form:

```
A   Do you have today's paper?
B   Sure, would you like to have a look?
A   If I may, thanks.
```

where B in the example above offers the preferred second pair part (agreement) to the pre-request. Ida's response in line 2, particularly the elongation of the first vowel and the change of pitch mid-utterance – 'ye:::↑ah' – and the one-second slot at the end of Ida's turn, suggests that the pre-request is heard, correctly, as a prelude to a second part rather than as an unmotivated asking. Further, this (dispreferred) response to a pre-request *displays* Ida's appreciation of, and reluctance to accede to, the projected upcoming request (compare, for example: Jenny: 'Ida do you know how to cook rice?' Ida: 'Sure Jenny, do you want me to do that?'). That Ida has correctly identified Jenny's first turn *as* a pre-request, and that her utterance made her reluctance clear to Jenny, is visible sequentially, in both the dispreference markers (hedge + pause × 2 + account) at the start of Jenny's turn and in the subsequent structure of the turn itself. As the standard pre-request + request device has been derailed by

Ida's turn, Jenny offers an account of the reasons for her request (she and Jim have prepared most of the meal) as a second trailer to its issue and then does not directly *ask* or *instruct* Ida to cook the rice, but rather offers a softened 'we're going to *let* you cook the rice'. This formulation is, then, both nicely recipient designed (Ida has claimed knowledge of rice cookery) and also finely sequentially tuned (Ida has declined Jenny's previously issued request that she cook the rice) to accomplish Jenny's project of nominating Ida for a specific role in dinner preparations.

On the face of it, then, this should have been sufficient for Jenny to leave the rice cooking to Ida, however she goes on (in line 7) to say: 'and *I'll* show you how much rice to put in'. What are we to make of this utterance, with the stress on *I'll*, in the sequential position it occupies here? It seems plausible to suggest that this *apparent* offer of instruction in the details of rice cookery has less to do with Ida's need for training, than it has to do with accomplishing the reassertion of the position Jenny occupies in domestic activity – as both more *capable* than Ida, and also as *having the authority* to determine the respective contributions to domestic activity of various household members.

Extract 63 again takes place in the kitchen: Karen is cooking dinner when Sherie, a staff member, enters. Karen opens this sequence in line 1, employing what Kuder and Bryen (1993) described as a 'conversational encourager' – an initiation which, ordinarily, it would be impolite to ignore – with the inclusive 'we': 'what shall *we* have for sweets?' (my emphasis). Sherie, however, does not immediately respond to Karen's opening turn (and in so doing does not take the opportunity to establish common ground or indeed Karen's offer to involve her in decision making about sweets). Rather, after a long pause, Sherie's first utterance (in line 3) is a topic shift, which opens with 'right', a token which is deployed to mark the beginning of the task, and goes on to issue a series of instructions about the ongoing cooking, starting with a two part direction ('right, you need to get the um potatoes and vegies out (2.5 seconds) and turn them over').

Extract 63: KW/SB/1998

```
1   KAREN    For ↑sweets (.) ↑what shall we have for ↑sweets Sherie
2            (2.5)
3   SHERIE   Right (0.2) you ↑need to (.) get the um (.) potatoes and vegies
4            ↑out (2.5) and turn them o↑ver
5   KAREN    Yep
6   SHERIE   O↑kay (Karen begins to remove vegetables from oven)
7   KAREN    I need ↑to I need a ah (0.5) ↑mitten
8            (4.0)
9   SHERIE   Two ↓hands
```

Sherie's utterance in lines 3–4 includes both two micro-pauses punctu-
ating the key clauses in the utterance, and a noticeably extended, 2.5
second pause, separating the instruction to get the vegetables out and the
subsequent instruction to then turn them. This prosody is reminiscent
of that which may be employed in giving directions to someone whose
first language is not English or who is hard of hearing. While Karen's
promptly delivered 'yep' indicates an acceptance of both this instruction
(and of her position as someone who requires such instruction) Sherie's
next utterance ('okay' in line 6) reinforces her prior demand for agreement. Noticeably, Karen does not issue a further agreement token but
instead carries out the task, and in doing so demonstrates both her ability
to accomplish it, and (in line 7) *also* demonstrates her awareness of what
is required to carry out the task safely and efficiently ('I need to I need
a ah mitten'). Not content to accept this demonstration, after a further
lengthy pause of 4 seconds Sherie offers a final instruction ('two hands'),
producing herself as the more knowledgeable of the two of them on how
many mittens were appropriate in the given situation.

In extract 64 support worker Sarah is sitting watching Peter cooking
dinner. Mike is sitting next to her also watching Peter. Peter goes to the
cupboard, looks for something, and brings out a small colander. Sarah
issues an instruction to stop in line 1 ('no'), before going on ask a 'question' which functions to indicate a preferred option ('well that's not the
one you usually use you've got a big colander haven't you').

Extract 64: PP/MK/SS/1998

1	SARAH	No (.) well ↑that's not the one you ↑usually use you've got a big
2		↑colander haven't ↑you like a big-
3	PETER	⌈I can't ↑find it
4	MIKE	⌊cor↓ner ((pointing))
5	SARAH	Well (.) would you get up and help ↑Peter (0.2) cause you seem
6		to know where it ↑is
7		(1.5)
8	MIKE	Yep

In line 3 Peter cuts Sarah off when she begins to offer an explanation of
what a big colander may look like in line 2 ('like a big-') and, with 'I can't
find it', displays both that he knows what such an implement looks like,
and offers an *account of the reason* why he is proposing to use the (smaller)
colander. In verbalising the 'facts of the matter' Peter thus orients to
the fact that the issue of his competence is in question, and accordingly
provides evidence of his ability to make rational decisions. In doing so he
also displays his recognition of, and resistance to, staff attempts to instruct
him. Mike's overlapping one-word turn ('corner' in line 4) similarly works

to demonstrate his knowledge of domestic arrangements, noticeably *not* by offering a description of the colander, but simply by indicating its location. As we also saw in extracts 62 and 63, Sarah's response to this collaborative demonstration of ability from Peter and Mike is to reassert staff control by making a direct request to Mike that he assist, a turn which reasserts her position that Peter's status is not that of someone who can manage matters by himself but, rather, is in need of 'help'.

In the final extract for this section we see an example of staff instruction that is acceptable to, and accepted by, house residents. In extract 65, Joan and Marie have been writing a shopping list and, in finishing, Joan checks with Marie that everything needed has been included.

Extract 65: MW/JB/1998

```
1   JOAN    So (.) have you got ↑enough can I ↑just check the cup↑boards to
2           see what you've got and what you haven't ↑got (0.5) or have you
3           already ↑done ↑that (1.0) well there you ↑go ↓then (0.5) lots of
4           ↑cooking you've got to ↓do ((Joan gets up from the table))
5           (0.5)
6   MARIE   O::h ((Gets up and stretches))
7   JOAN    (   )
8   MARIE   ((Goes to the pantry))
9   JOAN    Do you ↑need any more cere↑al (0.5) do you think you ↑need
10          any more cere↑al or any  ⌈↑thing
11  MARIE                            ⌊Mm
12  JOAN    Do you want to write that down ↑then
13  MARIE   ((Walks to table))
```

That Joan's opening utterance in the extract (lines 1–4) is received by Marie as an instruction that she should check in the pantry for possible omissions from the shopping list is made evident in her accession to this suggestion (lines 6–8). Joan's utterance is notable for the inclusion of the 'or have you already done that?' component which, unlike many of the extracts we have seen so far, does not propose an absence of competence on the part of the resident; rather such a component provides for the possibility that the ability to complete the task in question is already within Marie's capacities. Similarly Joan's prompt about the possible omission of cereal (lines 9–10) is shaped not as a directive, but rather as an enquiry about whether Marie *thinks* she needs cereal *or anything else*. Such a turn again is careful *not* to identify a *specific error* on Marie's part (she has forgotten the cereal) and simultaneously is attentive to buttressing Marie's agency and intellectual capacities (what does she, Marie, 'think'). Marie's underplayed receipt ('mm' – line 11) acknowledges her oversight and is matched by a further downgraded instruction from Joan to add cereal to the list ('do you want to write that down then') – which instruction Marie accepts and in line 13 she returns to the table to comply.

Collaboration/Pedagogy

The final section of this chapter examines staff–client interaction which demonstrates that it is entirely possible for staff practices to involve house residents in decision-making, offer suggestions rather than instructions, allow and encourage house residents to make choices, and a lexicon and symmetry of turn-taking more associated with two interlocutors of equal status. We have 'met' some of the residents in the following extracts in previous sections where they have been produced as incompetent by staff actions. However, with different staff, or with the same staff using different interactional practices, house residents can – and do – not only display a mundane interaction competence but also demonstrably participate in mutually comprehensible conversation. In many of the extracts there is some evidence of teaching, or instructing, going on, however the way that this is managed – *by both parties* – is much more in keeping with attention to supporting resident competence.

Extract 66 takes place in the dining area of one of the community homes, where staff members Anne and Colin are discussing the purchase of a clothesline for the house. Kylie is seated at the table watching the conversation and Susan is standing with the two talkers. This extract makes explicit that the 'rules' that govern the community based homes studied are well appreciated by the people who live in them, and here Kylie establishes herself as the one to relay them to the new staff member Colin, who did not understand usual procedures when working in the house for the first time. Here, both Kylie and Anne collaboratively take on the role of educating Colin about the house, its procedures and the division of available facilities. Anne issues Susan with a direct instruction (line 3) in overlap with Kylie's opening of a collaborative – information providing – conversation with Colin (line 4).

Extract 66: KA/SK/AB/CA/1998

1	ANNE	↑Marilyn is the one with the money so (.) even (.) ↑even if you
2		take it out of <u>our</u> ↓money it doesn't make much differ↓ence (.)
3		⌈Sus↓an ((Susan is hugging Colin))
4	KYLIE	⌊Colin
5	ANNE	Sus↓an (0.5) not too many ↓hugs
6	KYLIE	Colin
7	ANNE	It's a bit embarrass↓ing for Col ⌈in ↑isn't it
8	KYLIE	⌊We (0.5) we got a red note
9		on ↓there

```
10   COLIN    Yep   ⌈I didn't ↑see that fridge
11   KYLIE          ⌊That's me that's me and (.) ↓Susan
12   COLIN    ⌈Yep
13   KYLIE    ⌊So she ↑cannot go in the ↓fridge
14   COLIN    I under ⌈stand ↓now (.) I didn't ↑realise ↓before
15   ANNE              ⌊No (.) well we've ↑put a note on it now   ⌈ (hhh)
16   KYLIE                                                        ⌊And the
17            of↑fice and the and the toi↓let (.) that's for staff ↑only (.) not for
18            ↓her
19   COLIN    Right
```

Colin is involved in two sequences in this extract, the one started by Kylie, and the other one preceding that, started by Anne in line 1. Following the attention getting device 'Susan' in line 3, in line 5 Anne issues an instruction to Susan ('not too many hugs'), to which Colin had attended briefly before resuming his previous activity. When Susan does not immediately desist, a follow-up instruction – this time formed as a 'question' which in practice offers an account of reasons why hugging should be discontinued (the ramifications for Colin of her display of affection) – is issued, and is so shaped as to project the relevance of agreement with the proposition that, as making people embarrassed is not a 'nice' thing to do, it should be avoided. Clearly the issuing of instruction in these terms carries with it (and conveys) the presupposition that Susan, despite 'needing to be told' to stop hugging Colin, is sufficiently aware of the operative cultural prohibition not to require a direct instruction such as 'stop'. That is, Susan is produced in this utterance as a member of a *shared cultural order*.

Colin chooses to attend to Kylie's talk, initiated in line 6 with her nomination of him as next speaker. Colin collaboratively takes up the opportunity provided by Kylie to talk about the mistakes he made (for example: 'yep I didn't see that fridge'). Kylie continues to offer additions to her previous account of house management techniques (red notes, their meaning and their intended recipients). Of particular note here is the way that Kylie skilfully takes the floor at the transition relevance place (overlapping Anne's possible place-holding inbreath) at the end of Anne's turn in line 15 (which has reiterated Kylie's earlier note material) with an upgrade, describing the *other* places in the house where Susan cannot go. Compare the competence of the contributions Kylie makes here to the near silent, acquiescent, interlocutor in extract 44 when confronted with her mother's complete dominance of the floor. It would seem that any analysis of Kylie's competence based upon parental completion of an adaptive behaviour checklist (recall, Kylie has 'no brains' according to her mother), despite being a routinely used methodology in appled intellectual disability research, may mislead. Likewise, to attribute a 'strong disposition' to acquiescence to Kylie would be remarkably tempting on the basis of the interaction between her and her mother. Once again this would offer an artificial, uni-dimensional, and entirely inaccurate account of her interaction competence. Communicative environments, as Leudar and Fraser (1985) observe, may have an important bearing on the display, or otherwise, of competence.

In extract 67 Joan and Gordon negotiate over who will take the rubbish out in an exchange which illustrates delicate management of issues of autonomy and agency. Note the way in which Gordon proposes that, as he is going to stay and look at the paper, it should be Joan who takes the rubbish bag out in lines 4–5; that after a side-sequence on the fullness of the bag, Joan's account of the reason why a half-full bag should be taken out *serves as a preface* for her to gently nudge responsibility for disposal towards the non-specific 'we' (line 8). When this is receipted with an agreement token by Gordon in line 10, it is in overlap with Joan's counter-proposal that Gordon should take the rubbish out.

Extract 67: GH/JB/1998

```
1   JOAN     You've got a day before you go away (.) on your holi↓day
2   GORDON   Yeah
3   JOAN     (   )
4   GORDON   I'm gonna sta: y and look at ↑paper (1.5) O::h take the rubbish
5            (.) bag ↑out
6   JOAN     Yeah ↑how full is ↓it
7   GORDON   Half ↓full
8   JOAN     You've ↑got some food in it so we will have to put it ↓out or it's
9            going to be smel↓ly
10  GORDON   ⌈Yeah
11  JOAN     ⌊Would you like to do that ↑then and then put a new bag
12           ↑in
13  GORDON   I've seen this ↑one ((Closing newspaper))
```

Note how exquisitely attentive Gordon's turn at line 13 ('I've *seen* this one') is to the issue of his status: that is, 'I've seen this one' works to produce Gordon as being happy to comply with Joan's request, despite his earlier avowal of his intention to 'stay and look at paper', *on account of the fact* that the paper is one that he has already seen (implying that he had the option of refusal at his disposal – and may well have not complied had the paper been one he *hadn't* seen). Gordon is thus producing a version of himself as a reasonable man who is prepared to accede to staff requests on his terms: he is not simply a 'resident' who will meekly do as he is told.

Gerald uses a similar style of interaction with William in extract 68 when he arrives to help with dinner preparation. He arrives to find dinner underway and the extract commences with a mundane greeting + return + evaluation sequence between he and William in lines 1–3. This pre-sequence serves then to frame (Goffman, 1974) the upcoming interaction or to set up a pair of cover identities (NOT-STAFF + NOT-CLIENT) under which the interaction can be prosecuted *before* Gerald goes on to establish where the cooking has got to after a pause which, in context, serves as a topic-shift marker in line 3 ('(2 secs) what you into *mate*' – my emphasis). Here, in contrast with extract 3 for example, the interaction appears to be prosecuted *by both parties* in line with the cover identities proposed by Gerald ('mates') in line 3 and reiterated in lines 10 and 15. That is, even though here it is clear who is the one with greater knowledge – for example Gerald's turn in line 6; 'oh you can cook it with the bones in it' – these knowledge displays are met not with resistance or submissive acquiescence, but are receipted *as* knowledge displays. In the case of the information about cooking chicken with the bones in, for instance, Gerald's turn is receipted by William not as a correction (Schegloff *et al.* 1977), an instruction or a directive, but rather as a neutral *piece of information* ('can you'). That *this* receipt is met in line 8, in overlap, with 'oh well you (.) you're nearly there now . . .' plus an understated positive evaluation of William's performance is in marked contrast to earlier extracts we have seen where staff third turns in such circumstances frequently worked to reassert staff control of ongoing activity.

Extract 68: WM/GS/1998

```
1    GERALD    How's it going Will↑iam
2    WILLIAM   All right
3    GERALD    That's ↑good (2.0) what you ↑into ↑mate
4              (3.0)
5    WILLIAM   The ↑bones still in the chicken
6    GERALD    ↑O::h you can ↑cook it with the bones ↑in it
7    WILLIAM   Can ⌈↓you
8    GERALD         ⌊Oh well you (.) you're nearly there now (0.2) may as well
9              keep ↑going you're doing an alright ↑job (1.0) did you (.) do
10             your hands ↑mate
11             (2.0)
12   WILLIAM   Yeah
13   GERALD    You did ↓oh well ↑I'll do mine
14             (10.5)
15             watcha ↑cookin' tonight ↑mate (.)
16             Chicken obvious↑ly
17             ((William holds up jar))
18   GERALD    Ssa:↓tay
```

Similarly, both the immediately following sequence (lines 9–13) on hand-washing, and the final adjacency pair (lines 15–17) on satay, work to establish reciprocally co-equal footings. In the handwashing sequence both interlocutors establish cooking hygiene as a *mutual responsibility*, with Gerald's utterance in line 13 in particular serving to underline these statuses both semantically and, via symmetrical stress, prosodically ('you *did* oh well *I'll* do mine'). Likewise in line 15 Gerald displays both *knowledge gleaned from his observation of William's activity* and also *his ignorance* of the dish under preparation, which deficit William promptly repairs by brandishing a jar of cook-in sauce. The exchange here then, I suggest, is supportive of William's competence rather than constraining of it and, further, conveys a respectful relationship in which *both parties* orient to their shared, intersubjective, understanding that knowledge (here of cooking) is a commodity that is *co-constructed*.

Extract 69 further illustrates the way in which staff–client interactions may be prosecuted in such a manner as to both orient to client competences and also to support, rather than to undermine, displays of mundane competence. Again, dinner is underway and Carol and Leanne are deciding how many potatoes are needed. Here it is noticeable that Carol's opening turn in line 1 is receipted by Leanne with a second pair part *marked for its tentativeness* (the elongation of wel:l and the 'maybe' serving so to do). Here Leanne's turn does not issue direction or instruction but rather leaves open the possibility that the number of potatoes required is a decision within Carol's competence to make.

Extract 69: CH/LE/1998

```
1    CAROL    ↑How many spuds we ↓want Gwyn (.) ah::m Le↑anne how
2             many ↑spuds
3    LEANNE   Wel:l maybe one potato ↑each
4    CAROL    Yeah (.) ↑I need more than one got↑ta  ⌈eat-
5    LEANNE                                          ⌊Yeah but ↑when it's cut
6             u↑p (.) it makes ↓more (.) so ↑if ↑if ↑if you cut each pota↓to in half
7             and then half a↓ga↑in (.) that means you get four pieces of potato
8             so it's ↑like you get one big po↓tato (0.2)
9             ↑You can have more if ↓you ↑want
10   CAROL    ⌈No
11   LEANNE   ⌊That's (.) that's enough ↓for me:↑:
12   CAROL    That's e↑nough (.) that be e↑nough ↑cut (.) all cut ↑up
13   LEANNE   Have you got ↑three there ↓have ↑you
14   CAROL    Yeah
15   LEANNE   Yeah ↑that should be ↓fine ↑when you cut ↓it (.) if you ↑don't
16            think it ↑does (.) look e↓nough then=
17   CAROL    =You get get one more
18   LEANNE   Can get ↓more ↓yeah
```

Similarly we see, in the elaboration offered by Leanne (in lines 5–9) on Carol's complaint (line 4) about the insufficiency of a single spud, that this hearably instructional sequence does *not* close with a reassertion of staff control over decision-making, but rather with the utterance 'you can have more if you want', which hands back the responsibility for making the final decision to Carol. That Carol receives Leanne's proffered instruction as collaborative throughout the extract is evident in her anticipatory turn completion (cf. Lerner, 1996; Sacks, 1992) of Leanne's turn at lines 15–16 with a recycle ('you get get one more' in line 17) of her prior utterance in line 9 '↑*you* can have more if ↓you ↑want'.

In the final extract considered here Gerald comes into the kitchen to see how William is faring with preparing dinner on another evening. Again we note a greeting pre-sequence (lines 1–4) which proposes the identities under which the interaction to come is to be prosecuted, and which is separated from the business in hand by a long pause before Gerald's first 'business' turn in line 6 which opens with the news-mark 'oh'.

Extract 70: WV/GS/1998

```
1   GERALD     How you goin' there ↑Wills
2   WILLIAM    All right ↑Gerald
3   GERALD     Getting it together ↑mate
4   WILLIAM    Yep
5              (5.0)
6   GERALD     O:oh hang on ↑Wills
7   WILLIAM    ↑Mm
8   GERALD     You've actually gotta ↑break (0.5) from a solid ↑block ↑see
9              how that's really so↑lid
10  WILLIAM    Yeah 'tis solid    ⌈block
11  GERALD                        ⌊Solid as a ↓rock (.) isn't ↓it
12  WILLIAM    Yeah
13  GERALD     It's ↓frozen so (.) we gotta thaw it ↓out by putting it in the
14             micro↑wave
15  WILLIAM    Yeah in micro    ⌈wave
16  GERALD                      ⌊We gotta thaw it ↓out
17             (2.0)
18  WILLIAM    Yeah
19  GERALD     So (1.0) ((Clears throat)) (2.5) what do you reckon we should
20             do with it (.) to thaw it ↓out
21  WILLIAM    Mm put it in the micro↓wave
22  GERALD     ↑ Yep (.) good think↓ing
```

Note in line 6 that the newsmark is accompanied by a non-specific alerting via the attention getting device 'Wills'. William is alerted to the need to 'hang on', but no *direct* identification of error on his part is offered. Instead, Gerald waits until William's response ('↑mm') fails to display an immediate awareness of what the 'news' at issue is (that the sausages are a frozen block in need of breaking up) before he draws William's attention to the need to rectify the situation.

The following two sequences (the 'solid as a rock' material in lines 8–11 and the 'microwave' material in lines 12–18) show the classic markers of collaborative pedagogic, or 'classroom', talk (McHoul, 1978): that is they follow the pattern of teacher formulation of the PROBLEM + STUDENT recycle of the PROBLEM + TEACHER confirmation (with possible upgrade). Like the effects of interviewers using 'expansion-questions' in Antaki *et al.*'s (2002) study, or the 'clueing' and 'contextual-ising' devices in classroom interaction (Edwards and Mercer, 1987), here Willliam 'comes up, apparently spontaneously, with the right answer, or the full answer, without the original answer being challenged explicitly as wrong' (Antaki *et al.* 2002: 451). Schematically the exchange can be represented as follows:

1. Teacher formulation   You've actually gotta ↑break (0.5) from a solid
                         ↑block ↑see how that's really so↑lid
2. Student recycle   Yeah 'tis solid ↓block
3. Teacher confirmation Solid as a ↓rock (.) isn't ↓it

Of particular note in this extract is the closing sequence. Again in contrast to other extracts discussed earlier, in the final three turns it is to William that Gerald, the staff member, hands responsibility for the decision about thawing.

Extract 70: WV/GS/1998 (detail)

19	GERALD	So (1.0) ((Clears throat)) (2.5) what do you reckon we
20		should <u>do</u> with it (.) to thaw it ↓out
21	WILLIAM	Mm put it in the micro↓wave
22	GERALD	↑Yep (.) good think↓ing

While clearly 'what do you reckon we should do with it to thaw it out' (line 19) is a 'test question' (there is absolutely no reason for us to believe that Gerald does not know what should be done), it is also evident that by both soliciting a competent response from William, which he offers in line 21, and then offering a positive acknowledgement of it, Gerald is here supporting and underpinning William's abilities rather than constraining them. As such this sequence reflects the organisation of interaction identified by Schegloff *et al.* (1977) in that the correction is instructional and competency *building*, rather than otherwise.[4] In this regard this sequence is indeed relevant to 'those who are still learning or being taught to operate in a system which requires that, for its routine operation, they be adequate self-monitors and self-correctors as a condition of competence' (1977: 381).

[4] Similar correction sequences have been identified in aphasic–spouse interactions (Lindsay and Wilkinson, 1997); second language learning (Gaskill, 1980) and adult–child interaction (Drew, 1981).

6   A deviant case . . .

with Alec McHoul

Who are the mental defectives?

(Wechsler, 1958: 49)

At one stage in his lectures Sacks (1992: 312–19) addresses the issue of 'omni-relevant devices' for categorising persons. He refers in particular to devices that contain pairs of categories such as THERAPIST + PATIENT(S) and TEACHER + STUDENT(S). By 'omni-relevant' he does not intend that any given person carries with them, at all times, incumbency in that device. Hence, because one is a therapist (for certain purposes) that does not mean that belonging in that category (from the paired device) would necessarily be relevant at, say, a barbecue or a concert. What it does mean is that, in particular, in therapy sessions, that one is the therapist and the others are the patients is a classification of persons that can be invoked, depended upon and hearably mentioned or implied under pretty much any circumstances during such sessions. That is, along with other such categorisation devices, even the 'omni-relevant' varieties are locally occasioned, and indeed may be indirectly proposed (see, for example Gerald and Will's management of the omni-relevance of the NOT-STAFF + NOT-CLIENT device in chapter 5). As we have seen earlier, in discussion of Simmons-Mackie and Damico's (1999) study of an aphasia therapy session, it can be plausibly suggested that it is precisely the omni-relevance of devices such as THERAPIST + PATIENT that made the in-session transition from this pairing to that of COMPETENT CONSUMER + INADEQUATE SERVICE PROVIDER so problematic (and indeed Simmons-Mackie and Damico (1999) address this point, albeit under the rubric of the notion of 'social roles').

Specifically, the omni-relevance device is an available resource in particular *single conversations*; for example, in the talk analysed by Sacks, where a group therapy session is being conducted. Hence it is the therapist and not the patients that, for example, introduces a new member to the group and that affords the opportunity for anticipatory turn completion of therapist utterances by patients as a site for the doing of humour. Or, in other cases, it's incumbent on a teacher (rather than any of the students) to announce that the seminar is over.

The question then remains: how could an all-parties orientation to a local rule such as 'there is an omni-relevant device operating in this talk' be seen to be occurring for any given empirical case? In early ethnomethodology, one way would be to construct a 'breach study' (Garfinkel, 1967) where, for example, one party (teacher, therapist, etc.) was deliberately instructed to act as something other than an incumbent of that category in interaction with the others (students, patients . . .). Today, such research techniques are regarded as unethical (Mehan and Wood, 1975) – since deliberately structured breakdowns of local social relations can have (and, in the past, have had) far-reaching consequences. The best that could be hoped for would be a naturally occurring breach study where an incumbent of a locally possible category in an omni-relevant device simply did not act as if the rule for such devices were in force for a particular stretch of talk – and, moreover, without announcing that fact. How the other or others in the interaction worked with its absence and/or to bring the rule into operation, or how they might not, may then demonstrate its local operativity.

Such instances would be where, for example, teachers or therapists, for whatever reason, went into a classroom or consulting room without 'doing being teachers' or 'doing therapy' and rather, conducted themselves such that what 'officially' was supposed to be a seminar or a therapy session was 'mere chat' between non-incumbents of the categories TEACHER + STUDENTS or THERAPIST + PATIENT. In the data that follow such an event is apparent: a professional – here, an administrator of a psychological assessment instrument – conducts the business at hand in a manner that is describable (at the very least) as delaying or (at the most) hearable as showing little apparent interest in getting the formal business of the talk (the assessment) underway.[1] The question is, then, as follows: if omni-relevance is pertinent to this setting (and a major part the analysis in this chapter turns on showing whether or not it is), how does that omni-relevance *actually appear* in the materials when the 'professional' (who should, if it is operational, clearly be the initiator of the business-at-hand – since it's his reason for being there at all) does not orient the talk in that (the appropriate) direction but, on the contrary, does anything but, as it were, take his proper place? If the omni-relevance device appears

---

[1] The psy-complex (Rose, 1985) rejoinder here might be to gloss the pre-initiation section of the talk as 'rapport-building' or some such other professional activity. Of course if it is accepted that the asssessor's apparent lack of interest in formal business is, in fact, the doing of a variant of formal business, then the perspicacity of his interlocutor is that much more apparent, and the breach, when it comes, that much more startling.

under these (presumably rare) circumstances, then this offers empirical evidence for holding that such a rule actually exists as a concrete social object. And if it does so exist, there are clearly consequences for how at least one other possible categorisation of persons: that which provides for persons to be (called) 'intellectually disabled' or 'mentally retarded' is conceptualised.[2] The specific concern here is with what can be learnt about the capacities of persons described as 'intellectually disabled' from a what appears to be a 'deviant' case. That is, via an analysis of the operationalisation of Sacks's conjecture regarding the candidate social scientific object he described as an 'omni-relevant device', it is possible to see more clearly precisely the subtlety and sophistication of the grasp that definitionally 'incompetent' members have of structures of social action. Sacks defines an 'omni-relevant device for conversation' thus:

An 'omni-relevant device' is one that is relevant to a setting via the fact that there are some activities that are known to get done in that setting, that have no special slot in it, i.e. do not follow any given last occurrence, but when they are appropriate, they have priority. Where, further, it is the business of, say, some single person located via the 'omni-relevant device', to do that, and the business of others located via that device, to let it get done. (1992: 313–14)

If, in the following transcript, then, it can be shown that there are indeed (a) 'some activities that are known to get done' in this setting which (b) 'have no special slot' but do (c) 'have priority', and such that (d) it is one of the parties' business to do those activities. If all four features are provably oriented to by the participants, then an omni-relevant device is operating. Conversely, if any one feature of the array (a) to (d) is not provably oriented to in the transcribed talk, by the participants in the talk, it cannot be confidently asserted that the omni-relevance device is present.

In the extract that follows we again meet Mike (a clinical psychologist) who is visiting Bob (a man described as 'moderately intellectually disabled' by the agency which provided his supported housing) as part

---

[2] The preamble to the QOL.Q begins by noting that it is specifically designed for use with 'persons with mental retardation'. Accordingly, for at least one of the parties to the talk (the assessor), that categorisation of the other party (the assessee) is at least *possibly* relevant. To pre-empt the analysis perhaps a little, it appears from the data that this identity is not locally relevant to any great extent. That is, neither party appears *directly* to orient as such to the possibility that one of the speakers is formally describable as 'retarded'. That is to say, there is no absolutely unambiguous NORMAL + RETARDATE device apparent in the transcript. (However, as at least one reader of the transcript has noticed, it is possible to hear a note of over-done praise in some of Mike's remarks to Bob – thanks to Karen Tracy for this noticing. Much turns here on how one hears such items as, for example, 'oh very good' in line 10.) This highly problematic matter (and its connection to the omni-relevance phenomenon) is returned at the end of the chapter.

of an audit of the service. As will become clear later, it is important to note that the written record of this visit confirms that it occurred on 24 December 1994.

Extract 71: Code HB/MR/TT

```
1    Bob    (———this) in 'e:re (2.0)
2    Mike   [^t] w'll it's in a state >isn't it<
3    B      eh?=
4    M      =eh? (.) >when you got ⌈(—)<
5    B                          ⌊for Chris:mas
6           (2.0)
7    M      °oh°
8           (2.0)
9    B      (we got er:::) (.) we got from Asda
10   M      oh very good (. .) lots of chocolate
11          (2.0)
12   B      >(there's me- there's me)< (cake up there).h
13   M      you save it up for Christmas
14   B      yeah
15          (7.0) ((shuffling and chair scrapings))
16   B      do y' take sugar
17   M      oh there's some here on the table (. .) Bob
18   B      d'y' take (.) do you take sugar
19   M      yes please (.) >let us have<=
20   B      =how many?
21   M      just one of them (.) °please° (. .)
22   B      (——————————) I take two you   ⌈see
23   M                                     ⌊do you? (. .)
24   B      ((sniff)) hh I (—) do us a drink later (. .)
25          later on when:: (. .)
26   M      when we're done
27          (5.0)
28          (?) ((choking syllable))
29          (1.0)
30   B      whereabouts do you: come from
31   M      I come from Marlington (. .) >this morning<
32   B      what part (.)
33   M      erm (.) >well I've got an office< at the County
34          Castle (.)
35   B      office at th- so you go back there (when:)
36          you've bee:n
37   M      yeah
38   B      .hh when you've finished 'ere:
39   M      yeah
40          ((Bob can be heard breathing for 16.0))
41   B      I went to Portugal last June
42   M      did you? (.) whereabouts?
```

```
43   B      yeah (. .) Algar:
44   M      Algarve?
45   B      (eah) yeah
46   M      I've been to Lisbon (. .)
47   B      eh?
48   M      I've been to Lisbon
49   B      been to Lisbon
50   M      <yeah> that was nice
51   B      that's that's where they have all the
52          big ships in it?=
53   M      =yeah (.) that's right (. .) yeah (.) ˍyeahˍ
54   B      (—) we couldn't go to where the: (the bo–) (. .)
55          we couldn't go to where the: >th– the< docks
56          was cos it was a mile off you see
57   M      right (.) so (.) did you sit on the beach (. .)
58   B      ye– yeah
59   M      yeah?
60   B      (no) we went in that (.) went on that (. .) (—)
61          (.) (—) went to that 'ut (1.0) >y'know< that
62          like a café (bur) it's a hut
63   M      oh right (. .) no I °don't° (. .) >I've not I've
64          not< been to the Alga:rve (.) I've only (.)
65          when I went to Portugal I only went to
66          ⌈Lisbonˍ
67   B      ⌊(————)?
68   M      °er° no I don't >I don't< know that (. .) Bob
69   B      that's in Port:ugal
70   M      (oh)? (. .)
71   B      (————) been to Lisbon though have yer (. .)
72   M      where are you going (. .) next time (.)
73   B      J– (.) next year J– Jer:sey
74   M      Jersey (. .) oh that's nice (.) have you been
75          before (.)
76   B      yeah
77   M      >yeah< whereabouts
78          (2.0)
79   B      Saint Helier
80   M      yeah I know it (1.0) >ˍyeahˍ< I know it well
81          (. .) have some friends who live there (.)
82   B      (now:) (there's a por:t ⌈there————)
83   M                            ⌊°yeah° (.) (yeah) are
84          you interested in boats (.) Bob (>ˍare youˍ<)=
85   B      =ye– yeah
86   M      yuh?
87          (4.0)
88   B      (we) got (to) take the pla:ne=
89   M      =hmm (. .) to Jersey
90   B      from Manchester yeah=
```

```
 91   M     =yeah
 92         (4.0)
 93   M     how long will you go for (. .)
 94   B     just a wee:k=
 95   M     =°huh° (1.0) and who you gonna go with
 96         (2.0)
 97   B     °Henry° (. .) Ste:ven: ('t) (1.0) the other
 98         Steven (.) Rod >(no– no)< Steven Pallister (. .)
 99         you wouldn't know 'im ⌈°would you°=
100   M                          ⌊no::
101   M     =°no° is he staff? (. .)
102   B     eh?
103   M     is he staff?=
104   B     =no: (.) °err° res:ident
105   M     hmmm
106   B     .hhh he lives >er he lives< on: Dane Green:
107         (1.0)
108   M     ⌈right
109   B     ⌊°.hhh° (. .) (————) as th the bus tur– (.) the
110         buses turn round to get (.) into Marlington
111   M     mm hm?
112   B     °.hh hhh .h° <ahh> da da da di di di dum: (. .)
113         <daa> da di di di di di dah: (. .) I ma' I made
114         this cup a while ago: (1.0) >I ma'< I made
115         (this) (—) (.)
116         ((2 quiet knocks)) (1.0)
117   M     you made that? (. .) that's very good=
118   B     =(————) but err (1.0) at Wes:ton Roa' long
119         before i' (. .) shut (.) long before the: (1.0)
120         the class shut down.
121   M     hmm: (. .) so pottery classes hm?
122   B     there is a pottery class yeah but >th th< it's
123         not (now) I go to Green Lane now (. .)
124   M     that's quite a trip isn't it?
125   B     eh?
126   M     that's quite a trip
127   B     .hh yeah
128   M     °yeah°
129         (7.0) ((2 knocks and  ⌈pouring sound))
130   B                          ⌊((sings)) °Sa:nta Claus
131         is comin' to town (.) Sa:nta Claus is co:ming
132         to town .h San:ta Claus is co:::ming: to:::
133         tow::n:°
134         ((stirring sound)) (16.0)
135   B     there y'are
136   M     thank you
137   B     (Rod) made this
138         ((tapping noise))
```

```
139   M    yeah? (. .)
140        ((scraping noise for 2.0))
141   M    >that was nice<
142        (5.0) ((2 scrapes))
143        (?) ((whistles))
144   B    hhh (do you know more) than the residents
145        there?
146   M    erm?
147   B    (at the County Castle)
148   M    I think so ⌈yeah (. .) I know quite a lot of them
149   B           ⌊((slurping noise)) eh?
150   M    I know quite a lot of them (.) there's not many
151        people left there now though
152   B    no: (.) °er° .h >most of< um:: died didn't
153        they?
154   M    hmm died or moved out (. .) °hm?° did you used
155        to (. .) °hhh° be at the Castle
156   B    yeh=
157   M    =°yeh°
158   B    I didn't like it much
159   M    no:?
160   B    .hhh I'd sooner be 'ere
161   M    yeah (.) how long have you been here Bob
162   B    since from nineteen eighty nine
163   M    (right) that's about >(so)< for five years now
164        (. .)
165   B    yeah
166   M    yeah (1.0) and you wouldn't wanna go back
167   B    <no> ((throaty syllable)) °y' can: sti–° (. .)
168        you know what you can do: with it?
169   M    what's that then
170   B    .hh stick it up °where° the monkeys keep their
171        nuts
172   M    °uh huh huh hu° ((sniff)) <yeah> it's not ter
173        (1.0)
174   B    er >sh we sh we< make a start then
175   M    yep (.) okay (1.0) erm=
176   B    =((slurping noise))
177   M    what >we're< what I'm trying to do is find out
178        (.) what people think about (. .) life (.)
179        really
180   B    yes
181   M    yeah? (.) er:m (. .) and so I got some (1.0)
182        questions which I'd like to ask you=
183   B    =questions
183   M    yeah? and (1.0) what I want you to (.) to do is
184   
185        think about (.) where you live and (.) what you
186        do and: (.) how you have fun and your
```

```
187              ⌈family and friends and staff
188   B          ⌊ye– yeah (.) yeah
189   M          (.) yeah?
190   B          yeah
191   M          erm (. .) there are quite a few questions an-
192              and there are (.) three choices of (.) answer::
193              (. .) okay?
194   B          yes:=
195   M          =if I read them out to you (.) and you tell me
196              which one you think's (.) best how you feel (.)
197              yeah?
198   B          YEAH
199   M          is that okay:?
200   B          yes
201   M          erm: (.) >there's °nothing°< it's not right or
202              wrong (.) °(this)° and it's not a test (.) it's
203              ⌈just just trying to find
204   B          ⌊no
205   M          out (.) erm how you (.) how you feel about
206              things
207   B          yer  ⌈yer
208   M               ⌊is that okay?
209   B          yeah
210              (1.0)
211   M          okay (.) can you tell me how old you are to
212              start with Bob
213   B          err (. .) fifty four
```

The business in hand here is the administration of a psychological testing instrument, the same Quality of Life Questionnaire (Schalock and
Keith, 1993) encountered throughout in this book, whose administration begins in the penultimate turn of the transcript. Yet, from the start,
with his discussions about topics such as the state of Bob's house and the
upcoming Christmas festivities, Mike (the assessor) appears to display
very little interest in getting that business underway. That this business
is expectable is, however, hearable in the various pro-terms for it that
are used early in the transcript: for example in the joint completion in
lines 25 and 26 ('later on when we're done') and in Bob's 'when you've
finished here' (line 38). Something that both parties know is, then, to be
'finished' or 'done' – and what that is cannot be other than the business-
at-hand, the assessment. No other candidates are available. One does
not, for example, in 'ordinary' conversation routinely advert to having to
'finish it' at the outset of its prosecution: a conversation is not that sort
of a thing.

It is also audible, then, that, at lines 27–9, *immediately following* mention of the current business's being, at some later point, 'done', Bob is offering Mike (via the six-plus second pause in which he chooses not to self-select) an entré into an initiation of the business that is to be, at some unspecifiable stage, 'done' (the test). An even more extreme example follows the second mention of the business ('when you've finished here', line 38) where Bob leaves a very long gap of 16 seconds. Consequently, it is plausible that Bob at least is orienting to the candidate identities ASSESSOR + ASSESSEE via the assumption that only the former (Mike) ought properly to initiate the test and that the most the latter (Bob) can do is to offer possible slots for that to happen, thereby producing his silences as hearable *invitations-to-initiate*. Bob makes similar uses of silence at lines 87, 129 and 142, offering five likely cases in all (along with some less definite candidates). What follows these relatively long pauses is not without its significance either.

In the first case (following lines 27–9), Bob offers a polite query: 'whereabouts do you come from?' This may possibly be formulated as concerning Mike's *place of origin* since '. . . do you come from?' rather than '. . . have you come from?' tends to do that kind of work. On the other hand, this is picked up by Mike as a query about his *current place of work* and Bob does not repair that interpretation. In the second case (following line 38), the invitation-to-initiate ('when you've finished here') is again not taken up, whereupon Bob starts out on a new topic – his holiday in Portugal the previous summer. In the third case (following line 87), Bob continues the topic of his projected summer holiday to Jersey. After the seven-plus second pause at line 129, Bob breaks into a festive song – and indeed, given the date, one that is highly seasonally relevant. And finally, following line 142, he returns to querying Mike about his job and whether he knows many ('more than'?) residents of the hospital from which Bob has been 'resettled'. So the pattern is:

1. Long pause + 'Where do you come from?' + Place of work (Hospital)
2. Long pause + New topic: holiday (Portugal)
3. Long pause + Topic continued: holiday (Jersey)
4. Long pause + Singing (Festive song)
5. Long pause + Topic: knowledge of hospital residents (being a psychologist)

Now while, with the possible exception of the singing (though as the interview was conducted the day before Christmas this is moot), these can be matters that are ubiquitous topics for chat (places of origin, one's holidays, one's job, persons possibly known in common) – and chat with pretty much anyone one happens to meet.[3] However, it's also the case (and this time including the singing) that they display a deep and abiding knowledge (on Bob's part) of the kind of encounter this is. To wit: the other is a psychology professional, at Bob's house to perform an assessment (which he should initiate, and is being repeatedly invited to initiate), and that assessment has to do with Bob's happiness and well-being. And all this such that, moreover, should he be found wanting in the 'quality of life' department, his place of residence could be officially altered – and, on his own estimation (lines 170–1), for the worse.[4] Accordingly, it is incumbent on Bob (if the assessment is not to proceed formally, as such, at least for now) to display, nevertheless, that he is indeed extremely happy: he takes overseas holidays, he's looking forward to Christmas, he sings, and so forth.[5] Add to this his other topics: taking an interest in shipping, being successful at pottery, having a sizeable group of friends, and so forth, and it becomes clear that this – *doing* having a great quality of life, or at least being content with his lot – is what is being accomplished in (or via) the chat. One further possible piece of evidence for this is that Bob does not resort to that ubiquitous topic *par excellence*, the weather. Being December in the North of England, of course, the weather is far from mentionable as contributing to *anyone's* happiness. On the contrary, it can only be a complainable. ('I really love all this rain and sleet and freezing wind' would, for example, clearly be prejudicial to the project of 'doing being happy'; it would also, surely, run the risk of producing Bob as a little odd to say the least).[6] It is also the case that the selection of Bob's conversational topics can be heard as performing the function of demonstrating his recognition and display, both early on (item 1 – workplace) and after several invitations to initiate (item 5 – knowledge of hospital residents), that the presumably somewhat puzzling reluctance of Mike to initiate *his* business-at-hand is an

---

[3] See the analysis of this in McHoul and Rapley (2000).

[4] That Bob is not in any way an anomaly in this regard is demonstrated by other interviews in the corpus. In one instance, as we have seen in chapter 3, the psychologist's post-preamble invitation to the testee to 'ask any questions that they have' is met with the blunt statement 'I like living here', twice repeated.

[5] Whereas Bob's singing could be construed (for example, under standard psychological descriptions) as a 'dis-inhibition' or as a 'psychotic break', note that this putative description is less than compelling for the following reasons. (1) The very seasonal topicality of the particular song he chooses to sing (he is very clearly oriented to time); (2) The absence of any evidence of similar behaviour throughout the interaction (which extends some one-and-a-half hours); (3) The utter cogency and interactional sophistication of Bob's interlocution throughout.

[6] Throughout his analyses of the Group Therapy Session materials, Sacks shows how the 'patients' work hard to avoid being heard as 'crazy'. This does not of course in any way afford the view that they were 'in denial' or 'invisible to themselves' (cf. chapter 4).

accountable that may be delicately repaired by the offer of a cognate topic. Whichever of these interpretations is accepted (and the former is taken up at more length below) such delicacy and artfulness is not routinely ascribed to persons described as 'intellectually disabled', in part at least – as has been argued throughout – because it is only extremely rarely that researchers, clinicians and therapists take the trouble to pay detailed attention to the practices by which (in)competence is realised in interaction.

Accordingly there is at least a strong suspicion that Bob, at certain points, by pausing for some seconds, is 'hearably' inviting Mike to get on with initiating the assessment (the activity which the possible omni-relevant device might be said to 'assign' him).[7] For all this, though, there are other possible ways of reading the pauses – such as that Bob is preparing cups of tea, or simply that he is trying to think of something else to say to this 'professional' who has come to his house to 'assess' him. But earlier work on this corpus has shown how 'cover identities' are clearly operating in this transcript. (See Antaki and Rapley, 1996a.) Sacks (1992) has shown how cover identities routinely work hand-in-hand with omni-relevant devices when such devices are, in fact, present. Accordingly, the conversational niceties, the tea-making, and the rest, can be seen as ways in which Bob and Mike (noting that Mike, too, initiates 'chat' sequences (e.g. line 46)) engage in the production of cover identities; making themselves over into 'acquaintances' – or as Antaki and Rapley (1996a) put it 'not-psychologist' and 'not-client' – who might easily engage in 'mere chat' (McHoul and Rapley, 2000) – or, here, NOT-PSYCHOLOGIST + NOT-CLIENT.

In this respect, the 'cover identities' and the 'cover topics' they invoke can be seen as ways of dealing with the situation in which these members find themselves: 'informally' working up to the formal 'business' of the visit (the assessment of Bob's 'quality of life') and so, in some 'covering' (*informal*) way, actually *doing* it. It is therefore worth noting that the point at which the assessment-proper is initiated (line 174) comes just when the talk has started to turn away from everyday niceties and towards professional-evaluational matters; as though the cover identities and topics had begun to fray or otherwise wear thin. If this is the case,

---

[7] We are very grateful to one of the anonymous reviewers of the first version of this analysis for pointing this out. That reviewer rightly notes that, without recourse to the question of cover identities, the analysis could involve a circularity: 'the authors suggest that an omni-relevant device *might* be operative in the talk, and then they interpret Bob's silences as invitations for Mike to start, which in turn demonstrates that the device *is* operative'. This part of the chapter relies extensively on a number of points taken almost verbatim from that reviewer's very useful comments.

then this is not a situation where the participants are, as it were, simply *waiting* for the omni-relevant device to show its face; rather, by invoking cover identities, they are mutually showing the device to be always potentially operable at any given moment. They are co-producing a similar process to the teenagers discussed by Sacks (1992) who systematically 'cover' the THERAPIST + PATIENT(S) device by using others such as TEENAGERS + ADULT(S). In parallel fashion, a topic like 'automobiles' can cover for the business of therapy *as such*. As Sacks puts it, 'an automobile discussion':

Is, for teenage boys, a very special kind of topic; one which is perhaps as ideal a one as could be had if one wanted not simply cover identification but a *'cover topic'*. [A]nd that's because of the range of matters which are expectable and in fact discussed at a place such as this, i.e. therapy topics, which can be discussed under the guise of 'an automobile discussion': Sex, guilt, independence, autonomy, authority, parental relations, the state of society, death, you name it. All can perfectly well be handled as sub-topics of 'an automobile discussion'. (Sacks, 1992: 320)

To put this simply: why else would 'cover identities' or 'cover topics' be needed by any speakers ('members', 'participants') unless there were *something to cover*? – and what would need covering more than an omni-relevant device and the other-than-cover identities (NORMAL + RETARDATE, PSYCHOLOGIST + PATIENT, and, ergo, topics) it entails? This is, arguably, why Bob is discussing holidays, singing, talking about his circle of acquaintances; why, in short, he is doing displaying 'happiness' (for want of a better term). All these topics are perfectly feasible for 'chit-chatters' or 'acquaintances'; they are, to be sure, mere 'niceties', but what ties them together is that they all, *and without exception* in the long preliminaries to the formal assessment, equally accomplish evidence of a strong and positive 'quality of life' on Bob's part.

Finally, note that Bob makes it perfectly clear to Mike that he understands the practical consequences of the up-coming test. He understands, that is, that test 'failure' (despite Mike's later assurances, in lines 201–3, that the encounter is *not* a 'test') can lead to a return to the institution: for, at lines 152–71, he graphically compares his current public-housing situation to the hospital (the 'Castle'), the latter being insertable 'where the monkeys keep their nuts' (lines 170–1). Immediately following this, as Mike finishes his laughter (marked as '°uh huh huh hu°') but not his turn, Bob again waits briefly (one second) and, perhaps because five invitations-to-initiate have passed without success, *he, Bob, the assessee, actually initiates the formal activity of the test* with 'Should we make a start then?' (line 174).[8] This is, again, both highly artful on Bob's part and augments (rather than diminishes) the evidence for an omni-relevant device being invoked and oriented to in this fragment.

That is items (a) to (d) *are* operational. To summarise:

(a) There are 'some activities that are known to get done': namely a psychological assessment has to take place and, therefore, has to be *initiated* or pre-announced as about to take place. Both Mike and Bob use a variety of pro-terms early on to invoke and orient to 'what it is we're here for' and project the (other) sorts of interaction which may be possible once that business is 'finished with'.

(b) Initiation (getting the test going) 'has no special slot': evidently, since initiation does not even follow (repeated) invitations-to-initiate. Therefore there is no particular place in the conversation where either party can easily predict when the assessment will actually start; initiations can – and in the instant case demonstrably do – follow on from *any* previous activity.

(c) These activities, the initiation, 'have priority': so much so that if they are not done by the one who should (see [d] below), then, in two-party conversations at least, *there is only one other* who can – and here does. In fact there is a clear sense in the transcript that, while there is no special slot for the assessment to get going, that does not mean that it can't be heard as 'late arriving' or that it's 'about time' a start was made. Further, once testing, *per se*, is unavoidably and unambiguously initiated, it *cannot but* be taken up, and promptly is.

(d) It is one of the parties' business to do those activities: the assessor ought *properly* to do the initiation.

It is item (d) that is particularly bolstered by Bob's 'Should we make a start then?' That is, it can be heard as (mild?) criticism of the adequacy of Mike's incumbency of the category of psychologist/assessor. Firstly, it uses the pro-term 'we' which, in this transcript and in transcriptions of many hours of similar assessment talk, is almost never used by the assessee/respondent, but frequently by staff or professionals, to refer to the two present parties. Accordingly, it can be clearly heard as an 'appropriation' of the assessor's position, given that any such 'appropriation' is simultaneously a *display* that the assessee must *know* the assessor's position. Secondly, it has the unusual sequential status of, for example, a school student asking a dithering teacher 'Can we start the lesson now, Sir?' or a job interviewee asking 'Aren't we going to talk about my qualifications?' and so on. All of these ('Should we . . .?,' 'Can we . . .?,' 'Aren't

___

[8] And/or perhaps because the topic has now (at Bob's delicate instigation) reverted to Mike's offical and professional status thereby making his duties in this encounter explicitly a mentionable.

we . . . ?') set up binary contrast classes: clearly implying a definite X (the formal business) as against an indefinite something else, Y, that we are now (hereby) being formulated as having been doing up until now (chat, gossip, idle banter, talk that anyone can do regardless of incumbency). How better, in its material effect then to show that a device should be present, and should be being oriented to, than by deliberately, artfully and symmetrically reversing one of its major features: namely feature (d), that it is (intersubjectively known) to be one of the parties' business to lead (into) the expectable activities and *utterly not* the other's – such that the other party should, to quote Sacks, merely '*let* it get done'. A rule such as this then may be even more audibly present in the breach than in the observance.

Two major implications flow from this analysis. The first concerns the omni-relevant device itself; the second – again – bears on conventional wisdom concerning the conversational status of 'intellectually disabled' persons.

Firstly, an omni-relevant device can be provably heard in this stretch of talk even when, for a considerable time, it is not explicity enacted by the expectable party but is demonstrably heard instead as *pertinently* absent by the other.[9] Moreover, in its absence, its work is achieved by various proxies for it in the form of 'cover identities' and 'cover topics'. This suggests confirmation of Sacks's conjecture about omni-relevant devices. Moreover, it does so by using something close to his own confirmation procedures – cf. 'He didn't even say hello' as a way of showing that absent greetings can be *pertinently* absent and have consequences for the moral, professional, etc. status of the perpetrator.

It also turns out that, in the instant case, the rule-required orientation to omni-relevance is, despite the professional assessor's apparent lack of interest in it, maintained and eventually *enforced* by Bob, the intellectually disabled lay assessee. It is crucial to recognise the import of this interven- tion on Bob's part. Here someone who, for all official purposes, is essen- tialised as an incompetent: a 'moderately intellectually disabled' person, a 'resident' (in his own terms) diagnostically defined *by virtue of* his sup- posed social and interactional incapacity. As we have seen repeatedly in

---

[9] Another possible reading is as follows. Sacks (1972) distinguishes between a Device-R (then a 'Collection-R'), a device with co-equal categories (such as FRIEND–FRIEND or STRANGER–STRANGER) and a Device-K (then 'Collection-K'), a device with- out such co-equality (such as POLICEMAN–SUSPECT or TEACHER–STUDENT). In the present materials, it is possible to hear Mike constructing himself and Bob, at least until line 177, as Device-R co-members, while Bob constructs himself and Mike as Device-K co-members throughout. Significantly, Bob's device-construction 'wins' any possible 'contestation' between the devices. See Sacks (1972) and the exegesis by Silverman (1998).

earlier chapters, if we accept the prevailing views in the various literatures Bob should, *inter alia*, also be so prone to acquiescence bias as to be an unreliable informant – saying 'yes' regardless of question content, agreeing to nonsensical propositions about matters such as his ethnicity or his flying abilities, or otherwise demonstrating a meek subservience to the demands of his 'unimpaired' interlocutor; he should be demonstrating that he is so experientially and/or cognitively deficient as to be incapable of understanding the meaning of his social status as 'intellectually disabled', indeed he should endeavour if at all possible to distance himself from any and all associations with members of that category; and finally he should clearly so lack the basics of social competence as to render meaningful interaction problematic at best. As is evident Bob displays none of these supposedly definitional characteristics of his professionally ascribed diagnostic status.

That such a (institutionally, officially, diagnostically) 'non-member' can, and evidently does, the delicate and sensitive interactional work seen in this interview more than suggests that rules such as that in question here (the omni-relevance device rule) are ubiquitous for talk – that is, where they are properly operational, they can be hearably oriented to *no matter what* the putative supra-local statuses of the parties to the talk (e.g. one a psychologist and one 'with an intellectual disabilty').

In this respect, the two points are linked. If so-called intellectually disabled persons can and must do such things, then anyone can and must, and also: if the intellectually disabled can and must, then they are vastly more competent, by any measure, than the psy-complex (Rose, 1990) literatures give credit for. If conversation, as a ubiquitous instance of sociality, displays such order (as in 'social order'), conversation displays it as being 'order at all points' (Sacks, 1992: 483–5) – including, as we have seen throughout, at those points where the (supposedly) least 'orderly' participants are located. And that says something important about both the order – and more pertinently for present purposes – about the participants.

7 Some tentative conclusions

Forms of life are always forms of life forming. Realities are always realities becoming.

(Mehan and Wood, 1975: 32)

Truth, that is to say, is always enthroned by acts of violence.

(Rose, 1999a: np)

Constructing 'the person with an intellectual disability' – 'the tutelage of experts'

We have examined how it is that psychology, and members of its allied trades, have come to constitute one of their key objects of study: the 'person with an intellectual disability'. The person under these descriptions is, *a priori*, socially and interactionally incompetent and suffers from cognitive deficits or conceptual impairments. Or in Alan's words, they are 'thick like'. Regardless of recent moves by professional associations and publishers of diagnostic manuals to stress the *interaction* between persons and their environments, and the specification of 'systems of supports', rather than the identification of 'levels' of retardation (AAMR, 2002), in practice the hypothetical construct 'intellectual disability' continues to be reified as a core, or essential, aspect of personhood: or rather, in much of the literature, an unambiguous identity that individuals *have*, whether they confess it or not. And as we have seen – in a remarkable exercise in circular reasoning – it is precisely the failure to fulfil the contemporary obligation to be the confessing subject, in the terms specified by the confessor, that is held up as confirmatory evidence of a truly incompetent identity, the trump card of moral disqualification.

Further, we have seen that, as Smith has noted,

The multiple and complex meanings of what is called 'mental retardation' is staggering. The only conceptual 'glue' that holds mental retardation together as a category of human beings is the typological notion that there is some fundamental essence to the universe of characteristics and the vastly differing needs of people identified by the term. Clearly, however, mental retardation is a term used to describe an aggregation of diverse human circumstances. (Smith, 2002: 62–3)

What the current psy 'diagnostic definitions' of intellectual disability have achieved since the 1800s, then, is to furnish the appearance – via the (rhetorical) adoption of scientific method and its trappings (statistics, the experiment, psychometrics, standardised interviewing) and the language of medicine – of an homogenous disorder, where, in practice there is heterogeneity, diversity and uniqueness. The work of the psy-complex here, as in the adjacent field of 'mental illness', then has been to actively construct a form of life as problematic but knowable, as identifiable (but only by specialist disciplinary techniques, not by lay recognition) and, hence as treatable (and again, only through the acquisition and deployment of a technical lexicon and an array of esoteric professional skills).[1] Through such newly constructed disciplinary knowledge, then, power may be exercised. Indeed, as Rose (1999a: np) notes 'psychology has been bound up with a transformation in the nature of social authority that is of fundamental importance for the kinds of society we live in in "the West"'. Central to this exercise of this social authority is the assiduous disguise of the practice of moral exclusion as solicitous attention to the 'needs' of the afflicted, the afflicted being visible in the extent of their deviation from what the same authorities tell us is the 'norm'. And we have seen the fashion in which such exclusion and control is both discreetly and 'scientifically', and occasionally, nakedly and coercively, exercised.

Discussing media and other reporting of the case of an unnamed (other than being a 'young woman labeled retarded') victim of sexual assault, Biklen and Schein (2001) observe that what we have seen played out in the relative privacy of the research interview, quality of life assessment or the domestic setting of the group home, also plays out on a broader stage. That is to say in the public sphere we see precisely the same individualising, atomising, 'experimental' approaches to questions of competence, capacity and status as a unique human being that is characteristic of the current psychologised regime of truth.[2]

Throughout the court proceedings and news coverage of the trial of her abusers, each of her utterances and each of her actions were examined and interpreted, often in a decontextualized way, by psychologists, psychiatrists, news media,

---

[1] Hence the routine appeals both to 'scientific progress' and the ready dismissal of what are condescendingly described as 'folk understandings' (cf. Davies and Jenkins, 1997: 99).

[2] See Hansen, McHoul and Rapley (2003) for a discussion, and Spinozan reformulation, of the hugely problematic notion of the psy-complex's 'individuality' as an adequate descriptor of subjectivity itself.

attorneys, family, and others. She became seemingly more and more isolated as a stereotypical case example of mental retardation, the object of other people's authority to judge her. (Biklen and Schein, 2001: 449)

That is, what the bulk of the literature presents us with is not an account which might allow for the recognition of the doing of competence by persons, but rather 'stereotypical case example[s] of mental retardation' which are, rhetorically, pressed into service (faithfully and veridically, we are assured) to represent the fixed and unchanging being-in-the world of all members assigned to the category (via, of course, the enactment of professional practices). But, to the contrary, as Mehan and Wood have it, 'forms of life are always forms of life forming. Realities are always realities becoming' (1975: 32). That is to say, the psy project seeks to deny flux and fluidity, situatedness and indexicality. Its project can only succeed if decontextualised utterances and actions are construed, histopatholog-ically, as definitive of – and defining – slices of 'reality': and as we have seen this is, overwhelmingly, the case. Where we are offered examples of the talk of people described as intellectually disabled they tend to be presented not as sites for detailed, disinterested, analytic scrutiny but as specimens or *exhibits*: they are flourished as exemplars, instances, or 'object[s] of other people's authority to judge'. That is, very little indeed of the mainstream literature is concerned either to understand or to demonstrate competence: rather it is organised so as to confirm what the researchers already know – that people are cognitively deficient; that they cannot 'validly' complete the simplest interview; that they are 'invisible to themselves'; that they cannot, adequately, define 'learning difficulties'. And, in keeping with the disciplinary project, in both of its senses, rhetor-ically these accounts serve to display the correctness – not to mention the power – of the psy-disciplines' 'authority to judge'.

But it is important also to remember that 'normality', as we currently understand it, is a notion that is *itself* the product of the psychological imagination and psychological techniques for its assembly. Rose (1999a: np) has suggested that:

[P]sychology has been bound up with the constitution of a range of new objects and problems over which social authority can legitimately be exercised, and this legitimacy is grounded in beliefs about knowledge, objectivity and scientificity. Notable here are the emergence of normality as itself the product of management under the tutelage of experts.

As Goode has pointed out, the effects of the beliefs in knowledge, objec-tivity and scientificity so strongly held by the psy-complex cannot but lead not only to a failure of imagination, but also to a demonstrable trained incapacity to see, for example, 'normality' in anything other than expert, statistical, terms. Thus we see how Sacks's demonstration that it is utterly normative, entirely mundane, and *every* member's business to attend to 'doing being ordinary' (in the ethnomethodological sense of being massively routinely to be encountered, in the doing of every day life, by everyday members) is bent and twisted – by social scientists who appear only to understand that, as people with an intellectual disability are, by their own definition, not 'normal', they are not the same as 'us' – into morally negative evaluations disguised as social scientific fictions such as 'denial' and 'passing'.

That is, there is nothing, in fact, which differentiates a man with HIV downplaying his status as such, a researcher resisting the suggestion that they perhaps smoke too much, or a robbery suspect from claiming to have been elsewhere, from someone described as intellectually disabled declining to accept without struggle the moral opprobrium which attaches to such 'identities'. What differs is that in the former cases (though debatably in the case of HIV) there is the possibility of the successful contestation of the legitimacy of the exercise of the power conferred on the psy professions, and their associated agencies of control, to name problematic conduct as pathology. That is we would not readily accuse a thief of attempting to 'pass' as 'normal' by virtue of proffering an alibi, nor a heavy smoker of being 'in denial' of their 'true' identity as an upshot of a refusal to confess chain smoking. Yet psy continues to suggest that 'being intellectually disabled' is an uncontestable identity inherent in the individual, in a way which it abandoned (if only temporarily) in the case of criminality with the discrediting of Eugenics. In these cases then, we seem to be prepared to accept that it is an unremarkable part of everyday life that persons attend to face and face threats, and yet once a diagnosis of 'intellectual disability' has been made, such mundane – dare one say it, normal – practices are pressed into service as a warrant for the discrediting of those who employ them. As I have argued throughout, if people with an intellectual disability can be seen, demonstrably, to attend to warding off the ascription of morally negative characteristics or identities this, surely, is testament to their competence – not its negation.

Similarly, we have seen that the psy professions are adept at setting up another neat, but 'scientific', Catch 22 for the objects of their gaze. That is, people are constructed in the extensive psychological and sociological literatures as, by default if not disposition, entirely unreliable and invalid reporters on their own experience. Once more the invention of a 'strong disposition' to 'acquiescence' as part-and-parcel of the professionally homogenised 'disorder' serves to discredit those who would, perhaps, object to their own objectification. Recall that we are told by the 'discoverers' of the phenomenon that 'the validity of answers given by mentally retarded people can *never* be assumed: it must be demonstrated' (Sigelman *et al.* 1982: 518). This, in practice, amounts to a supposedly scientific legitimation of the silencing of an entire class of citizens: moral disqualification via denial of co-membership in the category of the fully ethical, truthfully confessing, human subject. Or as Gergen puts it, 'a politics by other means' (Gergen, 2001: np).

Yet upon a close examination of both the original and the contemporary means of production of the phenomenon, we see that it is equally plausible to suggest, as did Binet (1905) that 'if a person is forced to give an absurd reply by making use of an alternative pronounced in an authoritative voice, it does not in the least prove that he is lacking in judgment'. Rather, what inspection of the talk of people with intellectual disabilities in social contexts ranging in formality (and enacted power asymmetry) from official testing; through semi-structured interviews with researchers; to the doing of everyday life in group homes shows, is that 'acquiescence' is perhaps best understood as an entirely local response to what often amounts to blunt coercion, and hence reflects a highly acute judgment of the way things stand with 'being intellectually disabled'. Further, what we have seen is that even in situations where, for local interactional reasons (ranging from the demands of canonical testing protocols to explicit efforts by staff at the control of important decisions in people's lives), submission is actively *demanded,* that people with intellectual disabilities are more than capable of resisting the requirements of staff – and others in positions of authority – that they acquiesce to their will.

That is to say, in discursive psychology's central borrowing from ethnomethodology, if we look at real circumstances, where real issues matter to real people, then we will see rather different things to the artifacts we find if we ask people ridiculous or trick questions in formal testing encounters. If we remove the blinkers of pseudo scientificity, and adopt a slightly humbler and more respectful approach to persons described as intellectually disabled, then perhaps we will not be so quick to describe them as 'active but odd' or to summarily dismiss an inventory of possessions in response to questions about happiness with material circumstances as an 'irrelevance' furnishing only further evidence of constitutional incompetence. That is to say, if we begin to see (and to question) the walls of the regime of truth that demand the utterances of persons described as intellectually disabled be fashioned in terms of standardised psychometric measures, arbitrarily designed by the 'engineers of the human soul', we might just recognise that standardised measures (as Mehan and Wood (1975) showed us) cannot capture the complexity of what it is that persons can know or do.

Another look?

What this suggests is that second wave disability studies must look again at its unquestioning acceptance of the proposition that what psy has confected as an essentialised, interiorised, intellectual disability amounts to a 'real' impairment. As Joseph (2003) has noted, the inventors of the psychometric intelligence test were refreshingly frank about the arbitrariness of their measures, and the explicit design features which *intendedly* produced blacks, other 'non-Nordic' populations and the 'lower orders' as inferior. That is to say, rather than being the neutral scientific instruments that psy today proclaims them to be, IQ tests had built into them, by design, a deliberate reflection of the pre-existing class structures of early twentieth century western societies. It is a short scientistic step, it seems, from being identifiable as an 'idiot' by virtue of 'disgusting' or 'depraved' conduct, to being diagnosed as 'intellectually disabled' in consequence of failing to recall, on demand, the author of *Faust*; of providing a morally suspect account of what one might do with an unopened envelope chanced upon in the street; of offering an original (but not professionally ratified) narrative about a series of badly drawn cartoons; or of finding jigsaw puzzles, children's blocks and yet more badly drawn cartoons less than compelling (Wechsler, 1981).[3] That is to say we have come to take for granted that knowing about Goethe, being conventionally 'honest' (at least when so required by our authoritative confessors), offering conventional rather than imaginative narrative accounts and the 'successful' completion of a range of rather odd tasks is, actually, an accurate reflection of our global competence. This is, itself, a rather bizarre belief and one only sustainable if, again, we trap ourselves within the walls of the psychological imagination. Thus, in summarising his extensive ethnographic study of the Duke family, Taylor suggests that:

Finally, competence is a relative concept (Goode 1994). Although the Dukes and other members of their network may not perform well on standardized tests, in school programs, or in traditional jobs in the mainstream marketplace, they are competent to meet the demands of day-to-day life as they experience it. Bill not only knows the best junking routes, but where to sell junk at the best price. Winnie

---

[3] The persistence of negative moral evaluation as a central component of the identification of the 'defective' – which guided the design of contemporary measures of 'intelligence' – is shown by Wechsler, who notes that 'a mental defective is no longer defined merely as one who . . . is unable to handle himself or his affairs with ordinary prudence, etc., but in addition, as an individual whose lack of intellectual endowment is such as to render him incapable of attaining a minimum score or rating (M.A. or I.Q) on certain standardized intelligence tests' (Wechsler, 1958: 49).

knows where to turn for help when food is scarce. Sammy learned about junk cars from his father. Cindy's 'IEP' in her special education program listed 'Increase Community Awareness' as an annual goal; yet she was very aware and competent to function in stores and other settings within her immediate neighborhood. (Taylor, 2000: 88)

As we have seen throughout this book – whether we look at formalised quality of life assessments conducted by psychologists; informal interviews (at least from the perspective of the researchers – it would seem that their interlocutors may often have disagreed); or at the mundane interaction of staff members and the people they support in community-based homes – that what is to count as (in)competence is negotiated and *constructed* locally, and for local purposes, by local means. In the case of standardised tests what we have also seen is that the nature of the encounters required by them *produce* interactions that are not only shot through with power asymmetry, but also inevitably – in consequence – produce the 'impaired' party as 'happy' but incompetent. Yet, as Marlaire and Maynard (1993: 183) have pointed out: 'testing and assessment procedures upon which school organization and placement rely cannot distinguish language (and cultural differences) from ability differences', and as we have seen, the application of a standardised set of approaches both to *soi-disant* 'normals', and to those deemed *a priori* as deficient, not only cannot but miss displays of cultural competence, but also cements defect via a misappreciation of not only the way that language use is structured in talk-in-interaction, but also of what it actually means to be human (McHoul and Rapley, 2001). And, remarkably, we have seen that this was apparent to none other than Alfred Binet, the inventor of the intelligence test.

That is to say, competence is *very much* a relative concept, and moreover one which is, in actual social practices, actively negotiated. Disability studies theorists can, it appears, see this point clearly when it comes to buses and wheelchairs, microfiches and visual impairment, or ATMs and quadriplegia, but in the case of so called 'intellectual disability' we see a failure of imagination. The error of both 'mainstream psychology', and disability studies to date, is in the dogged insistence on treating capacities to act as if they were fixed, internal, *mental* attributes, of which people may sensibly be said to have quanta: and that not only are these quanta deterministic, they are context-independent. Careful examination of the moment-to-moment conduct of talk-in-interaction (a precaution mainstream psychology studiously avoids, and whose account seems to be taken on trust in disability studies), as we have seen in this book, leads inevitably to the conclusion that such accounts cannot, sensibly, be entertained. The essentialised incompetence of persons described as intellectually disabled is then, as Rose puts it: a 'truth . . . enthroned by . . . violence'.

The upshot of all of this, then, is that what we currently accept (and have since the middle-to-late 1800s) as the truth of an internalised defect of individuals may be, rather, a constraining discursive formation which re-speaks idiocy in newly minted, scientistic, terms. We cannot, without engaging in historicist fallacy, assume that the happy idiots working in the fields of Massachusetts in the 1840s (*American Journal of Insanity*, 1847) bear much resemblance to those today described as intellectually disabled nor, with any certainty, speculate upon the competences or capacities of Swinburne's (1590) 'naturall fooles'. Indeed, given the immense variation – even over the course of the twentieth century – in the range of persons encompassed by the term 'defective', it would probably be rash to assume any relationship of identity. What *does* appear to be the case, however, is that while they may have varied in their details, certain forms of moral conduct have, since the 1800s and the rise of reason at least, continuously attracted reprobation.[4] That is, we may indeed, as Trent has suggested, have merely replaced an outright moral condemnation with a self-proclaimedly scientific reformulation. That is to say, the insistence on the scientificity of 'intellectual disability' today, for all of its supposed diagnostic certainties, may be not so much 'chasing shadows' (Stainton and McDonagh, 2001) as nothing other than the re-invention of the 'feeble-mind'. And such a reformulation is not peculiar to intellectual disability. Rather, as Simmons-Mackie and Damico (1999; ms 31) suggest their aphasia therapy session data show, what we have in the present-day research literatures is: 'an example of [the] potential problems associated with institutionalized therapy routines. Specifically the failure to appreciate potential communicative competence in our clients, the undermining of a client's communicative confidence, and the potential dissolution of a therapeutic relationship.' They go on to ask does the institution of therapy prevent us from viewing the interactive competence of individuals cast as 'disordered'? It would seem that – with 'therapy' understood in its broadest sense, as professionalised psy understandings of, and interactions with, 'those cast as disordered' – the answer must be an emphatic yes.

In this regard Goodey and Stainton note that:

Explaining human nature has always tended to be a job for the elite . . . what is true of the substitution story is also true of most street talk: the etymology of words such as fool, idiot, imbecile, dunce, mong, moron and retard shows that

---

[4] Though see Stainton (2001) for a consideration of the influence of the thought of classical antiquity in contemporary constructions of intellectual disability.

abusive language comes not from the streets but from an exceptionally intellectual subculture as an imagining and construction of its own antithesis . . . Much psychiatry shares with the elite theologies . . . a zest for pathology and a zealous divisiveness in its understanding of human nature – characteristics which it projects both upon its own predecessors and upon the lay public'. (Goodey and Stainton, 2001: 233–4)

We see then that professionalised understandings of people with intellectual disabilities not only collapse 'people' and 'intellectual disabilities' in such a fashion as to reduce personhood, simply, to 'intellectual disability', but with 'a zest for pathology and a zealous divisiveness', also work to discredit, invalidate and de-legitimise any form of understanding other than those prosecuted within its own terms: that is to say 'commonplace intelligibilities are altogether suppressed' (Gergen, 1998: np). We are thus told that all that one needs to know is that someone is describable as 'intellectually disabled' in order to know the person in their entirety, whether or not we deign to attribute such knowledge of themselves, to themselves. And so we see a professionally produced literature which confects persons not only as identical with an authoritatively prescribed diagnostic and social category, but also provides the conditions of possibility for 'care staff', in interaction, to produce such persons as the moral equivalents of dogs and infants. But as discursive psychology argues, and as the data and analysis presented in this book has demonstrated, the pre-eminent psychological imagination simply misunderstands the way that both morality and identity work, and are put to work, in actual interactions. Shakespeare and Watson have it thus:

To assume that disability will always be the key to [their] identity is to recapitulate the error made by those from the medical model perspective who define people by their impairment. Any individual disabled person may strategically identify, at different times, as a person with a particular impairment, as a disabled person, or by their particular gender, ethnicity, sexuality, occupation, religion, or football team. Identity cannot be straightforwardly read off any more, it is, within limit, a matter of choice. (Shakespeare and Watson, 2002: 22)

If 'identity cannot be straightforwardly read off any more' from appearances, so too competence. All of the persons whose talk has been reproduced in this book (bar Connie and Jimmy in chapter 1) are, formally, officially, described – or diagnosed – as intellectually disabled in various 'degrees': as definitionally interactionally incompetent and cognitively deficient. And yet what we have seen is not an homogenous display of inherent incapacity, foolishness and stupidity but rather a frequently sophisticated appreciation of discrimination, an awareness of negative moral evaluations, and – where possible – resistance to the efforts of their interlocutors to exercise authority and control. This exercise of power by the psy professions in the production of persons as a subordinate class may be naked but it is more usually disguised: it is important to recognise that we are not simply dealing with the exercise of 'sovereign' power (Foucault, 1977). Thus in chapter 5 we saw a direct appeal by staff member Jenny to the importance of the accession by Mary to the entirely 'postmodern' project of the governing of her self, despite the fact that were a revision of the WAIS to ask 'who wrote *Discipline and Punish?*' *both* parties would likely fail this particular test of 'intelligence'.

That is, we see that the social construction of incompetence can also proceed via the deployment of strategies which, on the surface, appear entirely benign. Thus it is that, in their study of untrained interviewers administering a quality assurance interview, Antaki *et al.* (2002) found that interviewers could be seen to act 'helpfully' – by celebrating positive responses; suggesting improvements to answers and offering advice; shepherding the respondent's answer into more acceptably official shape; offering helpful candidate answers and prompting recollections of concrete examples as the basis for answering difficult or abstract questions. They suggest that: 'these interviewers are, if you like, embodying their general institutional mission of care' (452–3). Indeed. But of course such practices, while simultaneously producing the interviewers as 'carers', also produce their interlocutors as candidate incompetents *in need of care*, even where it can be seen, in both the data presented by Antaki *et al.* and this book, that such assistance is, often, superfluous.

Re-theorising intellectual disability?

How then might we re-theorise 'intellectual disability'? Perhaps most effectively by refusing to do so. To theorise intellectual disability *as such* is to confer solidity and permanence on that which is nothing but a habit of speech, an hypothetical construct which homogenises and totalises that which its proclaimers promise to pick apart.[5] This is by no means to deny that some persons do, it appears, require a substantial degree of assistance with managing the affairs of everyday life. Nor is it to gainsay suggestions that certain gene sequences and having difficulty with what psy terms 'conceptual thought', or even particular behavioural phenotypes, appear regularly to go together – but at the same time, to talk of 'intellectual disability' in the terms currently hegemonic in the social sciences is, fundamentally, of no assistance in developing a deeper appreciation of these circumstances, nor of acquiring a detailed understanding

---

[5] See McClimens (2002) for an alternative, continuum-based, take on this position.

of the capacities that persons may display. In truth 'intellectual disability' is little more than a translation of 'imbecility' accompanied by pseudo-scientific trappings and, as such, has no more 'scientific' merit than the nonce term of the 1800s. Indeed given that the most compelling reasons for changing nomenclatures in the psy disciplines have always been political and moral, there seems little reason, other than of simple courtesy to those who are professionally called 'self-advocates', not to return to such archaic usages. That is to say, to retain the concept of 'intellectual disability' as currently conceptualised in the professional literatures as some form of diagnostic, explanatory, construct is to fall victim to all of the problems caused by the practice in the pseudo-sciences of asking questions about lived human experience in the form: *'what is x?'* That is, if we read 'intellectual disability' for 'hearing voices' in the account below, it is difficult to escape identical conclusions.

The timeless and universal question 'what is hearing voices? period' is therefore not a happy one – it impoverishes the phenomenon studied. It impoverishes it because it treats as incidental and unimportant its context-contingent aspects. In psychology, which aims at biological and evolutionary explanations of mind, the timeless question implies there is a basic, raw experience of hearing voices. . . . This position is clearly not supported by the materials. . . . As there are no mechanical behaviours (except in abstractions) which become intentional conduct when combined with psychological phenomena, so there are no raw experiences which become meaningful under descriptions but can be lived without them. . . . So the general conclusion is really that local concepts are constitutive of local experiences and there cannot be a psychology or psychiatry which can do without them. (Leudar and Thomas, 2000: 209)

Schegloff (1999: 427) has suggested that: 'instead of thinking only or primarily of types and categories of persons and identities, mediated by evanescent lines of communication, perhaps we can also – or instead – think of structures of interaction as the recurrent structures of sociality, which recruit constantly shifting cohorts of participants to staff the episodes of conversation and other forms of talk-in-interaction which they organize'. Adopting such a form of thought would, inevitably, remove the focus upon internalised deficit assumed by psychology and, instead, replace it with a much more useful account of how it might be that the staffing of episodes of interaction by professionals and 'intellectually disabled people' might be more equitably accomplished. So, then, what can we say about the competence of those diagnosed as irredeemably incompetent by the standardised procedures and practices that the psy professions have honed over the last two centuries? What I hope to have shown is that if competence is re-specified in ethnomethodological terms as an intersubjectively negotiated, situated, accomplishment, and if evidence of competence is sought by examining the details of interaction rather than by scoring utterances or quantifying categories of conduct, that people described as intellectually disabled demonstrate, in interaction, that they can readily lay claim to the predicates of membership in the category of ordinary member – as long as pre-given, negative, moral evaluations are not imported under the guise of social scientific analysis.

That is, we have seen people demonstrably manage all of the normatively expectable accomplishments of ordinary members, from fine-grained sequential, syntactic and semantic analysis and anticipatory completion of the turns of 'unimpaired' speakers from their initial projection; the normative management of argument as sequentially structured conversational object; the deployment of intuitively non-apparent (Sacks, 1992) conversational devices such as kinship misidentification as insult; the demonstrable identification and use of culturally normative conversational rules for the provision of preferred second pair parts ranging from agreements to upgrades; the policing and eventual instatement of omni-relevant devices for conversation; the delicate management of identity ascription via understatement; the management of claims to membership via the avowal of category predicates rather than the making of simple bald claims; the real-time accomplishment of membership by the use of 'expert talk'; strategically organised attention to 'institutional agendas' via topic selection; the deployment of delicate pre-sequences and pro-terms for talk about potentially troublesome institutional matters; the recognition of variations in power asymmetry in different communicative environments and the consequential differential management of interaction in respect of these; the repair and, where locally advantageous, non-repair of dominant interlocutors' formulations; the employment of socially significant others as warrants for argumentative positions; a pervasive refusal, in communicative environments where a (relative) symmetry holds, to simply 'say yes' to any and all questions complemented by a strategic – and entirely sensible – deployment of agreement where both the preference structure of everyday interaction, and the demands set up by the quite separable demands of the interview *qua* interview, demand it; to, on occasions, the wrong-footing of interviewers in their own terms by appeal to the very institutional warrants – others (doctors, schools) authorised to conduct the moral management of troublesome actors – that their interviewers deploy to assert authority and control.

In this book I have argued that the employment of discursive psychology, with its roots in ethnomethodological and conversation analytic thinking, may offer a more detailed, and much more positive, account of the competences of persons described as intellectually disabled than that provided by contemporary psychology, sociology and disability studies.

Rather than view such persons as – *a priori* – non-members, I have argued that membership is a culturally, interactionally, achieved social status and, moreover, one which is routinely witheld from intellectually disabled people by virtue of the practices of the psy community.

That is, I think that it is reasonable to suggest that what we have become used to thinking as an essentialised condition afflicting persons is, in Taylor's words, nothing but a 'social construct and cultural artifact'. As he notes, 'differences among people in intellectual ability . . . do[es] not prove the objective existence of the construct of mental retardation or the utility of dividing humanity into two groups, the retarded and non-retarded' (Taylor, 1997: np). If, as members of those disciplines concerned with 'the retarded', we are to gain a better understanding of what it is that people can do, and be, and what it is that they may like to do (or be), but which may require assistance from others (and after all, this is at least one of the self-proclaimed *raisons d'être* of the psy professions) then perhaps we might start by making the effort to go and look. And, in the looking, we might, usefully, remember that 'what and who others, as well as we, are *depends on our relationships with them* and what we choose to make of us' (Bogdan and Taylor, 1989: 146, my emphasis).

Intellectual disability is, then, not a thing-in-the-world awaiting discovery, but rather is a disreputable moral status socially constructed, by psy, as a speakable truth about such persons. The analyses offered here, via the reading of post-structuralist thinking in terms of EM/CA and vice versa, both show in operation the reflexive relations of power/knowledge (Foucault, 1977) and also allow the respecification of 'intellectual disability' not as a totalising diagnostic outcome of the exercise of detached scientific observation, but rather as the upshot of 'locally managed' 'modes or practices of subjectification . . . rituals and routines which produce human natures' (Wetherell, 1999: 402).

So what might this mean for the psy disciplines and for disability studies? For the psy disciplines the strong argument would be that Wittgenstein's appeal – that we do away with explanation and let description alone take its place – actually be heeded. That if a respectful and helpful account of the competences and capacities of persons is to be achieved, then we must begin by abandoning typological thinking, empty diagnostic categories and pseudo-science. Instead, psy might usefully develop modes or practices of accurate description to replace morally laden, pre-emptive, evaluation. Discursive psychology offers both the conceptual and analytic tools to accomplish precisely that. The task has barely begun. For disability studies, particularly for 'second-wave' thinking, the upshot is that much more positive. It is, I think, clear that if intellectual disability is reconceptualised in the manner advocated here – with the abandonment of an uncritical acceptance of realist accounts of internal defect – that this analysis adds weight to the arguments of disability studies theorists about the essentially social character of disablement *in toto*. The task is – as Goodley, Taylor and others have also argued – to incorporate a detailed understanding of the lived reality of 'intellectual disability' into a newly written social model.

If the notion of 'intellectual disability' must be retained – and, given its conceptual emptiness and the tautological 'explanation' of 'incompetence' it offers, I would argue for its abandonment – then for both fields, if a clearer explication of competence is to be achieved, an explicit recognition of the inescapably moral nature of the category, and its inextricable binding to the project of the governing of souls is an essential starting point. The development of a comprehensive descriptive account of this nexus, and its upshots, promises to be a substantial task.

That is, rather than accepting the story that psy has trained us to tell ourselves about ourselves – and about people with intellectual disabilities – and attempting to develop an understanding of persons and their capacities from within its confines, we might, with Foucault, instead start this task more profitably by simply saying:

Do not ask me who I am, and do not ask me to remain the same: leave it to our bureaucrats and our police to see that our papers are in order. (Foucault, 1990: ix)

Appendix 1 Current definitions of mental retardation/intellectual disability

According to the Manual of Diagnosis and Professional Practice in Mental Retardation (American Psychological Association, 1996):

Mental retardation (MR) refers to (a) significant limitations in general intellectual functioning; (b) significant limitations in adaptive functioning, which exist concurrently; and (c) onset of intellectual and adaptive limitations before the age of 22 years. (p. 13)

The ICD-10 (World Health Organization 1992) and DSM-IV (American Psychiatric Association, 1994) use the same definition of mental retardation.

According to the Diagnostic and Statistical Manual of Mental Disorders, Fourth Edition: Diagnostic criteria for Mental Retardation:

A. Significantly subaverage intellectual functioning: an IQ of approximately 70 or below on an individually administered IQ test (for infants, a clinical judgement of significantly subaverage intellectual functioning).
B. Concurrent deficits or impairments in present adaptive functioning (i.e., the person's effectiveness in meeting the standards expected for his or her age by his or her cultural group) in at least two of the following areas: communication, self-care, home living, social/interpersonal skills, use of community resources, self direction, functional academic skills, work, leisure, health and safety.
C. The onset is before age 18 years.
Code based on degree of severity reflecting level of intellectual impairment:
317 Mild Mental Retardation: IQ level 50–55 to approximately 70
318.0 Moderate Mental Retardation: IQ level 35–40 to 50–55
318.1 Severe Mental Retardation: IQ level 20–25 to 35–40
318.2 Profound Mental Retardation: IQ level below 20 or 25
319 Mental Retardation, Severity Unspecified: when there is strong presumption of Mental Retardation but the person's intelligence is untestable by standard tests. (64)

The most recent definitions endorsed by AAMR and the American Psychiatric Association (DSM-IV) have recently been published (APA, 1994; Luckasson et al. 1992). The 1992 AAMR definition of mental retardation reads:

Mental retardation refers to substantial limitations in present functioning. It is characterized by significantly subaverage intellectual functioning, existing concurrently with related limitations in two or more of the following applicable adaptive skill areas: communication, self-care, home living, social skills, community use, self-direction, health and safety, functional academics, leisure, and work. Mental retardation manifests before age 18. (Luckasson *et al.* 1992, p. 1)

According to *'Did I Say That?' Articles and Commentary on the Try Another Way System* (Gold, 1980):

[Alternative definition]

Mental retardation refers to a level of functioning which requires from society significantly above average training procedures and superior assets in adaptive behavior on the part of society, manifested throughout the life of both society and the individual. (p. 148)

The mentally retarded person is characterized by the level of power needed in the training process required for her to learn, and not by limitations in what she can learn ... The height of a retarded person's level of functioning is determined by the availability of training technology and the amount of resources society is willing to allocate and not by significant limitations in biological potential ... (p. 148)

Greenspan's Definition (Greenspan, 1997).
Greenspan's proposed definition is as follows:

Persons who are MR [mentally retarded] are widely perceived to need long-term supports, accommodations or protections due to persistent limitations in social, practical and conceptual intelligence and the resulting inability to meet intellectual demands of a range of settings and roles. These limitations are assumed in most cases to result from abnormalities or events occurring during the developmental period, and which have permanent effects on Brain development and functioning. (p. 186)

Source: Adapted from Schroeder, Gerry, Gertz and Velasquez (2002: 27)

Appendix 2　Frequently asked questions about mental retardation and the AAMR definition

THE AAMR DEFINITION

WHAT IS THE OFFICIAL AAMR DEFINITION OF MENTAL RETARDATION?

Mental retardation is a disability characterized by significant limitations both in intellectual functioning and in adaptive behavior as expressed in conceptual, social, and practical adaptive skills. This disability originates before the age of eighteen.

WHERE CAN I FIND THE UPDATED AAMR DEFINITION OF MENTAL RETARDATION?

The new 10th edition of *Mental Retardation: Definition, Classification, and Systems of Supports* discusses the updated AAMR definition and classification system in detail. It presents the latest thinking on mental retardation and proposes tools and strategies to determine if an individual has mental retardation. Further, the book suggests what supports can be used to optimize functioning of persons with mental retardation.

WHAT FACTORS MUST BE CONSIDERED IN DETERMINING IF A PERSON HAS MENTAL RETARDATION AND CONSEQUENTLY, DEVELOPING A SUPPORT PLAN FOR THE INDIVIDUAL?

When using the AAMR definition, classification, and systems of supports, professionals and other team members must:
- Evaluate limitations in present functioning within the context of the individual's age, peers, and culture;
- Take into account the individual's cultural and linguistic differences as well as communication, sensory, motor, and behavioral factors;
- Recognize that limitations often coexist with strengths within an individual;
- Describe limitations so that an individualized plan of needed supports can be developed; and

- Provide appropriate, personalized supports to improve the functioning of a person with mental retardation.

KEY CONCEPTS IN DEFINITION

WHAT IS A DISABILITY?

A disability refers to personal limitations that are of substantial disadvantage to the individual when attempting to function in society. A disability should be considered within the context of the individual's environmental and personal factors, and the need for individualized supports.

WHAT IS INTELLIGENCE?

Intelligence refers to a general mental capability. It involves the ability to reason, plan, solve problems, think abstractly, comprehend complex ideas, learn quickly, and learn from experience. Although not perfect, intelligence is represented by Intelligent Quotient (IQ) scores obtained from standardized tests given by a trained professional. With regards to the intellectual criterion for the diagnosis of mental retardation, mental retardation is generally thought to be present if an individual has an IQ test score of approximately 70 or below. IQ scores must always be considered in light of the standard error of measurement, appropriateness, and consistency with administration guidelines. Since the standard error of measurement for most IQ tests is approximately 5, the ceiling may go up to 75. This represents a score approximately 2 standard deviations below the mean, considering the standard error of measurement. It is important to remember, however, that an IQ score is only one aspect in determining if a person has mental retardation. Significant limitations in adaptive behavior skills and evidence that the disability was present before age eighteen are two additional elements that are critical in determining if a person has mental retardation.

WHAT IS ADAPTIVE BEHAVIOR?

Adaptive behavior represents the conceptual, social, and practical skills that people have learned to be able to function in their everyday lives. Significant limitations in adaptive behavior impact a person's daily life and affect the ability to respond to a particular situation or to the environment.

Limitations in adaptive behavior can be determined by using standardized tests. On these standardized measures, significant limitations in adaptive behavior are operationally defined as performance that is at least two standard deviations below the mean of either (a) one of the following three types of adaptive behavior: conceptual, social, or practical, or

(b) an overall score on a standardized measure of conceptual, social, and practical skills.

Conceptual skills
Receptive and expressive language
Reading and writing
Money concepts
Self-directions

Social skills
Interpersonal
Responsibility
Self-esteem
Gullibility (likelihood of being tricked or manipulated)
Naiveté
Follows rules
Obeys laws
Avoids victimization

Practical skills
Personal activities of daily living such as eating, dressing, mobility and toileting. Instrumental activities of daily living such as preparing meals, taking medication, using the telephone, managing money, using transportation, and doing housekeeping activities.

Occupational skills
Maintaining a safe environment

SUPPORTS AND MENTAL RETARDATION

WHAT ARE SUPPORTS?

Supports are resources and individual strategies necessary to promote the development, education, interests, and personal well being of a person with mental retardation. Supports can be provided by a parent, friend, teacher, psychologist, doctor, or by any appropriate person or agency.

The concept of supports originated about fifteen years ago and has revolutionized the way habilitation and education services are provided to persons with mental retardation. Rather than mold individuals into pre-existing diagnostic categories and force them into existing models of service, the supports approach evaluates the specific needs of the individual and then suggests strategies and services to optimize individual functioning. The supports approach also recognizes that individual needs and circumstances will change over time.

Supports were an innovative aspect of the 1992 AAMR manual and they remain critical in the 2002 system. In 2002, they have been dramatically expanded and improved to reflect significant progress over the last decade.

WHY ARE SUPPORTS IMPORTANT?

Providing individualized supports can improve personal functioning, promote selfdetermination, and enhance the well being of a person with mental retardation.

Supports also leads to community inclusion of persons with intellectual disabilities.

Focusing on supports as the way to improve education, employment, recreation, and living environments is an important part of a person-centered approach to providing care to people with mental retardation.

HOW DO YOU DETERMINE WHAT SUPPORTS ARE NEEDED?

AAMR recommends that an individual's need for supports be analyzed in at least nine key areas such as human development, teaching and education, home living, community living, employment, health and safety, behavior, social, and protection and advocacy.

WHAT ARE SOME EXAMPLES OF SUPPORT AREAS AND SUPPORT ACTIVITIES?

Human development activities
- Providing physical development opportunities that include eye–hand coordination, fine motor skills, and gross motor activities
- Providing cognitive development opportunities such as using words and images to represent the world and reasoning logically about concrete events
- Providing social and emotional developmental activities to foster trust, autonomy, and initiative

Teaching and education activities
- Interacting with trainers and teachers and fellow trainees and students
- Participating in making decisions on training and educational activities
- Learning and using problem-solving strategies
- Using technology for learning

- Learning and using functional academics (reading signs, counting change, etc.)
- Learning and using self-determination skills

Home living activities
- Using the restroom/toilet
- Laundering and taking care of clothes
- Preparing and eating food
- Housekeeping and cleaning
- Dressing
- Bathing and taking care of personal hygiene and grooming needs
- Operating home appliances and technology
- Participating in leisure activities within the home

Community living activities
- Using transportation
- Participating in recreation and leisure activities
- Going to visit friends and family
- Shopping and purchasing goods
- Interacting with community members
- Using public buildings and settings

Employment activities
- Learning and using specific job skills
- Interacting with co-workers
- Interacting with supervisors
- Completing work-related tasks with speed and quality
- Changing job assignments
- Accessing and obtaining crisis intervention and assistance

Health and safety activities
- Accessing and obtaining therapy services
- Taking medication
- Avoiding health and safety hazards
- Communicating with health care providers
- Accessing emergency services
- Maintaining a nutritious diet
- Maintaining physical health
- Maintaining mental health/emotional well-being

Behavioral activities
- Learning specific skills or behaviors
- Learning and making appropriate decisions

- Accessing and obtaining mental health treatments
- Accessing and obtaining substance abuse treatments
- Incorporating personal preferences into daily activities
- Maintaining socially appropriate behavior in public
- Controlling anger and aggression

Social activities
- Socializing within the family
- Participating in recreation and leisure activities
- Making appropriate sexual decisions
- Socializing outside the family
- Making and keeping friends
- Communicating with others about personal needs
- Engaging in loving and intimate relationships
- Offering assistance and assisting others

Protection and advocacy activities
- Advocating for self and others
- Managing money and personal finances
- Protecting self from exploitation
- Exercising legal rights and responsibilities
- Belonging to and participating in self-advocacy/support organizations
- Obtaining legal services
- Using banks and cashing checks

CAUSES OF MENTAL RETARDATION

WHAT ARE THE CAUSES OF MENTAL RETARDATION?

The causes of mental retardation can be divided into biomedical, social, behavioral, and educational risk factors that interact during the life of an individual and/or across generations from parent to child. Biomedical factors are related to biologic processes, such as genetic disorders or nutrition. Social factors are related to social and family interaction, such as child stimulation and adult responsiveness. Behavioral factors are related to harmful behaviors, such as maternal substance abuse. Educational factors are related to the availability of family and educational supports that promote mental development and increases in adaptive skills. Also, factors present during one generation can influence the outcomes of the next generation. By understanding inter-generational causes, appropriate supports can be used to prevent and reverse the effects of risk factors.

INSIDE AAMR

HAS AAMR ALWAYS HAD THE SAME DEFINITION OF
MENTAL RETARDATION?

No. AAMR has updated the definition of mental retardation ten times since 1908, based on new information, changes in clinical practice, or breakthroughs in scientific research. The 10th edition of *Mental Retardation: Definition, Classification, and Systems of Supports* contains a comprehensive update to the landmark 1992 definition and provides important new information, tools, and strategies for the field and for anyone concerned about people with mental retardation.

Extracted from AAMR (2003)

References

Abbeduto, L. (1984). Situational influences on mentally retarded and nonretarded children's production of directives. *Applied Psycholinguistics*. 5: 147–66.

Abbeduto, L. and Rosenberg, S. (1980). The communicative competence of mildly retarded adults. *Applied Psycholinguistics*. 1: 405–26.

Abberley, P. (1987). The concept of oppression and the development of a social theory of disability. *Disability, Handicap and Society*. 2, 1: 5–19.

Albrecht, G. (1992). *The Disability Business: Rehabilitation in America*. London: Sage.

Allen, D. (1989). The effects of deinstitutionalisation on people with mental handicaps: a review. *Mental Handicap Research*. 2, 1: 18–38.

American Association on Mental Retardation (2002). *Mental Retardation: Definition, Classification, and Systems of Supports* (10th edition). Washington, DC: Author.

(1992). *Mental Retardation: Definition, Classification, and Systems of Supports* (9th edition). Washington, DC: Author.

American Journal of Insanity (1847/2001). Asylums and schools for idiots. *American Journal of Insanity*. July. 76–9 (edited by M. Simpson). Retrieved from http://www.personal.dundee.ac.uk/~mksimpso/joinsanity.htm. Accessed 8 April 2003.

American Psychiatric Association. (1994). *Diagnostic and Statistical Manual of Mental Disorders* (4th edition). Washington, DC: Author.

American Psychological Association (1996). *Manual of Diagnosis and Professional Practice in Mental Retardation* (edited by John W. Jacobson and James A. Mulick). Washington, DC: Author.

Antaki, C. (2001). 'D'you like a drink?' Dissembling language and the construction of an impoverished life. *Journal of Language and Social Psychology*. 20: 196–213.

(2000). Simulation versus the thing itself: commentary on Markman and Tetlock. *British Journal of Social Psychology*. 39: 327–31.

(1994). *Explaining and Arguing: The Social Organisation of Accounts*. London: Sage.

Antaki, C., Billig, M., Edwards, D. and Potter, J. (2003). Discourse analysis means doing analysis: a critique of six analytic shortcomings. *Discourse Analysis Online*. 1, 1. Retrieved from http://www.shu.ac.uk/daol/previous/v1/n1/index.htm. Accessed 18 March 2003.

Antaki, C., Condor, S. and Levine, M. (1996). Social identities in talk: speakers' own orientations. *British Journal of Social Psychology*. 35: 473–92.

Antaki, C., Houtkoop-Steenstra, H. and Rapley, M. (2000). 'Brilliant. Next question . . .': high-grade assessment sequences in the completion of interactional units. *Research on Language and Social Interaction*. 33: 235–62.

Antaki, C. and Rapley, M. (1996a). 'Quality of life' talk: the liberal paradox of psychological testing. *Discourse and Society*. 7: 293–316.

Antaki, C. and Rapley, M. (1996b). Questions and answers to psychological assessment schedules: hidden troubles in 'quality of life' interviews. *Journal of Intellectual Disability Research*. 40: 421–437.

Antaki, C. and Widdicombe, S. (1998a). Identity as an achievement and as a tool. In C. Antaki and S. Widdicombe (eds.). *Identities in Talk*. London: Sage.

(1998b). (eds.). *Identities in Talk*. London: Sage.

Antaki, C., Young, N. and Finlay, M. (2002). Shaping clients' answers: departures from neutrality in care-staff interviews with people with a learning disability. *Disability and Society*. 7, 4: 435–55.

Argenterius, J. (1556). *In Artem Medicinalem Galeni*. Turin.

Atkinson, D. (1988). Research interviews with people with mental handicaps. *Mental Handicap Research*. 1, 1: 75–90.

Atkinson, J. M. and Heritage, J. (eds.) (1984). *Structures of Social Action: Studies in Conversation Analysis*. Cambridge: Cambridge University Press.

Barham, P. (1999). Mental deficiency and the democratic subject. *History of the Human Sciences*. 12, 1: 111–14.

Barlow, C. F. (1978). *Mental Retardation and Related Disorders*. Philadelphia, PA: Davis.

Barlow, D. H. and Durand, V. M. (2002). *Abnormal Psychology* (3rd edition). Belmont, CA: Wadsworth.

Barnes, C. (1991). *Disabled People in Britain and Discrimination: A Case for Anti-Discrimination Legislation*. London: Hurst and Co. in association with the British Council of Organisations of Disabled People.

(1997). A legacy of oppression: a history of disability in western culture. In L. Barton and M. Oliver (eds.). *Disability Studies: Past, Present and Future*. Leeds: The Disability Press.

Barnes, C. and Oliver, M. (1993). Disability: A sociological phenomenon ignored by sociologists. Retrieved from www.leeds.ac.uk/disability-studies/archiveuk/Barnes/soc%20phenomenon.pdf. Accessed 14 October 2003.

Baroff, G. S. (1999). General learning disorder: a new designation for Mental Retardation. *Mental Retardation*. 37: 68–70.

Bateman, F. (1897). *The Idiot: His Place in Creation and his Claims on Society*. Norwich: Jarrold and Sons.

Beach, W. A. and Metzger, T. R. (1997). Claiming insufficient knowledge. *Human Communication Research*. 23, 4: 562–89.

Beadle-Brown, J. and Forrester-Jones, R. (2003). Social impairment in the 'Care in the Community' cohort: the effect of deinstitutionalization and changes over time in the community. *Research in Developmental Disabilities*. 24: 33–43.

Benjamin, A. C. (1937). *An Introduction to the Philosophy of Science*. New York: Macmillan.

Bergmann, J. R. (1992). Veiled morality: notes on discretion in psychiatry. In P. Drew and J. Heritage (eds.). *Talk at Work: Interaction in Institutional Settings*. Cambridge: Cambridge University Press.

Biklen, S. K. and Moseley, C. R. (1988). 'Are you retarded?' 'No, I'm Catholic': qualitative methods in the study of people with severe handicaps. *Journal of the Association for Persons with Severe Handicaps*. 13: 155–62.

Billig, M. (1991). *Ideology and Opinions*. London: Sage Publications.

(1996). *Arguing and Thinking: A Rhetorical Approach to Social Psychology*. (Revised edition). Cambridge: Cambridge University Press.

(1999a). Whose terms? Whose ordinariness? Rhetoric and ideology in conversation analysis. *Discourse and Society*. 10: 543–58.

(1999b). Conversation analysis and the claims of naivety. *Discourse and Society*. 10: 572–6.

Binet, A. (1905). New methods for the diagnosis of the intellectual level of subnormals. *L'Année Psychologique*. 12: 191–244. Translation by Elizabeth S. Kite (1916) in *The Development Of Intelligence In Children*. Vineland, NJ: Publications of the Training School at Vineland. Retrieved from http://psychclassics.yorku.ca/Binet/binet1.htm. Accessed 17 March 2003.

Blount, B. G. (1977). Ethnography and caretaker–child interaction. In C. E. Snow and C. A. Ferguson (eds.). *Talking to Children: Language Input and Acquisition*. Cambridge: Cambridge University Press.

Bogdan, R. and Taylor, S. J. (1989). Relationships with severely disabled people: the social construction of humanness. *Social Problems*. 36, 2: 135–48.

Booth, T. and Booth, W. (1998). *Growing up with Parents who have Learning Difficulties*. London: Routledge.

Boyle, M. (1999). Diagnosis. In C. Newnes, G. Holmes and C. Dunn (eds.). *This is Madness*. Ross-on-Wye: PCCS Books.

(2002a). *Schizophrenia: A Scientific Delusion?* (2nd edition). London: Routledge.

(2002b). It's all done with smoke and mirrors, or how to create the illusion of a schizophrenic brain disease. *Clinical Psychology*, 12: 9–16.

Bradshaw, J. (2001). Complexity of staff communication and reported level of understanding skills in adults with intellectual disability. *Journal of Intellectual Disability Research*. 453: 233–43.

Brewer, J. and Yearley, S. (1989). On conversational competence: a case study of talk among mentally handicapped persons. *Sociolinguistics*. 17: 103–23.

Brinton, B. and Fujiki, M. (1994). Ability of institutionalized and community-based adults with retardation to respond to questions in an interview context. *Journal of Speech and Hearing Research*. 37: 369–77.

British Psychological Society (1904). Editorial. *British Journal of Psychology*. 1, 1: 1.

Brown, P. and Drugovich, M. (1995). 'Some of these questions may sound silly': humour, discomfort and evasion in the mental Status Examination. *Research in the Sociology of Health Care*. 12: 159–74.

Brown, P. and Levinson, S. C. (1978). *Politeness: Some Universals in Language Usage*. Cambridge: Cambridge University Press.

Bruininks, R. H., McGrew, K. and Maruyama, G. (1988). Structure of adaptive behaviour in samples with and without mental retardation. *American Journal on Mental Retardation*. 95: 265–72.

Budd, E., Sigelman, C. and Sigelman, L. (1981). Exploring the outer limits of response bias. *Sociological Focus*. 14, 4: 297–307.

Burt, C. (1955). *The Subnormal Mind* (3rd edn). Oxford: Oxford University Press.

Bury, M. (1996). Defining and researching disability: challenges and responses. In C. Barnes and G. Mercer (eds.). *Exploring the Divide*. Leeds: The Disability Press.

Button, G., Coulter, J., Lee, J. R. E. and Sharrock, W. (1995). *Computers, Minds and Conduct*. Cambridge: Polity Press.

Button, G. and Sharrock, W. (1993). A disagreement over agreement and consensus in constructionist sociology. *Journal for the Theory of Social Behaviour*. 23: 1–25.

Caporael, L. R. (1981). The paralanguage of caregiving: baby talk to the institutionalized aged. *Journal of Personality and Social Psychology*. 40: 876–84.

Caporael, L. R. and Culbertson, G. H. (1986). Verbal response modes of baby talk and other speech at institutions for the aged. *Language and Communication*. 6: 99–112.

Caporael, L. R., Lukaszewski, M. P. and Culbertson, G. H. (1983). Secondary baby talk: judgments by institutionalized elderly and their caregivers. *Journal of Personality and Social Psychology*. 44: 746–54.

Cattermole, M., Jahoda, A. and Marková, I. (1988). Leaving home: the experience of people with a mental handicap. *Journal of Mental Deficiency Research*. 32, 1: 47–57.

Chaplin, R. and Flynn, A. (2000). Adults with learning disability admitted to psychiatric wards. *Advances in Psychiatric Treatment*. 6: 128–34.

Chappell, A., Goodley, D. and Lawthom, R. (2001). Making connections: the relevance of the social model of disability for people with learning difficulties. *British Journal of Learning Disabilities*. 29, 2: 45–50.

Chomsky, N. (1968). *Language and Mind*. New York: Harcourt, Brace, and World.

Chong, I., Yu, D., Martin, G., Harapiak, S. and Garinger, J. (2000). Response switching to repeated questions by individuals with developmental disabilities during interviews. *Developmental Disabilities Bulletin*. 28, 1: 56–67.

Coleman, W. (1990). Doing masculinity/doing theory. In J. Hearn and D. Morgan (eds.). *Masculinities and Social Theory*. London: Unwin Hyman.

Corker, M. and Shakespeare, T. (2002). Mapping the terrain. In M. Corker and T. Shakespeare (eds.). *Disability/Postmodernity: Embodying Disability Theory*. London: Continuum.

Corker, M. and Shakespeare, T. (eds.). (2002). *Disability/Postmodernity: Embodying Disability Theory*. London: Continuum.

Coulter, J. (1979). *The Social Construction of Mind: Studies in Ethnomethodology and Linguistic Philosophy*. Totowa, NJ: Rowan and Littlefield.

(1999). Discourse and Mind. *Human Studies*. 22: 163–81.

Craig, J., Craig, F., Withers, P., Hatton, C. and Limb, K. (2002). Identity conflict in people with intellectual disabilities: what role do service-providers play in mediating stigma? *Journal of Applied Research in Intellectual Disabilities*. 15: 61–72.

Cullen, C. and Dickens, P. (1990). People with mental handicaps. In D. F. Peck and C. M. Shapiro (eds.). *Measuring Human Problems*. London: Wiley.

Cummins, R. (1997). *The Comprehensive Quality of Life Scale: Intellectual Disability* (5th edition). Melbourne: Deakin University.

Cunningham, C. C., Glenn, S. and Fitzpatrick, H. (2000). Parents telling their offspring about Down Syndrome and disability. *Journal of Applied Research in Intellectual Disabilities*. 13: 47–61.

Czislowski-McKenna, A. (2001). 'Some days are diamonds: an ethnomethodological account of social agency and severe intellectual impairment.' Unpublished PhD, Griffith University, Brisbane.

Dagnan, D. and Ruddick, L. (1995). The use of analogue scales and personal questionnaires for interviewing people with learning disabilities. *Clinical Psychology Forum*. 79: 21–4.

Danforth, S. (2002). New words for new purposes: a challenge for the AAMR. *Mental Retardation*. 40, 1: 52–5.

Danziger, K. (1990). *Constructing the Subject*. Cambridge: Cambridge University Press.

Das, J. P., Naglieri, J. A. and Kirby, J. R. (1994). *Assessment of Cognitive Processes: the PASS theory of intelligence*. Boston, MA: Allyn and Bacon.

Davies, C. A. and Jenkins, R. (1997). 'She has different fits to me': how people with learning difficulties see themselves. *Disability and Society*. 12, 1: 95–109.

Defoe, D. (1697). A hospital for natural fools, in *An Essay upon Projects. The Works of Danniel Defoe: Political and Economic Writings. Volume 8: Social Reform*. London: Pickening and Chatto.

DePaulo, B. M. and Coleman, L. M. (1986). Talking to children, foreigners and retarded adults. *Journal of Personality and Social Psychology*. 51: 945–59.

Domingo, R. A., Barrow, M. B. and Amato, J. Jr (1998). Exercise of linguistic control by speakers in an adult day treatment program. *Mental Retardation*. 36, 4: 293–302.

Drew, P. (1981). Adults' corrections of children's mistakes: a response to Wells and Montgomery. In P. French and M. MacLure (eds.). *Adult–Child Conversation*. London: Croom-Helm.

Dybwad, G. (1996). From feeblemindedness to self-advocacy: a half century of growth and self-fulfillment. *European Journal on Mental Disability*. 39, 11: 3–18.

Edgerton, R. B. (1967). *The Cloak of Competence*. Berkeley, CA: University of California Press.

(1993). *The Cloak of Competence: Revised and Updated*. Berkeley, CA: University of California Press.

Edgerton, R. B., Lloyd, B. and Cole, M. (eds.). (1979). *Mental Retardation*. Cambridge, MA: Harvard University Press.

Edgerton, R. B. and Gaston, M. (1990). *'I've Seen It All!'* Baltimore, MD: Paul H. Brookes.

Edwards, D. (1995). Sacks and psychology. *Theory and Psychology*. 5, 3: 579–96.

(1997). *Discourse and Cognition*. London: Sage.

(1998). The relevant thing about her: social identity categories in use. In C. Antaki and S. Widdicombe (eds.). *Identities in Talk*. London: Sage.

(1999). Emotion discourse. *Culture and Psychology*. 5, 3: 271–91.

Edwards, D., Ashmore, M. and Potter, J. (1995). Death and furniture: the rhetoric, politics and theology of bottom line arguments against relativism. *History of the Human Sciences*. 8, 2: 25–49.

Edwards, D. and Potter, J. (1992). *Discursive Psychology*. London: Sage.

(2002). Discursive psychology. In A. McHoul and M. Rapley (eds.). *How to Analyse Talk in Institutional Settings: A Casebook of Methods*. London: Continuum.

Ferguson, P. M., Ferguson, D. L. and Taylor, S. J. (eds.). (1992). *Interpreting Disability: A Qualitative Reader*. New York: Teachers College Press.

Fernald, A. and Mazzie, C. (1991). Prosody and focus in speech to infants and adults. *Developmental Psychology*. 27: 209–21.

Fernald, W. E. (1903). Mentally defective children in the public schools. *Journal of Psycho-Asthenics*. 8: 2–3, 25–35. Retrieved from http://www. disabilitymuseum.org/lib/docs/1423.htm?page=5. Disability History Museum, www.disabilitymuseum.org. Accessed 17 March 2003.

Finkelstein, V. (1980). *Attitudes and Disabled People: Issues for Discussion*. New York: World Rehabilitation Fund.

(1981). To deny or not to deny disability. In A. Brechin, P. Liddiard and J. Swain (eds.). *Handicap in a Social World*. Sevenoaks: Hodder and Stoughton.

(2001). The social model of disability repossessed. Paper presented at the conference of the Manchester Coalition of Disabled People.

Finlay, W. M. L. and Lyons, E. (1998). Social identity and people with learning difficulties: implications for self-advocacy groups. *Disability and Society*. 13: 37–51.

(2000). Social categorizations, social comparisons and stigma: presentations of self in people with learning difficulties. *British Journal of Social Psychology*. 39: 129–46.

(2002). Acquiescence in interviews with people who have mental retardation. *Mental Retardation*. 41, 1: 14–29.

Flathman, R. E. (2000). Wittgenstein and the social sciences: critical reflections concerning Peter Winch's interpretations and appropriations of Wittgenstein's thought. *History of the Human Sciences*. 13, 2: 1–15.

Flynn, M. C. (1986). Adults who are mentally handicapped as consumers: issues and guidelines for interviewing. *Journal of Mental Deficiency Research*. 30, 4: 369–77.

(1988). *Independent Living for Adults with Mental Handicap: 'A Place of my Own'*. London: Cassell.

Flynn, M. C. and Saleem, J. K. (1986). Adults who are mentally handicapped and living with their parents: satisfaction and perceptions regarding their lives and circumstances. *Journal of Mental Deficiency Research*. 30, 4: 379–87.

Foddy, W. (1993). *Constructing Questions for Interviews and Questionnaires*. Cambridge: Cambridge University Press.

Foucault, M. (1967). *Madness and Civilization. A History of Insanity in the Age of Reason*. London: Tavistock. Abridged edition of *Histoire de la Folie*. Traslated into English by Richard Howard. Introduction by David Cooper.

(1977). *Discipline and Punish: The Birth of the Prison*. Translated by Alan Sheridan. London: Allen Lane.

(1978). Politics and the study of discourse. *Ideology and Consciousness*. 3: 7–26.

(1990). *Politics, Philosophy, Culture: Interviews and other writings 1977–1984*. Translated by Alan Sheridan and others. Edited with an Introduction by Larence Kritzman. London: Routledge.

(1995). Madness, the absence of work. Translated by Peter Stastny and Deniz Sengel. *Critical Inquiry*. 21 (Winter): 290–8.

Fowler, F. J. Jr and Mangione, T. W. (1990). *Standardised Survey Interviewing: Minimising Interviewer Related Error*. Newbury Park, CA: Sage.

French, S. (1993). Disability, impairment or something in between? In J. Swain, V. Finkelstein, S. French and M. Oliver (eds.). *Disabling Barriers – Enabling Environments*. London: Sage.

Garfinkel, H. (1967). *Studies in Ethnomethodology*. Englewood Cliffs, NJ: Prentice-Hall.

Gelb, S. A. (2002). The dignity of humanity is not a scientific construct. *Mental Retardation*. 40, 1: 55–6.

Gergen, K. J. (1998). The ordinary, the original and the believable in psychology's construction of the person. Draft copy for B. Bayer and J. Shotter (eds.). *Reconstructing the Psychological Subject*. London: Sage. Retrieved from http://www.swarthmore.edu/SocSci/kgergen1/web/printer-friendly.phtml?id=manu4. Accessed 8 April 2003.

(2001). Psychology as 'politics by other means'. Paper presented at the International Society for Theoretical Psychology meetings, Calgary, Canada, June. Retrieved from www.swarthmore.edu/SocSci/kgergen1/web/printer-friendly.phtml?id=manu24. Accessed 8 April 2003.

Gergen, K., Hoffman, L. and. Anderson, H. (1996). Is diagnosis a disaster?: a constructionist dialogue. In F. Kaslow (ed.). *Handbook for Relational Diagnosis*. New York: Wiley.

Gilbert, G. N. and Mulkay, M. (1984). *Opening Pandora's Box: A Sociological Analysis of Scientists' Discourse*. Cambridge: Cambridge University Press.

Gillman, M., Heyman, B. and Swain, J. (2000). What's in a name? The implications of diagnosis for people with learning difficulties and their family carers. *Disability and Society*. 15, 3: 389–409.

Goffman, E. (1963). *Stigma: Notes on the Management of Spoiled Identity*. Englewood Cliffs, NJ: Prentice-Hall.

(1974). *Frame Analysis: An Essay on the Organization of Experience*. New York: Harper and Row.

Gold, M. W. (1980). An alternative definition of mental retardation. In M. W. Gold (ed.). *'Did I Say That?' Articles and Commentary on the Try Another Way System*. Champaign, IL: Research Press.

Goode, D. A. (1983). Who is Bobby? Ideology and method in the discovery of a Down's Syndrome person's competence. In G. Kleinofner (ed.). *Health Through Occupation*. Philadelphia: F. A. Davis.

(1994). *A World without Words: The Social Construction of Children Born Deaf and Blind*. Philadelphia, PA: Temple University Press.

Goodey, C. F. (1999). Politics, nature and necessity: were Aristotle's slaves feeble-minded? *Political Theory*. 27, 2: 203–24.

Goodey, C. F. and Stainton, T. (2001). Intellectual disability and the myth of the changeling. *Journal of the History of the Behavioral Sciences*. 37, 3: 223–40.

Goodley, D. (1997). Locating self-advocacy in models of disability: understanding disability in the support of self-advocates with learning difficulties. *Disability and Society*. 12, 3: 367–79.

(2001). 'Learning difficulties', the social model of disability and impairment: challenging epistemologies. *Disability and Society*. 16, 2: 207–31.

Goodley, D. and Rapley, M. (2001). How do you understand 'learning difficulties'? Towards a social theory of impairment. *Mental Retardation*. 39, 3: 229–32.

Gowans, F. and Hulbert, C. (1983). Self-concept assessment of mentally handicapped adults: a review. *Mental Handicap*. 11: 121–3.

Greenspan, S. (1994). Review of the 1992 AAMR Manual. *American Journal of Mental Retardation*, 98: 544–9.

(1997). Dead manual walking: why the 1992 AAMR definition needs redoing. *Education and Training in Mental Retardation and Developmental Disabilities*. 32: 179–90.

Gregory, N., Robertson, J., Kessissoglou, S., Emerson, E. and Hatton, C. (2001). Factors associated with expressed satisfaction among people with intellectual disability receiving residential supports. *Journal of Intellectual Disability Research*. 45, 4: 279–91.

Grice, P. (1975). Logic and conversation. In P. Cole and J. L. Morgan, (eds.) *Syntax and Semantics*, Vol. 3, *Speech Acts*, New York, Academic Press.

Grossman, H. J. (ed.). (1977). *Manual on Terminology and Classification in Mental Retardation* (1977 revision). Washington, DC: American Association on Mental Deficiency.

Gudjonnsson, G. (1986). The relationship between interrogative suggestibility and acquiescence: empirical findings and theoretical implications. *Personality and Individual Differences*. 7, 2: 195–9.

Gunzburg, H. (1970). Subnormal adults. In P. Mittler (ed.). *The Psychological Assessment of Mental and Physical Handicaps*. London: Methuen.

Hacking, I. (1992). World-making by kind-making: child abuse for example. In M. Douglas and D. Hull (eds.). *How Classification Works: Nelson Goodman among the Social Sciences*. Edinburgh: Edinburgh University Press.

(1995). *Rewriting the Soul*. Princeton, NJ: Princeton University Press.

Hamilton, H. E. (1996). Intratextuality, intertextuality, and the construction of identity as patient in Alzheimer's disease. *Text*. 16, 1: 61–90.

Hansen, S., McHoul, A. and Rapley, M. (2003). *Beyond Help: A Consumer's Guide to Psychology*. Ross-on-Wye: PCCS Books.

Hare, E. H. (1983). Was insanity on the increase? *British Journal of Psychiatry*. 142: 439–55.

Hatton, C. (1998). Pragmatic language skills in people with intellectual disabilities. *Journal of Intellectual Disability Research*. 23, 1: 79–100.

Havercamp, S. M. (2001). *Health Indicators 2000–2001: a part of the North Carolina Core Indicators Project*. Chapel Hill, NC: University of North Carolina Center for Development and Learning. Retrieved from http://www.fpg.unc.edu/~ncodh/HealthIndicatorsProjectSummary.html. Accessed 6 March 2003.

Heal, L. W. and Sigelman, C. K. (1990). Methodological issues in measuring the quality of life of individuals with retardation. In R. L. Schalock (ed.). *Quality of Life: Perspectives and Issues*. Washington, DC: AAMR.

(1995). Response biases in interviewees with limited mental ability. *Journal of Intellectual Disability Research*. 39, 4: 331–40.

(1996). Methodological issues in quality of life measurement. In R. L. Schalock (ed.). *Quality of Life: Volume 1 Conceptualization and Measurement*. Washington: AAMR.

Heber, R. F. (1961). *A Manual on Terminology and Classification in Mental Retardation* (2nd edn). Monograph Supplement to the *American Journal of Mental Deficiency*. Washington, DC: AAMR.

Hensel, E., Rose, J., Stenfert Kroese, B. and Banks-Smith, J. (2002). Subjective judgments of quality of life: a comparison study between people with intellectual disability and those without disability. *Journal of Intellectual Disability Research*. 46, 2: 95–107.

Hester, S. and Francis, D. (2002). Is institutional talk a phenomenon? Reflections on ethnomethodology and applied conversation analysis. In A. McHoul and M. Rapley (eds.). *How to Analyse Talk in Institutional Settings: A Casebook of Methods*. London: Continuum.

Hogg, J. and Raynes, N. V. (1987). Assessing people with mental handicap: an introduction. In J. Hogg, and N. V. Raynes (eds.). *Assessment in Mental Handicap: A Guide to Assessment Practices, Tests and Checklists*. Beckenham: Croom Helm.

Holmes, J. (1995). *Women, Men and Politeness*. London: Longman.

Holt, E. J. (1996). Reporting on talk: the use of direct reported speech in conversation. *Research on Language and Social Interaction*. 29: 219–46.

Hooton, E. A. (1937). *Apes, Men and Morons*. New York: G.P. Putnam's Sons.

Hooton, E. A. (1939). *The American Criminal*. Cambridge: Harvard University Press.

Hooton, E. A. (1940). *Why Men Behave Like Apes and Vice Versa*. Princeton, NJ: Princeton University Press.

Houtkoop-Steenstra, H. (1995). Meeting both ends: standardization and recipient design in telephone survey interviews. In P. tenHave and G. Psathas (eds.). *Situated Order: Studies in the Social Organization of Talk and Embodied Activities*. Washington, DC: University Press of America.

Houtkoop-Steenstra, H. (2000). *Interaction and the Standardised Survey Interview: The Living Questionnaire*. Cambridge: Cambridge University Press.

Houtkoop-Steenstra, H. and Antaki, C. (1998). Creating happy people by asking yes/no questions. *Research on Language and Social Interaction*. 30: 285–313.

Howe, S. (1848). *On the Causes of Idiocy Being the Supplement to the Report Made to the Legislature of Massachusetts upon Idiocy*. Boston: Collidge and Wiley. Retrieved from http://www.personal.dundee.ac.uk/~mksimpso/howe3.htm. Accessed 17 March 2003.

Hughes, E. C. (1945). Dilemmas and contradictions of status. *American Journal of Sociology*. 50: 353–9.

Jackson, M. (2000). *The Borderland of Imbecility: Medicine, Society and the Fabrication of the Feeble Mind in Late Victorian and Edwardian England.* Manchester: Manchester University Press.

Jacobson, J. W. (2001). Environmental postmodernism and rehabilitation of the borderline of mental retardation. *Behavioral Interventions.* 16: 209–34.

Jacoby, S and McNamara, T. (1999). Locating competence. *English for Specific Purposes.* 18, 3: 213–41.

Jefferson, G. (1984). Notes on the systematic deployment of the acknowledgement tokens yeah and mm hm. *Papers in Linguistics.* 17: 197–216.

Jenkins, R. (ed.). (1999). *Questions of Competence: Culture, Classification and Intellectual Disability.* Cambridge: Cambridge University Press.

Jensen, A. R. (1998). *The G Factor: The Science of Mental Ability.* Westport, CT: Praeger.

Joseph, J. (2003). *The Gene Illusion: Genetic Research in Psychiatry and Psychology under the Microscope.* Ross-on-Wye: PCCS Books.

Kernan, K. T. and Sabsay, S. (1989). Communication in social interactions: aspects of an ethnography of mildly mentally handicapped adults. In M. Beveridge, G. Conti-Ramsden and I. Leudar (eds.). *Language and Communication in Mentally Handicapped People.* London: Chapman and Hall.

Kovarsky, D., Duchan, J. and Maxwell, M. (eds.). (1999). *Constructing (In)Competence: Disabling Evaluations in Clinical and Social Interaction.* Hillsdale, NJ: Lawrence Erlbaum Associates.

Krosnick, J. A. (1991). Response strategies for coping with the cognitive demands of attitude measures in surveys. *Applied Cognitive Psychology.* 5: 213–36.

Kuder, S. J. and Bryen, D. N. (1993). Conversational topics of staff members and institutionalised individuals with mental retardation. *Mental Retardation.* 31, 3: 148–53.

Langness, L. L. and Levine, H. G. (eds.). (1986). *Culture and Retardation: Life Histories of Mildly Mentally Retarded Persons in American Society.* Dordrecht: Kluwer.

Lerner, G. (1991). On the syntax of sentences in progress. *Language in Society,* 20: 441–58.

(1996). Finding 'face' in the preference structures of talk-in-interaction. *Social Psychology Quarterly,* 59, 4: 303–21.

Leudar, I. (1989). Communicative environments for mentally handicapped people. In M. Beveridge, G. Conti-Ramsden and I. Leudar (eds.). *Language and Communication in Mentally Handicapped People.* London: Chapman and Hall.

Leudar, I. and Fraser, W. I. (1985). How to keep quiet: some withdrawal strategies in mentally handicapped adults. *Journal of Mental Deficiency Research.* 29: 315–30.

Leudar, I., Fraser, W. I. and Jeeves, M. A. (1981). Social familiarity and communication in Down Syndrome. *Journal of Mental Deficiency Research.* 25: 133–42.

Leudar, I. and Nekvapil, J. (2000). Presentations of Romanies in the Czech media: on category work in television debates. *Discourse and Society.* 11: 488–513.

Leudar, I. and Thomas, P. (2000). *Voices of Reason Voices of Insanity. Studies in Verbal Hallucinations.* London: Routledge.

Levinson, S. (1983). *Pragmatics.* Cambridge: Cambridge University Press.

Linder, S. (1978). The perception and management of 'trouble' in 'normal–retardate' conversations. Working Paper No. 5, Socio-Behavioral Research Group, Mental Retardation Research Center, University of Los Angeles, CA.

Lindsay, J. and Wilkinson, R. (1997). Repair in aphasic-spouse interactions: a renegotiation of competence. Paper presented at the 'Disorder and Order in Talk' Conference. University College London, 25–6 June 1997.

Locke, J. (1690/1975). *An Essay Concerning Human Understanding*. P. Nidditch (ed.). Oxford: Clarendon.

Lowe, K. and de Paiva, S. (1988). Canvassing the views of people with a mental handicap. *Irish Journal of Psychology*. 9, 2: 220–34.

Luckasson, R., Coulter, D. L., Polloway, E. A., Reiss, S., Schalock, R. L., Snell, M. E., Spitalnik, D. M. and Stark, J. A. (1992). *Mental Retardation: Definition, Classification, and Systems of Supports*. Washington, DC: AAMR.

Lynch, M. and Bogen, D. (1996). *The Spectacle of History: Speech, Text, and Memory at the Iran-Contra hearings*. Durham, NC: Duke University Press.

(1997). Lies, recollections and categorical judgements in testimony. In S. Hester and P. Eglin (eds.). *Culture in Action: Studies in Membership Categorization Analysis*. Washington, DC: University Press of America.

McClimens, A. (2002). The organization of difference: people with intellectual disabilities and the social model of disability. *Mental Retardation*. 41, 1: 35–46.

McDonagh, P. (2000). Diminished men and dangerous women: representations of gender and learning disability in early- and mid-nineteenth-century Britain. *British Journal of Learning Disabilities*. 28: 49–53.

McHoul, A. and Rapley, M. (2000). Still on holidays Hank?: 'Doing business' by 'having a chat'. M/C: *A Journal of Media and Culture*, 3 (4). Retrieved from http://www/api-network.com/mc/0008/holidays.html. Accessed 1 January 2001.

(2001). Ghost: Do not forget; this visitation / Is but to whet thy almost blunted purpose. Culture, psychology and 'being human'. *Culture and Psychology*. 7, 4: 433–51.

(2002). 'Should we make a start then?': a strange case of a (delayed) client-initiated psychological assessment. *Research on Language and Social Interaction*. 35, 1: 73–91.

(2003). What can psychological terms actually do? Or, if Sigmund calls, tell him it didn't work. *Journal of Pragmatics*. 35: 507–22.

McHoul, A. and Rapley, M. (eds.) (2002). *How to Analyse Talk in Institutional Settings: A Casebook of Methods*. London: Continuum.

MacKay, R. (1974). Standardized tests: objective/objectivized measures of 'competence'. In A. Cicourel, K. Jennings, S. Jennings, K. Leiter, R. Mackay, H. Mehan and D. Roth (eds.). *Language Use and School Performance*. New York: Academic Press.

McLennan, G. (2001). *Thus*: reflections on Loughborough relativism. *History of the Human Sciences*. 14, 3: 85–101.

McMillan, D. L., Gresham, F. M., Siperstein, G. N. and Bocian, K. M. (1996a). The labyrinth of IDEA: school decisions on referred students with subaverage intelligence. *American Journal on Mental Retardation*. 101: 161–74.

McMillan, D. L., Siperstein, G. N. and Gresham, F. M. (1996b). A challenge to the validity of mild mental retardation as a diagnostic category. *Exceptional Children.* 62: 356–71.

McMillan, D. L., Siperstein, G. N., Gresham, F. M. and Bocian, K. M. (1997). Mild mental retardation: a concept that may have lived out its usefulness. *Psychology in Mental Retardation and Developmental Disabilities.* 23, 1: 5–12.

McNamara, T. (1990). Item response theory and the validation of an ESP test for health professionals. *Language Testing.* 7, 1: 52–75.

Marková, I. (1991). Asymmetries in group conversations between a tutor and people with learning difficulties. In I. Marková and K. Foppa (eds.). *Aysmmetries in Dialogue.* Hemel Hempstead: Harvester Wheatsheaf.

Matikka, L. M. and Vesala, H. T. (1997). Acquiescence in quality-of-life interviews with adults who have mental retardation. *Mental Retardation.* 35, 2: 75–82.

Maynard, D. W. (1991). Perspective-display sequences and the delivery and receipt of diagnostic news. In D. Boden and D. H. Zimmerman (eds.). *Talk and Social Structure.* Cambridge: Polity Press.

(1992). On clinicians co-implicating recipients' perspective in the delivery of diagnostic news. In P. Drew and J. Heritage (eds.). *Talk at Work: Interaction in Institutional Settings.* Cambridge: Cambridge University Press.

Marlaire, C. L. and Maynard, D. W. (1990). Standardised testing as an interactional phenomenon. *Sociology of Education.* 63: 83–101.

(1993). Social problems and the organization of talk and interaction. In J. A. Holstein and G. Miller (eds.). *Reconsidering Social Constructionism: Debates in Social Problems Theory.* New York: deGruyter.

Maynard, D. and Marlaire, C. (1992). Good reasons for bad testing performance: the interactional substrate of educational testing. *Qualitative Sociology.* 15: 177–202.

Mittler, P. (1979). *People Not Patients: Problems and Policies in Mental Handicap.* London: Methuen.

Mehan, H. (1973). Assessing children's language using abilities. In J. M. Armer and A. D. Grimshaw (eds.). *Methodological Issues in Comparative Sociological Research.* New York: Wiley.

Mehan, H. and Wood, H. (1975). *The Reality of Ethnomethodology.* New York: Wiley.

Mercer, J. R. (1994). Historical and current perspectives of the definition of mental retardation. *AAMR Psychology Division Newsletter.* 26–7.

Missouri Developmental Disabilities Resource Center (1998). *Fast Facts on Developmental Disabilities: DDRCFast Facts #110 – Quality Assurance.* Retrieved from www.moddrc.com/Information-Disabilities/FastFacts/quality.htm. Accessed 23 March 2003.

Mitchell, R. W. (2001). Americans' talk to dogs: similarities and differences with talk to infants. *Research on Language and Social Interaction.* 34, 2: 183–210.

Mitchell, R. W. and Edmonson, E. (1999). Functions of repetitive talk to dogs during play: control, conversation, or planning? *Society and Animals.* 7, 1: 55–81.

Oelschlaeger, M. and Damico, J. S. (1998). Joint productions as a conversational strategy in aphasia. *Clinical Linguistics and Phonetics.* 12: 459–80.

(2003). Word searches in aphasia: a study of the collaborative responses of communicative partners. In C. Goodwin (ed.). *Conversation and Brain Damage*. New York: Oxford University Press.

Oliver, M. (1985). Discrimination, disability and social policy. In M. Brenton and C. Jones (eds.). *The Yearbook of Social Policy 1984/5*. London: Routledge and Kegan Paul.

(1986). Social policy and disability: some theoretical issues. *Disability Handicap and Society*. 1, 1: 5–18.

(1987). *Social Work with Disabled People*. London: Macmillan.

(1990). *The Politics of Disablement*. London: Macmillan.

(1992). Changing the social relations of research production. *Disability, Handicap and Society*. 7, 2: 101–14.

(1996) *Understanding Disability: From Theory To Practice*. Chatham: Mackays.

(1999). Capitalism, disability and ideology: a materialist critique of the normalization principle. Retrieved from www.independentliving.org/docs3/oliver99.pdf. Accessed 23 March 2003.

Paoletti, I. (1998). Handling 'incoherence' according to the speaker's on-sight categorization. In C. Antaki and S. Widdicombe (eds.). *Identities in Talk*. London: Sage.

Parker, I. (1992). *Discourse Dynamics: Critical Analysis for Social and Individual Psychology*. London: Routledge.

Parker, I. and Burman, E. (1993). Against discursive imperialism, empiricism, and constructionism: thirty-two problems with discourse analysis. In E. Burman and I. Parker (eds.). *Discourse Analytic Research: Repertoires and Readings of Texts in Action*. London: Routledge.

Perry, J. and Felce, D. (2002). Subjective and objective quality of life assessment: responsiveness, response bias, and resident:proxy concordance. *Mental Retardation*. 40, 6: 445–56.

Pomerantz, A. M. (1984a). Descriptions in legal settings. In G. Button and J. Lee (eds.). *Talk And Social Organisation*. Clevedon: Multilingual Matters.

(1984b). Agreeing and disagreeing with assessments: some features of preferred/dispreferred turn shapes. In J. M. Atkinson and J. Heritage (eds.). *Structures of Social Action: Studies in Conversation Analysis*. Cambridge: Cambridge University Press.

Potter, J. (1996). *Representing Reality: Discourse, Rhetoric and Social Construction*. London: Sage.

(1998). Cognition as context (whose cognition?). *Research on Language and Social Interaction*. 31: 29–44.

(2000). Post cognitivist psychology. *Theory and Psychology*. 10: 31–7.

Potter, J. and Wetherell, M. (1987). *Discourse and Social Psychology: Beyond Attitudes and Behaviour*. London: Sage.

Price-Williams, D. and Sabsay, S. (1979). Communicative competence among severely retarded persons. *Semiotica*. 26: 35–63.

Prior, M., Minnes, P., Coyne, T., Golding, B., Hendy, J. and McGillivary, J. (1979). Verbal interactions between staff and residents in an institution for the young mentally retarded. *Mental Retardation*. 17: 65–9.

Puchta, C. and Potter, J. (1999). Asking elaborate questions: focus groups and the management of spontaneity. *Journal of Sociolinguistics*. 3: 314–35.

(2002). Manufacturing individual opinions: market research focus groups and the discursive psychology of attitudes. *British Journal of Social Psychology*. 41: 345–63.

Purcell, M., Morris, I and McConkey, R. (1999). Staff perceptions of the communicative competence of adult persons with intellectual disabilities. *The British Journal of Developmental Disabilities*. 45, 88: 16–25.

Rapley, M. (1998). 'Just an ordinary Australian': self-categorisation and the discursive construction of facticity in 'new racist' political rhetoric. *British Journal of Social Psychology*. 37: 325–44.

Rapley, M. and Antaki, C. (1996). A conversation analysis of the 'acquiescence' of people with learning disabilities. *Journal of Community and Applied Social Psychology*. 6: 207–27.

Rapley, M., Kiernan, P. and Antaki, C. (1998). Invisible to themselves or negotiating identity? The interactional management of 'being intellectually disabled'. *Disability and Society*. 13, 5: 807–27.

Reindal, S. M. (1999). Independence, dependence, interdependence: some reflections on the subject and personal autonomy. *Disability and Society*. 14, 3: 353–67.

Richardson, K. (2002). What IQ tests test. *Theory and Psychology*. 12, 3: 283–314.

Robson, B. (1989). *Pre-School Provision for Children with Special Needs*. London: Cassell Educational.

Rose, N. (1985). *The Psychological Complex*: London: Routledge and Kegan Paul.

(1996). *Inventing Our Selves: Psychology, Power and Personhood*. Cambridge: Cambridge University Press.

(1999a). Power and subjectivity: critical history and psychology. Retrieved from http://www.academyanalyticarts.org/rose1.html. Accessed 8 March 2003.

(1999b). *Governing the Soul: The Shaping of the Private Self* (2nd edition). London: Free Association Books.

Ross, L. (1977). The intuitive psychologist and his shortcomings: distortions in the attribution process. In L. Berkowitz (ed.). *Advances in Experimental Social Psychology*. Vol. 10. New York: Academic Press.

Ryan, J. and Thomas, F. (1998). *The Politics of Mental Handicap*. London: Free Association Books.

Ryave, A. L. (1973). Aspects of story-telling among a group of 'mentally retarded'. Unpublished PhD thesis, University of California at Los Angeles: Department of Sociology.

Ryave, A. L. and Rodriguez, N. (1989). The sequential organization of correcting others' talk: a case study of mentally retarded adult male interaction. Paper presented at the Annual Meeting of the Pacific Sociological Association, Reno, Nevada.

Ryle, G. (1949). *The Concept of Mind*. Chicago: University of Chicago Press.

Sabsay, S. and Platt, M. (1985). *Weaving the Cloak of Competence*. Working Paper No. 32, SocioBehavioral Research Group, University of Los Angeles, CA: Mental Retardation Research Center.

Sacks, H. (1972). An initial investigation of the usability of conversational data for doing sociology. In D. Sudnow (ed.). *Studies in Social Interaction*. New York: Free Press.

(1984). On doing 'being ordinary'. In J. M. Atkinson and J. Heritage (eds.). *Structures Of Social Action: Studies in Conversation Analysis*. Cambridge: Cambridge University Press.

(1992). *Lectures On Conversation*. Vols. 1 and 2 (ed. G. Jefferson). Oxford: Basil Blackwell.

Sarbin, T. and Mancuso, J. C. (1980). *Schizophrenia: Medical Diagnosis or Moral Verdict?* New York: Pergamon.

Sattler, J. M. (1992). *Assessment of Children* (3rd edition). San Diego, CA: Jerome M. Sattler.

Saunders, J. (1988). Quarantining the weak-minded: psychiatric definitions of degeneracy and the late-Victorian asylum. In W. F. Bynum, R. Porter and M. Shepherd (eds.). *The Anatomy of Madness: The Asylum and its Psychiatry*. London: Routledge.

Schalock, R. and Keith, K. (1993). *Quality of Life Questionnaire*. Worthington: IDS Publishing Corporation.

Schegloff, E. A. (1972/1990). Notes on a conversational practice: formulating place. In D. Sudnow (ed.). *Studies in Social Interaction*. New York: Free Press. Reprinted in J. Coulter (ed.). *Ethnomethodological Sociology*. Aldershot: Edward Elgar.

(1982). Discourse as an interactional achievement: some uses of 'uh huh' and other things that come between sentences. In D. Tannen (ed.). *Analysing Discourse: Text and Talk. Georgetown University Round Table on Language and Linguistics*. Georgetown: Georgetown University Press.

(1988). Presequences and indirection: applying speech act theory to ordinary conversation. *Journal of Pragmatics*. 12: 55–62.

(1989). From interview to confrontation: observations on the Bush/Rather encounter. *Research on Language and Social Interaction*. 22: 215–40.

(1992). Introduction. In H. Sacks (1992). *Lectures On Conversation*. Vols. 1 and 2 (ed. G. Jefferson). Oxford: Basil Blackwell.

(1997). Whose text? Whose context? *Discourse and Society*. 8: 165–87.

(1998). Reply to Wetherell. *Discourse and Society*. 9: 413–16.

(1999). Discourse, pragmatics, conversation, analysis. *Discourse Studies*. 1, 4: 405–36.

(1999a). 'Schegloff's texts' as 'Billig's data': a critical reply. *Discourse and Society*. 10: 558–72.

(1999b). Naivete vs sophistication or discipline vs. self-indulgence: a rejoinder to Billig. *Discourse and Society*. 10, 4: 577–82.

Schegloff, E. A., Jefferson, G. and Sacks, H. (1977). The preference for self-correction in the organization of repair in conversation. *Language*, 53, 2: 361–82.

Schenkein, J. N. (1978). Identity negotiation in conversation. In J. N. Schenkein (ed.). *Studies in the Organisation of Conversational Interaction*. New York: Academic Press.

Schiffrin, D. (1990). Conversation analysis. In W. Grabe (ed.). *Annual Review of Applied Linguistics*. Cambridge: Cambridge University Press.

Schroeder, S. R., Gerry, M., Gertz, G. and Velazquez, F. (2002). *Usage of the Term 'Mental Retardation': Language, Image and Public Education Final Project*

Report. Kansas University Center on Developmental Disabilities: University of Kansas.

Schütz, A. (1962). *Collected Papers I: The Problem of Social Reality.* The Hague: Martinus Nijhoff.

Scudder, R. R. and Tremain, D. H. (1992). Repair behaviors of children with and without mental retardation. *Mental Retardation.* 30: 277–82.

Scull, A. T. (1977). *Decarceration: Community Treatment and the Deviant: A Radical View.* Englewood Cliffs, NJ: Prentice-Hall.

—— (1979). *Museums of Madness: The Social Organization of Insanity in Nineteenth Century England.* London: Allen Lane.

Seguin, E. (1846). *Traitement moral: Hygiène et éducation des idiots et des autres enfants arriérés.* London: Baillière Tindall.

—— (1866). *Idiocy: and its Treatment by the Physiological Method.* New York: William Wood and Co. Retrieved from http://www.personal.dundee.ac.uk~mksimpso/SegIdio.htm. Accessed 14 March 2003.

Shakespeare, T. W. (1994). Cultural representations of disabled people: dustbins for disavowal? *Disability and Society.* 9, 3: 283–99.

Shakespeare, T. and Watson, N. (1997). Defending the social model. In L. Barton, and M. Oliver (eds.). *Disability Studies: Past, Present and Future.* Leeds: The Disability Press.

—— (2002). The social model of disability: an outdated ideology? *Research in Social Science and Disability.* 2: 9–28.

Sigelman, C. K. and Budd, E. C. (1986). Pictures as an aid in questioning mentally retarded persons. *Rehabilitation Counselling Bulletin.* 29: 173–81.

Sigelman, C. K., Budd, E. C., Spanhel, C. L. and Schoenrock, C. J. (1981a). When in doubt, say yes: acquiescence in interviews with mentally retarded persons. *Mental Retardation.* 19: 53–8.

—— (1981b). Asking questions of retarded persons: a comparison of yes–no and either–or formats. *Applied Research in Mental Retardation.* 2: 347–57.

Sigelman, C. K., Budd, E. C., Winer, J. L., Schoenrock, C. J. and Martin, R. W. (1982). Evaluating alternative techniques of questioning mentally retarded persons. *American Journal of Mental Deficiency.* 86: 511–58.

Sigelman, C. K., Schoenrock, C. J., Spanhel, C. L., Hromas, S. G., Winer, J. L., Budd, E. C. and Martin, P. W. (1980). Surveying mentally retarded persons: responsiveness and response validity in three samples. *American Journal of Mental Deficiency.* 84, 5: 479–86.

Silverman, D. (1994). Describing sexual activities in HIV counselling: the cooperative management of the moral order. *Text.* 14, 3: 427–53.

—— (1998). *Harvey Sacks: Social Science and Conversation Analysis.* Cambridge: Polity Press.

—— (2001). *Interpreting Qualitative Data: Methods for Analysing Talk, Text and Interaction* (2nd edition). London: Sage.

Simmons-Mackie, N. N. and Damico, J. S. (1999). Social role negotiation in aphasia therapy: competence, incompetence, and conflict. In J. Duchan, D. Kovarsky and M. Maxwell (eds.). *Studies in Normal and Pathological Discourse.* New York: Erlbaum.

Simpson, M. K. (2000a). *Bibliography of the History of Idiocy.* Retrieved from http://www.personal.dundee.ac.uk/~mksimpso/histories.htm. Accessed 10 March 2003.

(2000b). Idiocy as a regime of truth: an archaeological study of intellectual disability through the work of Edouard Seguin, William Ireland, and Alfred Binet and Th. Simon. Unpublished PhD Thesis, University of Dundee.

Sisson, L. A. and Barrett, R. P. (1983). Review of non-speech communication systems with autistic and mentally retarded individuals. In S. E. Breuning, J. L. Matson and R. P. Barrett (eds.). *Advances in Mental Retardation and Developmental Disabilities*. Vol. 1. London: JAI Press.

Smith, J. D. (2002). The myth of mental retardation: paradigm shifts, disaggregation, and developmental disabilities. *Mental Retardation*. 40, 1: 62–4.

Smith, J. D. and Mitchell, A. L. (2001). 'Me? I'm not a drooler. I'm the assistant': is it time to abandon mental retardation as a classification? *Mental Retardation*. 39, 2: 144–6.

Sokal, A. (1996). Transgressing the boundaries: toward a transformative hermeneutics of quantum gravity. *Social Text*, 46/7 (Spring/Summer 1996): 217–52.

Sokal, A. and Bricmont, J. (1999). *Intellectual Impostures: Postmodern Philosophers' Abuse of Science* (2nd English edition). No translator named. Profile Books: London.

Spitz, H. (1983). Critique of the development position in mental retardation research. *The Journal of Special Education*. 17, 3: 261–94.

Stainton, T. (2001). Reason and value: the thought of Plato and Aristotle and the construction of intellectual disability. *Mental Retardation*. 39, 6: 452–60.

Stainton, T. and McDonagh, P. (2001). Chasing shadows: the historical construction of developmental disability. *Journal on Developmental Disabilities*. 8, 2: 8–15.

Stancliffe, R. (1995). Assessing opportunities for choice-making: a comparison of self-reports and staff reports. *American Journal on Mental Retardation*. 99: 418–29.

Stone, E. and Priestley, M. (1996). Parasites, pawns and partners: disability research and the role of non-disabled researchers. *British Journal of Sociology*. 47: 699–716.

Suchman, L. A. and Jordan, B. (1990). Interactional trouble in face-to-face survey interviews. *Journal of the American Statistical Association*. 85: 232–44.

Szivos, S. E. and Griffiths, E. (1990). Group processes involved in coming to terms with a mentally retarded identity. *Mental Retardation*. 28: 333–41.

Taylor, R. L. (ed.). (1997). *Assessment of Individuals with Mental Retardation*. San Diego, CA: Singular Publishing Group, Inc.

Taylor, S. J. (1997). Disability studies and mental retardation. *Disability Studies Quarterly*. 16, 3: 4–13. Retrieved from www.soeweb.syr.edu/thechp/dsmr.htm. Accessed 18 March 2003.

(2000). 'You're not a retard, you're just wise': disability, social identity, and family networks. *Journal of Contemporary Ethnography*. 29, 1: 58–92.

Taylor, S. J. and Harris, P. (1997). Selected annotated bibliography: disability studies and mental retardation. *Disability Studies Quarterly*. 16, 3: 4–13.

Taylor, T. J. and Cameron, D. (1987). *Analysing Conversation: Rules and Units in the Structure of Talk*. Oxford: Pergamon.

tenHave, P. (1999). *Doing Conversation Analysis*. London: Sage.

Thomas, C. (1999). *Female Forms: Experiencing and Understanding Disability*. Buckingham: Open University Press.

Thomas, C. and Corker, M. (2002). A journey around the social model. In M. Corker and T. Shakespeare (eds.). *Disability/Postmodernity: Embodying Disability Theory*. London: Continuum.

Thomson, M. (1998). *The Problem of Mental Deficiency: Eugenics, Democracy and Social Policy in Britain, c. 1870–1959*. Oxford: Clarendon Press.

Tizard, J. (1964). *Community Services for the Mentally Handicapped*. Oxford: Oxford University Press.

Todd, S. (2000). Working in the public and private domains: staff management of community activities for and the identities of people with intellectual disability. *Journal of Intellectual Disability Research*. 44, 5: 600–20.

Todd, S. and Shearn, J. (1995). *Family Secrets and Dilemmas of Status: Parental Management of the Disclosure of 'Learning Disability'*. Cardiff. Welsh Centre For Learning Disabilities – Applied Research Unit.

(1997). Family dilemmas and secrets: parents' disclosure of information to their adult offspring with learning disabilities. *Disability and Society*. 12, 3: 341–66.

Tredgold, A. F. (1908). *Mental Deficiency – Amentia*. London: Baillière Tindall.

(1937). *A Textbook of Mental Deficiency*. Baltimore, MD: Wood.

Trent, J. W., Jr (1994). *Inventing the Feeble Mind: A History of Mental Retardation in the United States*. Berkeley, CA: University of California Press.

UPIAS (1976). *Fundamental Principles of Disability*. London: Union of Physically Impaired Against Segregation.

Voelker, S. L., Shore, D. L., Brown-More, C., Hill, L. C., Miller, L. T. and Perry, J. (1990). Validity of self-report of adaptive behaviour skills by adults with mental retardation. *Mental Retardation*. 28, 5: 305–9.

Walmsley, J. (2000). Women and the Mental Deficiency Act of 1913: citizenship, sexuality and regulation. *British Journal of Learning Difficulties*. 28: 65–70.

Watson, R. (1982). The presentation of victim and motive in discourse: the case of police interrogations and interviews. *Victimology: An International Journal*. 8, 1–2: 31–52.

Wechsler, D. (1958). *The Measurement and Appraisal of Adult Intelligence* (4th edition). Baltimore, MD: The Williams and Wilkins Company.

(1981). *Wechsler Adult Intelligence Scale – Revised: Manual*. Cleveland, OH: The Psychological Corporation.

Wehmeyer, M. L. (1994). Reliability and acquiescence in the measurement of locus of control with adolescents and adults with mental retardation. *Psychological Reports*. 75: 527–37.

Weinberg, D. (1997). The social construction of non-human agency: the case of mental disorder. *Social Problems*. 44, 2: 217–35.

Wetherell, M. (1998). Positioning and interpretative repertoires: conversation analysis and post-structuralism in dialogue. *Discourse and Society*. 9: 387–412.

(1999). Beyond binaries. *Theory and Psychology*. 9, 3: 399–406.

(2002). *Discourse as Data*. Buckingham: Open University Press.

Wetherell, M. and Potter, J. (1992). *Mapping the Language of Racism: Discourse and the Legitimation of Exploitation*. Hemel Hempstead: Harvester Wheatsheaf.

Wickham, P. (2001). Images of idiocy in puritan New England. *Mental Retardation*. 39, 2: 147–51.

Widdicombe, S. (1998). Identity as an analyst's and a participant's resource. In C. Antaki and S. Widdicombe (eds.). *Identities in Talk*. London: Sage.

Widdicombe, S. and Wooffitt, R. (1995). *The Language of Youth Subculture*. Brighton: Harvester.

Williamson, G. (2003). Instructor Restatements in Conversations with Learning Disabled Interlocutors. Retrieved from http://homepage.ntlworld.com/graham.williamson77/papers/restate.htm. Accessed 14 October 2003.

Willis, T. (1672). *De Anima Brutorum*. Oxford.

Wing, L. and Gould, J. (1978). Systematic recording of behaviours and skills of retarded and psychotic children. *Journal of Autism and Childhood Schizophrenia*. 8: 79–97.

(1979). Severe impairments of social interaction and associated abnormalities in children: epidemiology and classification. *Journal of Autism and Childhood Schizophrenia*. 9: 11–29.

Wittgenstein, L. (1926). Lecture on Ethics. *Philosophical Review*. 74: 3–26.

(1958). *Philosophical Investigations*. Oxford: Blackwell.

(1969). *On Certainty*. Oxford: Blackwell.

Wootton, A. J. (1990). Pointing and interaction initiation: the behaviour of young children with Down's Syndrome when looking at books. *Journal of Child Language*. 17: 565–89.

Wright, D. and Digby, A. (eds.). (1996). *From Idiocy to Mental Deficiency: Historical Perspectives on People with Learning Disabilities*. London: Routledge.

Yates, S., Taylor, S. and Wetherell, M. (2001). *Discourse as Data: A Guide for Analysis*. London: Sage.

Yearley, S. and Brewer, J. (1989). Stigma and conversational competence: a conversation analytic study of the mentally handicapped. *Human Studies*. 12: 97–115.

Young, I. M. (2002). Foreword. In M. Corker and T. Shakespeare (eds.). *Disability/Postmodernity: Embodying Disability Theory*. London: Continuum.

Zigler, E., Balla, D. and Hodapp, R. (1984). On the definition and classification of mental retardation. *American Journal of Mental Deficiency*. 89: 215–30.

Zigler, W. E. and Harter, C. L. (1969). Outer-directedness. In D. A. Goslin (ed.). *Handbook of Socialization Theory and Research*. Chicago, IL: Rand McNally.

Index